Books That Have Made History: Books That Can Change Your Life
Part III

Professor J. Rufus Fears

THE TEACHING COMPANY ®

PUBLISHED BY:

THE TEACHING COMPANY
4840 Westfields Boulevard, Suite 500
Chantilly, Virginia 20151-2299
1-800-TEACH-12
Fax—703-378-3819
www.teach12.com

ISBN 1-59803-026-4

J. Rufus Fears, Ph.D.

David Ross Boyd Professor of Classics, University of Oklahoma

J. Rufus Fears is David Ross Boyd Professor of Classics at the University of Oklahoma, where he also holds the G. T. and Libby Blankenship Chair in the History of Liberty. He rose from Assistant Professor to Professor of History at Indiana University. From 1986 to 1990, he was Professor of Classics and Chairman of the Department of Classical Studies at Boston University.

Professor Fears holds a Ph.D. from Harvard University. He has been a Danforth Fellow, a Woodrow Wilson Fellow, and a Harvard Prize Fellow. He has been a Fellow of the American Academy in Rome, a Guggenheim Fellow, and twice a Fellow of the Alexander von Humboldt Foundation. His research has been supported by grants from the American Philosophical Society, the American Council of Learned Societies, the National Endowment for the Humanities, the Kerr Foundation, and the Zarrow Foundation. He was chosen as Indiana University's first Distinguished Faculty Research Lecturer. He is listed in *Who's Who in America* and *Who's Who in the World*.

Professor Fears is the author of more than one hundred articles, reviews and historical plaques on Greek and Roman history, the history of liberty, and the lessons of history for our own day. His books and monographs include *Princeps A Diis Electus: The Divine Election of the Emperor as a Political Concept at Rome*, *The Cult of Jupiter and Roman Imperial Ideology*, *The Theology of Victory at Rome*, and *The Cult of Virtues and Roman Imperial Ideology* and *Selected Writings of Lord Acton*. He has also lectured widely in the United States and Europe, and his scholarly work has been translated into German and Italian. He is very active in speaking to broader audiences, and his comments on the lessons of history for today have appeared on television and been carried in newspapers and journals throughout the United States and abroad. Each year, he leads study trips to historical sites in the United States and Europe.

On 21 occasions, Dr. Fears has received awards for outstanding teaching. In 1996, 1999, and again in 2000, students chose him as the University of Oklahoma Professor of the Year. In 2003, he received the Excellence in Teaching Award from the Great Plains Region of the University Continuing Education Association. In 2005 he was named the national winner of the Excellence in Teaching Award from the University Continuing Education Association. The Senior Citizens Great Books Course, which he teaches at the University of Oklahoma, was cited prominently in this National Excellence in Teaching Award.

Books That Have Made History: Books That Can Change Your Life is the fifth course Professor Fears has produced with The Teaching Company. His other courses include *Famous Greeks*, *Famous Romans*, *A History of Freedom*, and *Churchill*.

Table of Contents

Books That Have Made History:
Books That Can Change Your Life
Part III

Books That Have Made History:
Books That Can Change Your Life

Scope:

This course, *Books That Have Made History: Books That Can Change Your Life*, is a companion to my earlier Teaching Company courses: *A History of Freedom*, *Famous Greeks*, *Famous Romans*, and *Winston Churchill*. Like these courses, *Books That Have Made History* rests upon the conviction that history is made by great individuals, great events, and great ideas. This course explores these great ideas through a discussion of some of the most seminal writings in history, books that have shaped the minds of great individuals and events of historic magnitude.

Our earlier courses, *A History of Freedom*, *Famous Greeks*, *Famous Romans*, and *Winston Churchill*, have all discussed some of the great books that have made history. In those contexts, we have studied such works as the *Apology* of Socrates, *Oedipus the King*, the *Iliad*, the *Odyssey*, the *Aeneid*, and the magisterial histories of Herodotus, Thucydides, Polybius, Gibbon, and Churchill. We will return to some of these treasured books from entirely new perspectives, but for the most part, we will strike off on new paths with new books.

The books we will discuss range in time from the 3rd millennium B.C. to the 20th century. Our geographical scope will carry us from Mesopotamia and China to Europe and America. It is the ideas that are important, and our course will be organized thematically around eternal questions that endure throughout history and that every thoughtful person must seek to answer. Either by conscious choice or by omission, nations, groups, organizations, and corporations, as well individuals, answer these questions:

- Question 1: God. Does God or do gods exist? What is the nature of the divine? Does God or do the gods care about humans and their actions? This is the first question with which every thoughtful person must come to grips. The other questions and some of the answers will flow from it.

- Question 2: Fate. What is fate? Do events, great and small, happen because they are predetermined by divine will or simply by chance and random occurrence? Do humans have free will? Do you determine your life, or is it already predetermined? Are you free to choose, or has your DNA already made the choice for you?

- Question 3: Good and evil. What do we mean by good and evil? Are there consequences for our actions, whether freely chosen or predetermined? If there are consequences for our actions, does this mean that there are standards by which to judge these actions? Who or what determines those standards? Are those standards enduring for all time? Or are there no absolute standards? Do circumstances determine what is right and wrong at any particular moment and for any particular individual, group, or nation? Does evil exist? Can we speak of evil as a real force that affects events and lives?

- Question 4: How should we live? Our answers or failures to answer or even to ask these questions have consequences. They determine how we, individuals, groups, nations, live our lives. They give us the values or absence of values to determine how we act toward others. Our great books course examines our actions under the following eternal human conditions, emotions, and challenges:
  - The meaning of life
  - Truth
  - Duty and responsibility
  - Law, government, and social justice
  - Love, jealousy, and hate
  - Courage, honor, and ambition
  - Beauty
  - Nature
  - History and the past
  - Education.

These themes will provide the context in which we discuss the books that have made history and books that can change our lives. It is the hallmark of a great book that it may offer us insights into many of these conditions and emotions. Thus, the same great book may be brought into our exploration of several of these themes.

We have repeatedly used the term *great book*. What do we mean by a great book? Can we even speak of great books?

The answer is yes. *Great book* is an unfashionable, even controversial term today, because it implies value judgments. As a society, we do not wish to make value judgments. *Judgmental* is an expression of reproach. However, great books are great precisely because they challenge us to make value judgments.

A great book has the following three essential qualities:

- Great theme. A great book is concerned with themes and issues of enduring importance.

- Noble language. Great books are written in noble language, language that elevates the soul and ennobles the mind. It is not the specific language, say Latin or English, that is noble. Any language can be used in such way that it conveys ideas and emotions powerfully and memorably.

- Universality. A great book is "a possession for all time" (Thucydides). It speaks across the ages, reaching the hearts and minds of men and women far removed in time and space from the era and circumstances in which it was composed. Thus, a great book summarizes the enduring values and ideas of a great age and gives them as a legacy to generations to come.

For us, in this course, what ultimately makes a great book is its ability to speak to you as an individual. You can read a great book many times, and each time, you read it with new eyes. At each stage of your life, you will find new messages to address new concerns. A great book gives you the personal wisdom to be better, better as an individual and better as the citizen of a free nation, empowered with the awesome responsibility of self-government.

Ultimately, great books are an education for freedom.

Lecture Twenty-Five
Plato, *Republic*

Scope:

Plato's *Republic* might be called the greatest book on politics, on education, and on justice ever written. As the *Divine Comedy* embodies the values of the Middle Ages and the *Aeneid* embodies the ideals and values of Rome, the *Republic* embodies the ideals and values of classical Greece. In the dialogue, Socrates raises a supreme question for us in this course: What makes a person happy? To prove that only a just person and, thus, a good person is happy, Socrates leads us to explore the meaning of justice, what sort of political organization can achieve justice, and how we can educate citizens for justice. These questions are as relevant for our democracy as for the democracy of Athens.

Outline

I. This lecture continues the theme of government and justice, especially the moral values that are essential to a good government. The model of Socrates, who insisted that terms be defined, can guide us through the great books. What do we really mean about the nobility of dying for one's country? How can *nobility* be defined?

   A. Socrates, through Plato, would say that nobility is related to justice and to defining the concept of justice. Justice is one of a number of essential qualities, or virtues, that every individual should have. Socrates explored these qualities in his discussion of the immortal soul in the *Phaedo*.

   B. These qualities are found in a variety of cultures and are reflected in such diverse literature as the *Bhagavad Gita* and in Confucius.

   C. These qualities include wisdom, justice, courage, and moderation.
   1. Courage is, of course, essential for those who go to war.
   2. An individual must have the wisdom to understand the difference between courage exercised in a just war and courage exercised in an unjust war. Without the wisdom

to understand that a nation is fighting for justice, courage is nothing more than brutality.

3. Moderation links the virtues. When any quality—even courage—is carried too far, it becomes unjust.

4. Courage, moderation, and wisdom—working together—produce true justice. That is the theme of Plato's *Republic*.

II. Plato's *Republic*, which is a magisterial discussion of what makes a good state, was probably composed during the 380s B.C.

   A. Plato was a pupil of Socrates and paid his teacher the greatest of compliments by putting all his own ideas into the mouth of Socrates, thereby indicating that none of his thinking would have existed without Socrates.

   B. Although Plato is called a philosopher, he was an intellectual. Philosophers, such as Confucius and Socrates, live their wisdom; intellectuals talk about ideas and try, from time to time, to put them into action.

   1. Plato, for example, went to Sicily and tried to help educate the young tyrant Dionysius. This attempt was a failure.

   2. Plato's contribution, in addition to his writings, was to create in Athens a university where lectures were held and young people were trained. Through this university, the ideas of Socrates were institutionalized.

   C. Alfred North Whitehead said, "All philosophy is but a series of footnotes to Plato."

III. The greatest of Plato's works is the *Republic*.

   A. Like *The Divine Comedy*, Plato's *Republic* is a difficult book to read.

   B. Like *The Divine Comedy*, it summarizes the values of a civilization at its apex. That civilization is the world of the *polis*, the city-state of classical Greece.

IV. Plato's *Republic* is concerned with how to create a constitution that ensures justice for all citizens. Plato puts this discussion into the form of dialogues.

   A. When the *Republic* begins, Socrates is returning from a religious festival in honor of the goddess Artemis. He stops to visit his friend Cephalus, who wonders about the afterlife, whether he has an immortal soul, what will happen to his soul, and whether good and bad behavior will have consequences. The two then begin to discuss justice.

B. The discussion starts with the conventional definition of justice, that is, rewarding friends and punishing enemies. Socrates, in the dialogues of Plato, often begins with a statement that everyone can accept.

C. Socrates then asks how a just man can do unjust things, even to his enemies. Socrates shows that the original definition is wrong. No good man would do harm to another.

D. One of the participants in the dialogue is Thrasymachus, a Sophist.

    1. The true Sophist in Athens educated their students to argue either side of an issue.

    2. To argue either side of a case successfully, an individual must be believe that the position is true. Therefore, the Sophist does not believe in absolute values.

    3. For the Sophist, unlike for Socrates, truth is whatever is expedient at the moment.

E. Thrasymachus argues that justice is power. Justice is what the powerful can get away with, and laws are what the powerful put in place to serve their own interests; thus, no such quality as justice can exist.

    1. This idea was accepted in Athens. Athenian foreign policy during the war with Sparta rested on the belief that might makes right.

    2. For example, in 416 B.C., Athens had demanded that the neutral nation of Melos join the Athenian coalition. When Melos refused, Athens launched a preemptive attack, captured it, put its men to death, and sold its women and children into slavery. Athenians justified the destruction of Melos by claiming that Athens had power and that Melos could choose to join Athens and live or resist and die. When Melos appealed to the Athenian idea of justice, the Athenians said that justice did not exist.

F. Socrates attempts to help Thrasymachus understand that if justice is whatever the strong can do, unjust acts will make weaker people hate them. Eventually, the weaker groups will band together and overthrow those in power. Therefore, it is expedient for those in positions of power to act justly.

G. Socrates says that to define justice, the idea should be examined in a larger unit, such as the state, or *polis*.

    1. Machiavelli was the first to use the term "state" (*il stato*) in its modern sense as a political unit separate from the people.

    2. As a true democracy, the Athenian government cannot be separated from the idea of the people.

H. Socrates said that the city is a collection of individuals, each of whom has certain qualities that reflect absolute values. In the transcendent world, absolute wisdom, courage, and moderation exist. These qualities, working together, will create true justice.

I. Socrates next asks how to bring these qualities together in the proper blend to make the *polis* just.

    1. Each person has a characteristic virtue, such as courage, moderation, or wisdom.

    2. A community in which every individual is able to exercise his or her characteristic virtue intelligently in the service of the *polis* will be a just *polis* that exists for the good of all.

    3. The state exists to serve the people, but the people must understand how the right kind of service is rendered.

J. Education is the means to bring about morality and to achieve the ideal government. Children must be examined at the earliest possible age to determine the qualities that they possess. They can then be educated. True education brings forth and cultivates the appropriate virtue of each citizen, educating each to suitable work in life.

    1. The strongest quality that most people possess is moderation. Those who possess moderation will form the basis of a community. They should be taught reading and writing, and they must understand that they should do whatever they do best and not aspire to other roles.

    2. The people who are warriors at heart should be soldiers. They must be taught poetry to awaken the soul and gymnastics to train their bodies.

    3. A few people have the ability to lead. These guardians should have a long and elaborate education.

Mathematics is an essential subject for these leaders, because they must keep their eyes fixed on absolute truth and justice. Numbers and geometry are ways to perfection.

K. Thus, the ideal republic rests on absolute values: absolute truth and absolute right and wrong. Absolute wisdom and absolute ignorance exist, as do absolute justice and injustice, absolute courage and cowardice, absolute moderation and intemperance.

L. Plato concludes his magnificent work on justice with the myth of Er, who could be Everyman.

  1. Er was killed in battle but was found alive 10 days later.

  2. He explained that his soul had left his body and gone to heaven, where he saw the afterlife and the souls of those who had done evil cast into the deepest pit, from which they would never be free. He saw others who could be redeemed. After paying their penalties, these souls came before the Fates, received a new life, drank from the River of Forgetfulness, and returned to this world.

  3. These souls made a choice through their free will about how to live their lives.

  4. Socrates ends his treatment of a just city with the belief in the immortality of the soul as the foundation of everything.

Essential Reading:

Plato, *Republic*.

Supplementary Reading:

Barker, *Greek Political Thought*.

Questions to Consider:

1. Why does Socrates end his treatment of the ideal government with a discussion of the immortality of the soul?

2. Would you want to live in Plato's Republic?

Lecture Twenty-Five—Transcript
Plato, *Republic*

In this lecture, we continue our discussion of the theme of duty and responsibility—and especially the duty and responsibility of a citizen. In our earlier lectures, we have looked at the *Aeneid* of Virgil; we have studied the two great wartime orations by two great democratic statesmen, Pericles and Abraham Lincoln; and we have examined what has been called—and I believe rightly—the greatest war novel ever written, *All Quiet on the Western Front* by Erich Maria Remarque. In the course of that, I have posed to you the question, "Is it the noblest thing that you can do to die for your country?"

Guiding us through the discussion of all of these great books, I believe, should be the model of Socrates, one of the greatest teachers ever. Socrates always insisted that you go back and define your terms. How can you know what you're talking about unless you define those terms? So, last hour we defined the term "education." How do we know what education is? What is the education of a citizen? How do we decide what we really mean by the nobility of dying for your country? Because if you're going to go out and die for your country, the thoughtful person will have examined this. To do that we want to continue with our discussions, building upon our discussion of Confucius—his *Analects*—of *The Prince* of Machiavelli, and going in this lecture to the *Republic* of Plato, and then in our next lecture into the wonderful work *On Liberty* by John Stuart Mill.

What, then, is nobility? How do we go about defining it? Socrates, through Plato, would say it is about justice and it is about defining the concept of justice. Justice is part of a series, as we shall learn further in the *Republic*, a series of essential qualities or virtues that every individual should have. We met them already in Socrates's discussion of the immortality of the soul in the *Phaedo*. I have suggested to you that we find them across a number of cultures, including classical India—the *Bhagavad Gita*—as well as Confucius: wisdom, justice, courage, and moderation.

Now, courage is certainly essential for those who go to war. However, what is the difference between courage exercised in a just cause—in a just war—and courage exercised in an unjust war? You see, without the wisdom to understand that your nation is fighting for justice, courage can be nothing more than brutality. Certainly the soldiers in the *Waffen S.S.* on the Eastern Front were brave men, but they were fighting for an evil cause.

Wisdom would have allowed them to understand that cause was evil, and true courage would have been to say, "No, this is wrong; I'm not going to do it," and that all must be linked together by moderation.

Any quality, even courage, if pushed too far, becomes "unwisdom." It can be unjust. So it is the working together of all of these elements—courage, moderation and wisdom—that produces true justice. That is the theme of Plato in one of the greatest books ever composed, and one of the most thoughtful essays on, "What is a good state?" The *Republic* of Plato was probably composed in the 380s B.C. Plato was the pupil of Socrates. We encountered him in the *Phaedo*. Socrates, as you know, and as I've told you, never wrote a book, but Plato paid him the greatest of compliments by putting all of his own ideas into the mouth of Socrates, as though to say, "Without Socrates, none of this would have existed." Now, Socrates was a true philosopher. He was a true lover of wisdom, and, as we saw in our lecture on Confucius, when we compared Socrates and Confucius, both of those lived their ideas. They lived their wisdom.

Plato, although we, of course, call him a philosopher today, is really an intellectual. Because I want to distinguish between the philosopher, which would include Jesus, who lives his ideas, and the intellectual, who talks about them, and may, from time to time, try to put them into action. Plato did that. He went to Sicily and tried to help educate the tyrant Dionysius. It was a total failure. Plato, of course, is one more of those who, if you can, do, if you can't—teach. What he then did, which was his great contribution outside of his magnificent works, was to create, in Athens, a university, where lectures were held and young people were trained. It was through this university that Socrates was institutionalized. Socrates' ideas by themselves were very revolutionary, very dangerous; got him executed. They needed to be put into a proper perspective; Plato did that. He institutionalized them; taught them through the university, and lived to a ripe old age. He was not, as Socrates was, put to death for his ideas.

In fact, it is very interesting. Socrates dies like a philosopher. Plato is absent from the last days of Socrates because he's sick. And Aristotle, who is the true professor, when the Athenians think about putting him to death for his ideas, goes into exile, and he gives a wonderful rationale: He cannot allow Athens to sin twice against philosophy.

But Plato is the most profound mind of the European world. It has been rightly said that all of philosophy is a series of footnotes to Plato. This is what the English educator Alfred North Whitehead quite rightly said. The greatest of Plato's works is the *Republic*. It is truly a great book. Like Dante's *Divine Comedy*, it is very difficult, and like Dante's *Divine Comedy,* it summarizes the values of a civilization at its apex, and that civilization is the world of the city-state, of the *polis* of Classical Greece.

It is concerned with how to create a constitution that would ensure justice for all citizens. Plato puts this discussion, as he always does, into the form of dialogues. Among his other great qualities, Plato is one of the most brilliant writers ever to compose. He has a gift of dialogue, of gathering you along in the discussion, that would do credit to any novelist.

So he creates a scene in which Socrates, who is always the central figure in these dialogues, is coming back from a religious festival, a religious festival to the goddess Artemis, a new festival that has been introduced for this goddess of wildlife and fertility. And, of course, he points out to you, how deeply religious Socrates really is. Remember, he is put to death for blasphemy, for not believing in the gods of Athens, but, in fact, he's always at religious festivals. Like Confucius, he has a deep respect for the traditional religious rites. He just wants them understood in the proper fashion. He is coming back and is urged to go to the house of Cephalus, an elderly man, about Socrates' age—they were contemporaries—just to spend the evening, having a meal and discussing. He always likes to go to see Cephalus. Cephalus is a man who is aging gracefully. Socrates says, "You know, I noticed how much he had aged since I saw him last, but he still had that sense of composure and calm, and I said to him, 'You know, it is just wonderful that you take your aging so well,' and he said, 'Yes, yes. I do.'" Then Socrates says, "Is there anything you miss in life?" "No, not really. In fact, you know that old Sophocles—a poet whom Socrates had very little respect for—came up to me and said, 'How are you still doing in the service of Aphrodite?' and I said to him, 'Oh, the gods be praised, those ideas are long away from my mind. Now I just want to think and be quiet,'" and Socrates says, "Well, what do you think about?" "Well, as I reach the end of my days, I keep coming back to the idea of, 'Is there an afterlife? Do I have an immortal soul?' and I know, Socrates, you believe that, but then what will happen to that immortal soul? Will there be consequences? Will I be rewarded for my just deeds, and will I be punished for my unjust deeds? I like to think that I am a man of justice and that I lived my life as much as I could with a sense of justice."

Socrates says, "You know, that's wonderful you're pondering justice in your last years. What is justice? Have you ever thought about that?" "Well, I don't know." Here's a man spending his last years pondering justice, but he's never really thought about it. Socrates says, "Well, let's think about what justice is." Cephalus says, "I always go with what the poets say." Socrates says, "That's a good start, to go with what the poets say, such as Homer. They are a source of much information for us, and many people take them very seriously. The poets say that justice lies in doing what is good to your friends and punishing your enemies, in other words, rewarding your friends and punishing your enemies. Wouldn't you think that's a reasonable idea of justice? Payback time for those who have done bad things to you and rewards for those who have helped you."

A good politician would say that, don't you think? I would think President Nixon, for example, would define that as an idea of justice, and he was a president with many, many good qualities. So justice is rewarding your friends and punishing your enemies. That was a standard, conventional definition of justice. That is how Socrates, in the dialogues of Plato, frequently likes to begin, with an idea that everybody accepts. Then he goes on and begins to discuss.

Well, how could a just man do unjust things, even to his enemies? Wouldn't the doing of an unjust thing to an enemy take away from his justice? Suddenly, one of the guests interrupts. He's a professor; Thrasymachus is his name. He is a sophist. They were the product of this Athenian democracy of the 5th century B.C., this age of freedom, of prosperity, in which intellectuals came from all over the Greek world to Athens. The same way that intellectuals and academics come from all over the world today to America, because they make good salaries. In Athens, they can teach at very high salaries. I have mentioned to you before, it is worth remembering, to study under a good professor, a good sophist, cost about as much, translated into the day's currency, as to earn a degree at Harvard; a year under a sophist was about the same as a year at Harvard. It would cost you around $40,000. That's what you would pay for your son, and your son would learn to speak well. That was a practical skill in the

©2005 The Teaching Company.

Athenian assembly. But in order to teach that young person to speak well, of course, you needed to teach them to argue either side of a case. Because it might be expedient in one political setting to argue for, let us say, a war against Sparta, and in another political setting, when the tide of public opinion had changed, to argue against it, don't you see? So you needed not only to be able to argue both sides, but you can't argue a side convincingly unless you believe in it. So you needed to teach that young person that there are no absolute truths. Nothing is absolutely true. It is just what is expedient at the moment. That is why Socrates was so totally different from these sophists. In the first place, he never took any money. In the second, he based his whole life upon absolute truths.

But Thrasymachus the professor breaks in, and you can almost hear him snorting, the way the whole professorial crowd does when you present an idea that's contrary to their current wisdom. Students are very respectful. They will listen. They are very open-minded, Professors never. They already know all the truth, and Thrasymachus just snorts, "All this is a lot of nonsense, talking about justice. Justice is one thing, simply. It is power. Might makes right." Exactly what Machiavelli told us in an earlier lecture. Justice is just exactly that thing that the powerful can get away with. Laws are what the powerful put in place to serve their own interests. So there is no such thing as justice.

This is a very widely spread idea in Athens. In fact, during the great war with Sparta, Athenian foreign policy had rested upon this belief that might makes right. In the year 416 B.C., the Athenians had gone to the small, neutral island of Melos, as we saw in our lecture on *Famous Greeks*. He demanded that this neutral island join their coalition. When that island refused, the Athenians launched a pre-emptive attack upon Melos, captured it, put every male citizen to death, and sold the women and children into slavery. That nation, that free nation, disappeared from history. In their justification, the Athenians said simply, "We have the power. You can either join us, Melians, and live; or resist us and die, and when the Melians the citizens of the island of Melos, appealed to the idea of justice, the Athenians snorted, There is no such thing as justice. The gods don't care anything about humans. You let us worry about the consequences. You just decide whether you're going to live or die."

That was a very widespread idea, that there is no such thing as justice. Simply, "might makes right." Socrates tries to argue patiently with the professor, and anyone who has tried to argue facts and reason with a professor knows how difficult that is. But Socrates is in a good humor, and never minds drinking a little bit, so he's mellow. He goes through and tries to get Thrasymachus, the sophist, to understand that if justice is nothing but what the strong can do, and that they can do anything they want to the weaker, that if they do unjust acts to them, those unjust acts will make the weaker people hate them. "Well, so what?" "Sooner or later, if you make enough people hate you, since they outnumber you considerably, they will overthrow you. So why would you go around consciously trying to make those who outnumber you and, in their collective mass, will have more power than you, if they cooperate and get together, hate you. So surely, it is in the interests—since you're such a big fan of expediency—for even those with power to act justly." "Bah. You don't know what you're talking about, Socrates. You're always coming up with these ideas. You're just like a lawyer. Well, all right. Let's just go along. I'll just sit here and listen to you, because you can't be right." Well, of course he is right, but a professor can't admit that he is ever wrong.

So Socrates then goes on and says, "But we have raised this question, haven't we, of 'What is justice?' So how are we going to go about defining justice? You know what I think we should do, instead of just worrying about the individual, as one person, maybe we will come to a clearer understanding if we look at justice as a whole inside a big unit, such as the *polis*, such as the state."

"State" is a word that I will use, but it is a difficult word to use in terms of the world of 5th century Athens. "State", as I understand it, first is used in Machiavelli, *il stato*, to mean a political unit separate from the people. That's how we refer to it today: The government did this, or The government gave me that, The government is taxing me. But for the ancient Athenians, as a true democracy, they were the government; hence, all of their official documents read, "The Athenians." The citizens, the Athenians, passed this law or passed that law, so we should not separate the idea of government from the people.

So how do we see the idea of justice in this great community, which is our city, our nation of Athens, the *polis?* In the Greek, Plato's work is called, the *Politeia*, which is the things, the way, the constitution of the city, of the *polis*. So we should turn and try to see what justice is in the city as a whole. The same way that if we want to understand a painting, we don't look at one little spot. We would look at the whole of it. Now, the city is a collection of individuals, and if we go around and look at every individual, each one has certain qualities. "I believe," Socrates says, "these qualities all reflect absolute values. I'm sorry," Socrates says, "that is what it always goes back to. It goes back to absolute goodness and absolute qualities. My whole thinking and approach is based on a belief in absolutes. I believe that there is, somewhere, in heaven, an absolute wisdom, there is an absolute courage; there is absolute moderation, by which we measure all other reflections of justice, moderation, wisdom, and courage, and that the working together of justice and courage and moderation and wisdom will create a true justice, when wisdom, moderation and courage all work together in their proper spheres, then we will have justice. So that's our definition of justice—when courage and moderation and wisdom all work together."

"But how are we going to bring about this proper blend that will make the polis just?" "We must look at every individual citizen and realize that you have a great abundance of courage. You're a very brave soldier. In fact, you're so brave that your moderation frequently is forgotten. You will rush into the very thick of battle and maybe throw away your life. That also means that maybe you're not wise all the time, but you are brave, and that's very useful. Now, he has a great deal of moderation. In fact, he almost never takes a stand for anything. So he's never going to come to real wisdom, and he's never going to live out his life. But that moderation is a sobering influence on you, don't you see? And she there, she has wisdom, but not the courage to put that wisdom into effect. She knows what is right, but she's not going to put it into effect, but that, too, is valuable, to have that wisdom.

"What we want, then, is for every individual to be able to exercise intelligently their own unique absolute truth or value. Now, once again, this rests on the fact that your courage is but a reflection of an absolute courage that exists, and would exist even if everyone on Earth denied its existence." Do you understand that?

It is the same—this is not coincidental—that two plus two is always four. That is the absolute truth. Even if the whole world denies it, as they did in *1984*, remember, with George Orwell, it is still true. So the whole world can say that there is no such thing as justice. There is no such thing as absolute wisdom, but it is true. What we want, then, is to bring all of this together. Once we have a polis in which every individual is able intelligently to exercise in the service of the community, the service of the polis or service of the state, their characteristic virtue, then we will have a just polis—one that exists for the good of all, for that is fundamental. The state, the polis, exists to serve the people, but the people must be made to understand this and to understand how the right kind of service is rendered. "Well, how are you going to do that Socrates? With people being the way they are." "It is only through education."

The *Republic* then turns to one of the greatest treatises ever composed on education, for a citizen. Socrates believes that we must take each individual at the earliest possible age, and at one point he even says, "You know, the only way you would ever truly bring this about is just have children. Get rid of all the grown-ups one way or another and just start with the children, so you have absolutely clean slates."

I don't know. I ponder that when I see an eager class of second-graders. I would rather lecture to second-graders than to eleventh-graders. Eleventh-graders are just impossible to reach. They've already been too absorbed into the world. But those eager second-graders, their little hands reaching up into the air, want to learn. Start with them, and what we do, then, is look at the qualities of each one of those, and educate them. The bulk of people have as their best quality, if we could bring it out in them through the proper education—sobriety—moderation. They just want to work hard, take care of things. They will form the real basis of our community, and they need to be educated so that they read and write, but also they have to understand that that is a good thing to do, that they should not aspire to be soldiers. They should not aspire to be leaders. They should just aspire to do very good jobs of what they do, whether they are farmers or cobblers or merchants or any of these. That is what their education should rest upon, a kind of vo-tech, where, instead of feeling that they had failed in society, they feel that they have succeeded and are being fulfilled.

But then there will be a certain number who are warriors at heart, who have that competitive drive, who will shed blood if they have to in a just cause. They need to be our soldiers. There needs to be a soldier class, and they, too, need to study poetry and gymnastics. What can make your soul more alive than to learn good, real poetry?

©2005 The Teaching Company.

These are they, who lay down the splendor of their young
lives,
Beside the Eurymedon.
By land and on swift sailing ships alike,
They fought with their spears against the foremost of the
bow-bearing Medes.
They are no more,
but they have left behind the fairest memorial to their valor.

Isn't that a good poem to learn? Yes or no? Of course! So the poetry
and music—stirring, martial music. We learned a song yesterday,
didn't we?

In the beauty of the lilies, Christ was born across the sea,
With a glory in his bosom that transfigures you and me.
As he died to make men holy, let us die to make men free…

Isn't that a great song? Yes. So that's what they would learn. And
gymnastics; they will train their bodies. They will not be weak and
out of shape; they will be trained to be warriors, so they will receive
a military education. They will believe that this is their role in life,
and they will not aspire to be political leaders. Nor will they be sorry
that they aren't shopkeepers. They will be happy in this, and by
carrying out their appointed task for their community, they will be
just in their souls because the quality they have best, courage, is
being used with wisdom. That will make them just people. But there
are a few—there are a few—who have the ability to lead, and they
must be our guardians. For them, the road is long and hard.

"Excuse me, Socrates. May I ask you something?" "Yes." "Cause
this is going to get the attention of later generations a whole lot,
What about women? What role do they play?" "Well, women have
the same abilities as men. They can undergo the same education."
"Oh. Okay." "And to make sure that everybody gets the right
qualities I think there should probably be a community of wives and
husbands, and a community of property. Now, can I please get on
with what's really important?" "Yes, yes."

"All right now. There will be a few who have the ability to lead, and
they will go through a long and elaborate education. They will pass
beyond gymnastics and music, to ponder the deepest of questions.
Essential to that education for leadership that only these few will
receive, is mathematics. This is the study of numbers and geometry.

Why? Because these, as guardians, must always keep their eyes fixed on the absolute truth and justice. Their eyes will be turned up towards heaven, and they will constantly contemplate the good and the true and the just. They will contemplate God, who is the embodiment of the truth and the justice and the wisdom, and the numbers, and the study of geometry, that is the way to this perfection. What did I tell you? Two plus two is four. Understand that. That is the very nature of an abstraction, and there is somewhere the perfect triangle of which every triangle on the Earth is but a reflection."

"This is a wonderful portrait that you have drawn for us. I am just speechless at the end of it. I still come back to this question, though, of justice. Even if we do all of these things, or don't do them, who cares? Who cares if we have a just state, and everybody in it fulfills their place?"

"Ah," Socrates says. "You know the story of Er, Er from Pamphylia, Er who could be any man? How he was killed in battle, and ten days later when they got ready to burn his corpse, he was still alive! He had not decayed at all, and they said, 'What are you doing?' He said, 'I'm alive! I'm not dead!' 'Well what have you been doing all this time, because you sure looked dead, even though you haven't been decomposing.' 'I had this most extraordinary experience. My soul left my body, and it went up to heaven. There the gods saw me and said, "Er, you must take this lesson back to the human race," and there I saw the afterlife. I saw the souls that had been so evil on Earth cast down into the deepest pit of punishment, and they would never be free. I saw others, who had done good things in life, but had made a few mistakes. I saw a few who had done a good many bad things, but could be redeemed, and after a thousand years, each paying their penalty, they came before the Fates. The lots were thrown out, and each one with all the knowledge of their past life, and what they had suffered and gained from it, could reach in and take a new life. I still saw people who, knowing everything that happens, wanted to be a tyrant, even a tyrant who would live only for five years, just to have that power. I saw Odysseus, who had suffered so much reaching and saying, "I just want the life of an ordinary person, without troubles." Then they drank from the river of forgetfulness and come back to Earth, where they live out their appointed lives. So they made their choice.' It was with free will that we then live out our lives." So with this statement, this belief in immortality of the soul, as the foundation of everything, Socrates ends his brilliant treatment of the just city.

Lecture Twenty-Six
John Stuart Mill, *On Liberty*

Scope:

Published in 1859, Mill's *On Liberty* is the classic statement of the liberal ideal of democratic government and social justice. This is the philosophical statement of the ideas of government put into effect by the great British Prime Ministers William Gladstone and Winston Churchill. For Mill, government exists to serve the individual. Individual liberty is the end of government, not a means to an end. Liberty is defined as the freedom of the individual to live as he or she chooses, unrestrained by government regulations as long as no harm is done to others. For Mill, the essence of true freedom lies in the individual's liberty, not in majority rule. Education, justice, economics must all be determined by how well they foster the freedom of the individual. Mill's themes remain as vital today as they were a century and a half ago. It is the eternal question of how much government regulation is necessary to secure these individual rights and whether the individual or the majority is the best judge of what is right.

Outline

I. The previous lecture continued the discussion of the ideals of government and justice and what is it means to be a good citizen or, in the words of Socrates, a just citizen. In Plato's *Republic*, Socrates defines the idea of justice to the individual in the framework of the larger concept of the state.

II. Much in Plato worried 19th-century thinkers, including John Stuart Mill.

    A. To people like Mill, Plato was disturbing because he reduced the ordinary citizen to the subjugation of the state; the state, in turn, might mislead the ordinary citizen in the name of a higher good that was determined by only a few people.

    B. As a student of Socrates, Plato understood the role of irony. Socrates frequently used irony to make people think.

    C. Sophists were guardians of the truth and had open minds. They sometimes challenged convention in the name of educating their students. However, the irony with which

Socrates depicted Sophists led them to be discredited into the 19th century.

    1. Socrates's students were so embittered by Socrates's death that they portrayed Athenian democracy as the worst possible form of government.

    2. Plato traces the degeneration of the ideal state into an Athenian-type democracy, in which each individual is free to live as he chooses without any restraint. In judging this depiction of democracy run amok, we must consider Socrates's use of irony.

D. The benefits of Athenian democracy were first recognized in the 19th century by British Liberals such as John Stuart Mill. Mill would argue that Athens was the first government to be based on the ideal of the greatest good for the greatest number and that it was a model form of government because of its concern for individual freedom.

III. *On Liberty*, published in 1859, was one of the culminating points in the life of a great intellectual.

A. The father of John Stuart Mill, James Mill, was closely associated with Jeremy Bentham and the Utilitarian movement.

    1. Utilitarianism sought to reform politics in England, to increase the number of English voters, and to create a democracy that rested on the rights of the individual.

    2. Utilitarians believed that the purpose of government was to achieve the greatest good for the greatest number of citizens; a government should be of, by, and for the people.

    3. Utilitarians believed that the test for any quality, virtue, or ethical principle was how well it worked, its usefulness.

B. James Mill wanted his son to be an intellectual who followed his father's philosophical ideas, and put his ideas into practice by becoming a civil servant.

C. John Stuart Mill described his education in his *Autobiography*, the story of his intellectual progress—both his failures and his success.

    1. In his *Autobiography*, Mill says that we should keep growing intellectually throughout our lives.

2. By the time Mill was 3 years old, according to his *Autobiography*, he could read Greek.

3. By the age of eight, he had read much classical literature and helped his father by summarizing his father's writing. He believed that one of the best ways to shape the mind was to summarize.

4. By the time he was in his teens, Mill was actively helping his father write.

5. At the age of 20, Mill suffered a complete nervous breakdown, which he later saw as a failure of will. A mundane book gave him the insight to understand what was going on and set him back on the track that he wanted to follow.

D. Mill turned political reformer. He worked in the civil service and became one of the leading intellectual lights of 19th-century England.

1. He wrote works on logic and on political economy.

2. He married Harriet Taylor, who was his true intellectual companion and who assisted him in his writings.

IV. In *On Liberty*, Mill defines *liberty* as the belief that every individual should be free to live his life untrammeled by other constraints, as long as he does not harm anyone else. The state has a right to interfere with an individual's life only when that individual is doing concrete harm to someone else.

A. This idea is the traditional concept of liberty.

B. Mill built on this concept an idea of a state and the relationship between the state and the individual. Mill believed that the individual is above the state and that the state exists to serve the individual.

1. Confucius, in contrast, believed that the government and its leaders should exercise benevolence toward ordinary people and that the state should play an important role in elevating ordinary people to morality. Confucius believed that few people were capable of being leaders and that they should be educated for that leadership role. The state should tax people in a fair fashion, and people were to live their lives under the beneficent rule of the state.

2. Machiavelli believed that people existed to serve the state and the leader. The qualities of leadership that Machiavelli described were necessary for the peace and prosperity of a nation. According to Machiavelli, the main goal of the leader should not be to help people but to maintain his power. In maintaining power, the leader would give the people reasonably prosperous lives. Machiavelli also believed that only a few people were qualified to be leaders.

3. In Plato's *Republic*, ordinary citizens possess the quality of moderation. Only a well trained few are capable of leadership.

4. Mill disagreed with all these ideas. He believed that the state should be as uninvolved in the lives of citizens as possible.

C. Mill believed that absolute freedom should rest on absolute freedom of thought and discussion. There must be complete freedom of the press, along with complete and unrestricted freedom of speech.

D. Mill believed that although words have the power to cause harm, state regulation can create far more serious problems. Regulation cannot be based on what a community believes to be appropriate or inappropriate. Mill cites the examples of Socrates and Jesus, who were put to death because they outraged public opinion. Although Socrates and Jesus went against public opinion, their beliefs did not harm people. Mill believed the individual should be free to expound ideas. The state could punish a crime, but not the idea that motivated the crime.

V. Many of Mill's ideas have relevance today.

A. Mill believed that society must be willing to tolerate eccentricity as long as it does not harm others. Mill asks where governmental intervention will stop after it begins.

B. He believed that governmental involvement in education presented a great danger to a free society. All education, he believed, should be private and should be the responsibility of the parents.

1. He believed that the only purpose of compulsory education by the state was to train citizens to do the bidding of the state: State education will not develop a conscience in its citizens and will remove conscience and values imparted by parents.

2. Although Mill did not support compulsory education, he believed that all people should read and write and that parents might be required to teach reading, writing, mathematics and certain facts.

3. According to Mill, government involvement in education means that the state will impose its values, perhaps in the form of national educational standards that ensure that every student knows the same things. By controlling educational credentials, the state effectively controls all aspects of education.

C. Mill opposed state regulation of drinking. A state mechanism to limit the drinking age had the potential for expansion. Mill believed that the state's ultimate aim is control, and any implement to achieve that control could create a police state.

D. Mill believed that taxes are dangerous. Taxes establish a mechanism that enables the state to control private life.

E. Mill believed that true liberal democracy will limit the role of government as far as possible. It will intervene to protect an individual who is being physically harmed and will have courts to ensure justice for those who are harmed, but giving the state the ability to intervene in the life of individual citizens is dangerous.

F. For the same reason Mill believed that allowing government to intervene in health matters is dangerous

G. Mill would argue that the reason we accept state intervention in our lives has to do with compulsory education which is designed to produce dutiful citizens. The state does not educate people in some noble, abstract, and eternal ideal of justice but in the name of government convenience.

H. Mill was opposed to Machiavelli and Plato in his defense of the right of the individual to live exactly as he chooses—in defense of what contemporary Americans view as the ideal today.

VI. *On Liberty* is a work of compelling intensity, which speaks across the ages.

Essential Reading:

Mill, *On Liberty*.

Supplementary Reading:

Mill, *Autobiography*.

Questions to Consider:

1. How does Mill's *On Liberty* fit into your definitions of *liberal* and *conservative*?

2. How do you think Mill would respond to some of our current debates, for example, on a national health care or abortion?

Lecture Twenty-Six—Transcript
John Stuart Mill, *On Liberty*

In our last lecture we continued our discussion of the idea of duty and responsibility, the duty and responsibility of a citizen. What do we mean by a "good citizen," or in the words of Socrates, a "just citizen?" We saw how, in the *Republic* of Plato, Plato—putting his ideas into the mouth of Socrates—defines the idea of justice for the individual within the framework of the larger concept of the state, of the *polis*. We wish to continue that theme in this lecture, looking at the 19th century and the liberal tradition of the relationship between the state and the citizen for there is much in Plato, and in the *Republic,* that worried 19th century thinkers, such as our figure, John Stuart Mill, in his work, *On Liberty*.

To them, to people such as Mill, Plato—for all his brilliance, was very disturbing. They saw Plato as reducing the ordinary citizen to the subjugation of the state. Even misleading the citizen in the name of a higher good was determined by only a very few people, these guardians.

Now, one thing we must always keep in mind in reading Plato is that, as a student of Socrates, he fully understood the role of irony, of teasing, in Socrates's dialogues. That is what made Socrates so engaging. In fact the great theologian and thinker of existentialist ideas, Soren Kierkegaard, wrote his doctoral dissertation on the concept of irony in Socrates. It is fundamental to an understanding of Socrates that he will say things, frequently, that are meant to be taken seriously, in the sense that they make you think. Unless something is put in a very forceful fashion, perhaps even as a complete opposite of what you believe, then people won't take it seriously. So he attacks the sophists again and again, as I made comparison of them with the professors. Socrates understood, just as I understand, that, in fact, the sophists were, like professors today, guardians of the truth; men with very open minds, who sometimes challenged convention in the name of educating their students as well as possible. But the very irony with which Socrates overlaid his portrait of these sophists led them to be discredited right down until the 19th century.

In the same way that the Athenian democracy put Socrates to death and so embittered his students, such as Plato, that they portrayed the Athenian democracy as the worst possible form of government. That is how it comes out in the pages of the *Republic* itself, when Plato traces the degeneration of an ideal state. The ultimate degeneration is democracy of the Athenian kind, where the individual is free to live as he chooses, without any restraints and, for the Athenians, this was not a bad comment. It was the celebration of their democracy, where Plato describes a democracy run amok, in which it is so multicultural and so diverse that he compares it to a great quilt that is of many, many colors, where people have such a sense of their rights that children do not obey their parents, that students do not obey their teachers, that even animals walk down the street and expect people to get out of the way because animals have rights. Now to us, that is not a very wrong description of a good democracy that is flourishing as it should. Where people are free to be individuals. But in judging that, we must always deal with the irony of Socrates and his desire to get us to sit up and think.

In fact, it would not be until the 19th century that not only were the sophists, true professors of intellectual freedom, but also the Athenian democracy would receive a fair hearing. It would be in England, and it would be in the minds that congregated around our figure, John Stuart Mill, that the Athenian democracy was first recognized, as Mill would say, as the first government to be based on the ideal of the greatest good for the greatest number of citizens. It was to be a very good form of government, which we should try to emulate in terms of its concern for the individual's freedom, and the freedom to live as you choose should be our definition of a modern, liberal democracy.

John Stuart Mill's *On Liberty* was published in 1859. It was one of the culminating points in the life of a truly great intellectual. He was raised to be an intellectual. His father was James Mill, closely associated with Jeremy Bentham in the Utilitarian Movement. That was the movement that set out actively to reform politics in Britain, to increase the franchise of the English voters, so that more and more people could vote, to create a democracy in England that rested upon the rights of the individual. They believed that the purpose of government was to achieve the greatest good for the greatest number of citizens. That would still be our definition today, don't you believe, "government of the people, by the people and for the people?" They also believed that the test stone of any quality or virtue or ethical principle was how well it worked, its usefulness not its abstract qualities, but how well it worked—its usefulness. Hence they were called the "Utilitarians."

From the time he was a baby, the father of John Stuart Mill, James Mill, wanted John Stuart Mill to be an intellectual. He wanted him to follow his father's philosophical ideals, and then, like his father, to put these into real practice by being a civil servant, by being part of the government. So, by the age of three, we are told by Mill in his *Autobiography*—which is a marvelous study of what he called his "mental progress"—his view that all through life you should keep growing intellectually. It is a very frank statement of some of his failures, as well as his ultimate progress. Mill tells us in his *Autobiography* that by the age of three, his father had taught him how to read Greek. Now, that seems astounding to us, and I never really believed it, until I read the letters of an early American classicist named Guildersleeve. Guildersleeve says that his father was a minister and home-schooled him, and he was never conscious of not knowing Greek. That was how early he had learned it, so it is possible. John Stuart Mill learned Greek, and by the time he was about eight he had read a good part of Classical literature. He had read Virgil and Homer and Tacitus and Livy and was helping his father by making summaries of his father's own writings. The elder Mill, like many home-schoolers in the 19th century, believed that one of the best ways to shape your mind was to summarize a Great Book to summarize it in a few pages. Then Mill went on, by the time he was a teenager, actively to help his father in terms of his father's writings and political thoughts.

At the age of twenty, he had a complete nervous breakdown, brought upon by overwork, but which he later saw simply as a failure of will, and he needed to be set back upon the right track. It was in reading a very mundane book that gave him the insight of what was going on with him and set him back upon the track that he wanted to follow. He became active in politics, in terms of pushing for reforms. He worked in the civil service. He became one of the leading intellectual lights of England in the 19th century. His books were discussed at Oxford. He wrote works on logic and political economy. He married, to Harriet Taylor, and she became, as she had been already before their marriage, his true intellectual companion. He talks about, in his book *On Liberty*, the powerful role that she had played in the writing and thinking about this work.

In *On Liberty* Mill, in the first pages, tells us exactly what he means by liberty, and it is worth quoting at some length. Mill tells us, "by 'liberty' I mean the belief that every individual should be free to live his life untrammeled by any other constraints insofar as he does not harm anyone else, and that the state has the right to interfere in a person's life only insofar as that individual is harming someone else in a concrete fashion." Now, that is the great traditional concept of liberty. We discussed it in our *History of Freedom*. It is the definition that the founders of our country would have accepted, and did accept as the ideal of liberty, the freedom to live as you choose, as long as you do not harm someone else.

Mill then goes on to build upon this concept, an idea of the state and the relationship of the state and the individual. In our ongoing dialogue, Mill is clearly on the side of the belief that the individual is above the state, in the sense that the state exists to serve that individual.

That was not the view of Confucius. Confucius believed that the government, the leaders, should act in a beneficial way, should exercise benevolence toward the ordinary people, but that the state had a very important role in elevating ordinary people to morality. Very few people, according to Confucius, should be leaders, and they should be those who were educated for that leadership role. The ordinary people just wanted to live. The state should tax them in a fair fashion. If the state had to lead them into war, it should be a just war, well explained to them; but the people were there to live their lives under the beneficent rule of the state.

Machiavelli turns that around. They are there to serve the state, and they are there to serve the leader. That's not a bad thing, for Machiavelli, and we must realize that in those qualities of the leader that Machiavelli described in our lecture, in *Il Principe*, in *The Leader*, these qualities are necessary if a nation is to have peace and be prosperous. It must have a strong leader, and that strong leader, it is sad to say, but it is a fact, will have to exercise these qualities in order to remain in power, and keep peace and prosperity. Now, his main goal should not be to help people. That's going to get him in trouble. His main goal should be to maintain power, but by maintaining power, he will give the people reasonable, prosperous lives.

Once again, for Machiavelli, like Confucius, only a very few people are qualified to be leaders. Democracy is not the goal of Machiavelli, and in Plato's *Republic*, the ordinary citizen has the quality of what? Moderation. They are content to live their lives with moderation. Only a very few, who are well trained, should be leaders.

For Mill, this is all wrong. It is all about the individual. The state should be as uninvolved as possible. How, then, do we put that into practice? That is what makes Mill so stimulating today. If we are going to have absolute individual freedom, then that freedom must rest on an absolute freedom of thought and discussion. There must be complete freedom of the press. There must be complete freedom to say anything that you want. We like to think that that is our goal, do we not? Nonetheless, there are things that you can say today, in our own society, that can harm other people, we believe. Words that you might use can harm someone. Mill says that may be true. They may harm people in the sense of hurting their feelings or even in creating an unjust climate for them, but for the state or society to intervene in that matter and to try to restrict freedom of speech in any way, is far more injurious. So you should be allowed to say anything that you wish, and so, too, every book should be allowed to be published, and every idea should be free. Well, you might say, what about pornography? Mill would say it's a terrible thing; however, for the state to try to intervene and set up laws that define what is appropriate, whether on—if he had it in his day—television or music, that again creates the far more serious problem.

What, you might ask, did Mill say about the opinion of the community? Should not the guide be what does the community feel to be inappropriate? Mill says, "You know, that has been tried before. The two greatest examples, he says, are Jesus and Socrates. Both of them lived in societies, which had a degree of freedom of speech. In fact, the Athenian democracy celebrated itself for its freedom of speech, and under the Roman Empire, individuals were free to say what they wanted to say. That was, again, one of the ideals on which Roman Emperors prided themselves. That was that individual liberty that was guaranteed by being under the rule of Caesar. Each one of these spoke words that did not harm anybody. Yet Socrates was brought up on trial for outraging the morality of the community. He taught gods that were different from the Athenian gods, and he corrupted the young. Thus he was put to death in a legal trial. "That's utterly wrong!" we say today, Mill tells us, but that is why he died. He outraged public opinion.

Jesus—he said he was the Son of God, the Messiah. Well, that outraged a significant body of public opinion, but did he harm anybody by saying that? Did he concretely go and harm anyone? "Well," you might say, "he was leading them away from their religious beliefs, the same way that Socrates had led Athenians away from their religious beliefs." "But did that harm them? Did that punch them in the nose and make them bleed?" Mill asked. It did not. "So if we want to learn from the examples of the past, we will say any idea, no matter how bizarre, how repugnant to us, ought to be allowed to be spoken, and there should be no punishment for it whatsoever." Punish a crime but not the idea that motivated that crime, he would tell us.

Moreover, we must be willing to tolerate eccentricity. Mill, like many English intellectuals had a great deal of eccentricity to him; he was a very eccentric person. He said, "You know, there is a person who walks down the street. They are dirty, and disheveled and they talk to themselves all the time. Should we take them in and forcibly restrain them? No. Again, even if somebody is an absolute minority of one, living a life that seems very bizarre to you, once again, as long as they do not go and punch somebody, then leave them alone. The very definition of a free society is the right of one person to have the most bizarre ideas, the most repugnant behavior, as long as it does not harm anyone else because once you step across that line, once government begins to intervene, then where does it stop?"

Well, we've followed Mill along with this and we don't see much to object to there. It seems like the way we live our lives through, but, he says, let's go on a little bit. What is the role of the government in terms of education? Because today, in 1859, we live in an age of increasing compulsory education. All over Europe and in the United State, we are learning from Prussia the value of a compulsory education to educate good citizens. We're learning words like "kindergarten", which comes from Prussia, so that we can begin at an early age to educate, because we do not want our children to grow up uneducated. How can they be good citizens? After all, the founders of our country believed, and said in the Northwest Ordinance, that education should be forever encouraged. They even set aside plots of public land so that there could be universities and schools, so the state has a very important role to play in education.

Mill says, "No it does not." That is the greatest possible danger to a free society, is to have the government involved in education. All education, if it exists at all, should be private, and entirely at the disposal of the parents. Because, according to Mill, the only purpose for compulsory education by the state is to turn out dutiful citizens who will do whatever they are told to by the state. They will become the slaves of the state, and that is the only reason that the state cares about educating them. It will not want to develop a conscience. In fact, it will do just the opposite. It will remove a sense of conscience from them. It will remove a sense of values that their parents might have imparted to them. It will remove any barrier between the control of the government and their thought.

Now, he said, of course it is important for people to learn how to read and write, and I would go only this far, he says, that the government might require of parents, that by a certain age, their child knows how to read and write. Maybe we could go so far as to say that they know how to do basic mathematics so that they can survive in society, and we can give them some basic facts, like, "there is a Constitution, and this is what is in the Constitution," but these must—and what you will appreciate—was that these must be multiple choice questions. Because once you get into any kind of interpretation, then the state is going to intervene and try to impose its values.

So if we do believe that children should receive some education, the parents themselves should be totally responsible for how that comes about, with the state only saying that by a certain age, that child needs to be able to read and write, and do multiplication and division and addition and subtraction, and perhaps know what is in the American Constitution or what is the British Constitution. That is it.

That is very far removed from our devotion to education today and our belief that the state should spend billions of dollars to have an educated citizen body. It is very different, and I'm not taking a stand on this issue, you understand, but it is very different from our idea of national standards. Not national standards about whether you can read or write, but national standards about interpretation of history, national standards that ensure that every student all over the country knows the same things. To Mill that would have only one purpose, again, I'm not taking a stand, but that would have only one purpose—of insuring an absolutely homogeneous citizen body that had learned everything from the state.

Mill would say, "Yes you allow home schooling, but nobody can progress in life unless they learn the things that are taught in schools. Nobody can go to a private school and not learn the things that are taught in the state-controlled schools if they are going to get into college." Without going to college, you're never going to have any kind of life in your country, so by controlling their credentials, the state effectively controls all aspects of education.

You might find his educational views disturbing. Let's take him another step. What about drinking? Alcoholism was a serious problem in the England of John Stuart Mill in 1859. Why, there were kids of five and six who would go in with a penny and buy a glass of gin and pour it off; they were already little alcoholics, and their lives were ruined. All around you were the results of the degradation brought about by alcoholism—the ruined families, the abused wives, what would lead, in our country, to Prohibition. It was a very great social ill. Mill says it is a social ill, but that the state has no business trying to control the consumption of alcohol. It is too bad if children of six want to drink. However, for the state to set up an apparatus to limit the age to drink is to create a mechanism for control that will expand to far greater limits. Because, believe me, the state really does not care about drunken children. What it wants is control, and any implement you put in place—this is John Stuart Mill speaking—to control in the name of a good, such as non-alcoholic children, will be used by it to create a police establishment that extends its tentacles far beyond alcohol, into all aspects of life—whether people smoke or not, whether they carry guns or not. All of this will then be controlled through this mechanism so better never to let it start. "Well, isn't there some way we can control alcoholic children? What if we make it impossible to get a penny glass of gin? What if we make it cost a dollar to get a glass of gin? Then those little kids can't beg on the street and then run in and buy a glass of gin."

No; even taxes are dangerous, because, once again, you are setting into place a mechanism by which the government controls. You are accepting the principle that the government has a role to control your private life, to control your health. So that is why, in a true liberal democracy, the government's role will be limited as far as possible. It will intervene to protect someone who has been physically harmed.

It will probably have courts to see that you receive justice if you are physically harmed or harmed in your property, but a broader interpretation of the right of society in the form of the government intervening in the private life of the individual is deeply dangerous. What would Mill think, for example, of seat belts, or anti-smoking laws?

Now we would say, yes, indeed, someone who smokes in a restaurant—and again, we are just deducing from John Stuart Mill; we're following his argument; we're not taking a stand on this, you understand—but someone would deduce from that if someone smokes in a restaurant, according to scientific evidence, that is harmful to you, the second-hand smoke. But Mill would intervene and say, "Well, that is not a physical harm that I can recognize. I distrust a science, based upon funding by the government, don't you see. This is how he would deduce that. How many of you have gone out and run those experiments and seen this effect? Now again, I am someone who has never smoked, and I'm not taking a stand on this, but we must challenge ourselves to think in the view of John Stuart Mill.

"Why," Mill would say to us, "if you are so worried about second-hand smoke, why do you, for example, still subsidize the growing of tobacco?" "Does that still exist?" we would ask. It certainly did exist at one point, when you were so vigorous in your attack upon smoking. Or why can a tax be collected from cigarettes, if the government is so concerned with your health? "No," Mill would say, "We must always go back to this fundamental issue—that government is something that exists only to serve the people, and the more limited its power, the better the people are."

Every attempt by a government to intervene in the name of your health or well being is dangerous. He would say, "What about your seat-belt laws?" Once again, you put on that seat belt, don't you, very, very dutifully and you click it and off you go. You are told that insurance rates will go up if everybody doesn't wear their seat belts. Mill would say this is the most specious of arguments—that your insurance rates will go up. You allow this infringement on your freedom in the name of a highly abstract possibility. Why do you so willingly accept all of this "intervention," Mill would say? It is, of course, because you have been educated in compulsory schools. For Mill the great danger was the very good idea of everybody being educated, but the result of this compulsory education, he has already warned, was just to make dutiful individual citizens. So that, from the moment you are in this kindergarten, you raise your hand in order to go to the bathroom. You are there for a large part of your day. You will learn exactly what is proscribed to you. You are taught to be obedient and dutiful. So from this greatest of good, educating the citizen body, you have created a nation in which everyone is willing to follow what they are told, taken to an extreme, not in our country, of course, but in an extreme. Have you not, Mill would say, done exactly what Plato told you you should do in terms of educating everybody, for his role in life, but not in the name of some noble, abstract and eternal idea of justice, but simply in the name of government convenience.

It's a very challenging book, John Stuart Mill. He stands absolutely opposed to Machiavelli or to Plato in his defense of your right to live exactly as you choose. In other words, in defense of what we say is our ideal today. It is a work that is of compelling intensity, despite its rather turgid language. I would say it is not written in a particularly noble style, but it has a very great theme—individual freedom and your duty to ensure that freedom, and it can, if you will sit down and let it be put into the context of your daily life today, speak across the ages.

Lecture Twenty-Seven
Sir Thomas Malory, *Morte d'Arthur*

Scope:

The totalitarian society of *1984* denies human love. Yet love, along with religion, may be the deepest wellspring of human feeling and the inspiration of its noblest literature and art. This was certainly true of medieval Europe. In both secular and religious life, love was elevated into a cult. Religious and carnal love, history and myth came together in the literary cycle of King Arthur and the search for the Holy Grail. King Arthur and his Knights of the Round Table, the love of Lancelot and Guinevere, and Sir Galahad and the Grail brought together the themes of chivalry, courtly love, and religious mysticism. Thomas Malory's *Morte d'Arthur* captures the passion, consequences, and contradictions of romantic and spiritual love. One of the first great works of English prose, it summarizes the civilization of medieval chivalry in its ideal form. The *Morte d'Arthur* has inspired poets as diverse as Alfred, Lord Tennyson and T. S. Eliot.

Outline

I. The lecture on John Stuart Mill concluded our discussion of the theme of government, justice, and the duty of a citizen toward that government.

    A. Our discussions of the role of government have ranged from the classical China of Confucius to the Renaissance Italy of Machiavelli, the England of John Stuart Mill, and the Athenian democracy of Plato's *Republic*.

    B. The lectures have described a fundamental dichotomy in how great books and great thinkers have approached the question of whether the individual exists to serve the state or whether the state exists to serve the individual. Profound minds are on both sides of the question.

        1. In the *Republic*, Plato says that the state exists to serve the individual, to make the individual just, but that the state must exercise control to achieve its aim.

        2. These lectures have tested whether a set of values exists to determine the character of a citizen who serves the state or is served by the state. Both Confucius and

Socrates spoke of fundamental values of wisdom, justice, moderation, and courage. John Stuart Mill presented a radical defense of the freedom of the individual and absolute refusal to accept any form of control.

    C. We now turn to what is perhaps the most radical of individual decisions. We leave the harsh strains of war and politics and move to the softer side of human nature, to the theme of love. Although Lord Acton asserted that religion and liberty were the causes for the greatest and worst acts in history, we might argue that love is really the cause.

II. Sir Thomas Malory's *Morte d'Arthur*, or "*The Death of Arthur*," summarizes the values of the Middle Ages.

    A. Malory was an English knight who served with distinction in the Hundred Years' War with France and was elected to Parliament.

    B. In 1459, he and a group of fellow knights beat up and robbed some monks.

    C. Malory was sentenced to jail, where he died in 1471.

    D. Malory used his time in jail to come to grips with the question of love and to write *Morte d'Arthur*.

III. *Morte d'Arthur* meets the definition of a great book.

    A. The theme, love, works on two levels; it deals with love and with the distinction between lust and true spiritual love.

    B. The work is written in noble language. It is the first long work of prose fiction in the English language.

    C. The story is a universal one. Each generation has new movies, new novels, and new comic books about King Arthur.

    D. *Morte d'Arthur* summarizes a culture—the world of the Middle Ages—at its apex.

        1. Dante's *Divine Comedy*, also written during the Middle Ages, focuses on love, but in the *Divine Comedy*, God's love, which will redeem Dante, is the true theme.

        2. For medieval society at the spiritual level, Christianity was the great religion of love. Gothic cathedrals, as previously mentioned, are a symbol of this idea of divine love. Malory composed *Morte d'Arthur* at the height of the Gothic era.

IV. King Arthur embodied the values of the Middle Ages, an era of great religious faith and marked by a code of chivalry and feudalism.

    A. The notions of trust and obligation were strong. Honor defined relations between people. Honor was a complex concept in which one had to have a reputation and a commitment to integrity and courage.

    B. This age was an era of courtly love. The object of love was frequently someone that the lover could not have; she was worshipped from afar. This ideal gives a sacred character to the courtly love of the Middle Ages. However, in reality, there was much seduction and infidelity. Carnal love plays a role in the story of King Arthur.

    C. King Arthur was a hero who came to epitomize England of the 15th century. In the story, he is a king who ruled the British Isles and became the emperor of Europe as well. In these tales, King Arthur and the Knights of the Round Table brought an age of justice and glory to England. This golden age was symbolized by the palace at Camelot.

    D. The story of King Arthur spread throughout Europe. Malory borrowed heavily from French works in his story of the death of King Arthur.

V. King Arthur actually existed.

    A. Arturus was a war leader in Britain in the dark days following the collapse of Roman rule, around 500 A.D.

    B. The Romano-Celtic population of Britain was being driven to the west by the Anglo-Saxons.

    C. For a brief period, the Roman Britains rallied and stopped the tide of the Anglo-Saxons in a series of battles.

    D. Arthur won a mighty battle over the Angles and Saxons at Mount Badon.

    E. A group of tales about King Arthur was kept alive by Celtic-speaking peoples. These legends began in Wales. Around King Arthur clustered a series of marvelous figures, including the magician Merlin, and wondrous events, including the story of the Holy Grail, an embodiment of salvation, which had been brought to England by Joseph of Arimathea.

VI. In *Morte d'Arthur,* Malory developed the story of the King Arthur of legend.

    A. King Arthur is the son of Uther Pendragon, a mighty ruler over the western part of the British Isles. He becomes infatuated with Igraine, the wife of the Duke of Tintagel. Merlin arranges for Uther Pendragon to assume the form of the duke of Tintagel and to be transported to the duke's castle. The duke is killed in battle, and Igraine marries Uther Pendragon. Their son is King Arthur, who is accepted as legitimate. Uther Pendragon dies.

    B. Arthur rides to an assembly in London. Word has gone out that the next king will be the man who can draw a great sword from a stone. Only the young Arthur can do so. The nobles agree that Arthur should be the king of England.

    C. A strange woman in a lake gives the sword Excalibur to Arthur. With that sword and his innate goodness, Arthur unifies Britain and the whole of Europe into one kingdom, with himself as emperor.

VII. Knights come to serve King Arthur at his capital city at Winchester, or Camelot. The knights sit at a round table because everyone is equal. King Arthur weds Guinevere. The knights serve the cause of good.

    A. The greatest of all the knights is Lancelot, who is brave, courteous, and bold. His only flaw is that he loves Queen Guinevere—and she loves him. Lancelot stays unwed to remain pure.

    B. On a journey, Lancelot arrives at the castle of King Pelleas, who says that he is a cousin of Joseph of Arimathea, the man who brought the Holy Grail to England. King Pelleas asks Lancelot to sleep with his daughter Elaine so that he will sire a son who will be the perfect knight. When Lancelot refuses, Pelleas changes his daughter's appearance so that she looks like Guinevere. Lancelot sleeps with Elaine and sires Galahad.

    C. Galahad truly is the perfect knight. He is raised by nuns, who eventually lead him to Camelot. He comes to the round table and moves to the one seat that has never been filled, the *Siege Perilous*. That seat had been designated for the person that God chose to find the Holy Grail. Anyone else who attempts to fill that seat will be struck dead immediately, but when Galahad sits in it, a chalice appears.

D. The knights decide that a young boy should not seek the Holy Grail by himself, and the entire Round Table sets off. Arthur is distraught. He believes that many of these men of honor, courage, and faith will die on this lonely journey.

E. After many months of travel, Lancelot comes to a tiny chapel in a far-off place and sees once again the vision of the chalice in his sleep. Lancelot's carnal love for Guinevere will prevent him from ever possessing the Holy Grail.

F. Galahad has remained pure, and with his friends Sir Perceval and Sir Bors, he continues his quest to find the Holy Grail. When they find it, they travel to Sarras, the city from which Joseph of Arimathea came, to return it.

G. Content to have achieved this goal, Galahad dies peacefully. Perceval stays with him and joins him in death. Sir Bors, after performing many wondrous deeds against the infidels, makes his way back to tell Arthur and Lancelot of these events and about Galahad's immediate ascension to heaven for his goodness.

VIII. In Camelot, as King Arthur foresaw, all is coming to ruin. Lancelot and Guinevere have been overcome by lust, and their affair is an open secret in the court. Arthur shuts his ear to these rumors.

A. Close advisers, such as Sir Modred, tell Arthur that he must show the world whether Guinevere is innocent or adulterous. Modred tells Arthur to test Lancelot by arranging a hunting trip. When Lancelot returns to Guinevere at nightfall, Arthur sees the truth. Guinevere and Lancelot go to Lancelot's castle, the Joyous Gard. Arthur, who has been shamed, must wage war against Lancelot. Lancelot leaves Britain.

B. Arthur, without Lancelot, faces the forces of revolt led by Modred. In a great battle between the forces of good, led by Arthur, and the forces of evil and rebellion, both Arthur and Modred are slain. As he is dying, Arthur requests that a knight throw his sword into the lake. When Arthur is told that a woman's hand reached up to take the sword, Arthur says that he can die.

C. According to Malory, many people believed that Arthur was taken away by queens to islands in the west, where he awaits the time when Britain needs him and he will return.

D. Lancelot and Guinevere regret all the misfortune their carnal love has caused. Guinevere becomes a nun and Lancelot, a monk, fasting and serving God until Lancelot learns that Guinevere has died. Lancelot can no longer eat or drink, and he wastes away and dies. He is buried by knights who fought beside him.

IX. This story of love, the search for the Holy Grail, becomes a story of redemption. Sinners, such as Lancelot and Guinevere, bring destruction to those they love. But God can take away their sin so that they die in peace. *Morte d'Arthur* is a great love story and a great religious story. The book speaks to the values of the Middle Ages—an era remote from us in both time and spirituality.

Essential Reading:

Malory, *Morte d'Arthur*.

Supplementary Reading:

Huizinga, *Waning of the Middle Ages*.

Matthews, *King Arthur, Dark Age Warrior, Mythic King*.

Weston, *From Ritual to Romance*.

Questions to Consider:

1. In the *Morte d'Arthur* is love portrayed as a positive or negative force? Is the difference that of pure, divine love or carnal love? How would you distinguish the two?

2. Do you regard love as one of the strongest forces motivating humans? Can you think of other instances, besides Marc Antony and the Duke of Windsor of public men or women who have thrown away everything for love? Does this have any relevance in your life?

Lecture Twenty-Seven—Transcript
Sir Thomas Malory, *Morte d'Arthur*

In our last lecture on John Stuart Mill and his great work, *On Liberty*, we brought to a conclusion our discussion of the theme of government, responsibility, and the duty of a citizen towards that government. I think we can draw several conclusions from that discussion, which ranged all the way from the Classical China of Confucius to the Renaissance of Machiavelli—his Italy and Florence—through John Stuart Mill and back to the Athenian democracy of Plato in the *Republic*. We saw a fundamental dichotomy in how great books and great thinkers have approached this question: Is the individual there to serve the state, or does the state exist to serve the individual? We found very profound minds on both sides of the question; and the more profound the mind the more difficult it is to place them. Because you might say that Plato in the *Republic* says, "Yes, the state is there to serve the individual, to make that individual just. But the state must exercise considerable control in order to make that person just."

We tested whether a set of universal values existed in determining the character of that citizen who serves the state or is served by the state, and we saw that both Confucius and Socrates spoke of these fundamental values of wisdom, justice, moderation and courage, as we continue in our pursuit of whether there are indeed universal values, accepted by all civilizations in all times. We saw with John Stuart Mill the radical defense of the freedom of the individual, the absolute refusal to accept any form of control. He was very disturbed, for example, that Plato wanted to banish poets like Homer from the republic, as immoral influences. Let the individual decide.

Our theme now is perhaps one of the most radical of individual decisions. It is love. Whom do you choose to love?

Now, I tell you, Lord Acton said that religion and liberty had been the reasons for the greatest and worst acts in all of history. I'm a great admirer of Lord Acton, but he was wrong. Love. Love is the greatest cause for good events and bad events. And while every one of us, on a regular basis, must deal with our government, and from time to time even with our conscience—if we have one—all of us deal every day with the question of love. Someone we loved once, still married to; someone we're married to we still love; someone we would like to have married; somebody that we really do not like.

There they are, love and hate. And, it has been the subject of very great literature.

Oh my goodness. We could do a Teaching Company course just on great love poetry and great love novels. We could take the *Romeo and Juliet*, or we could have looked at the *Aeneid* just from the point of view of Dido, that tremendous love story in which the dutiful Aeneas must say, "No, No," to Dido, and go on with his task of founding Rome.

I have chosen instead to look at the wonderful summary of the values of the Middle Ages that is *Le Morte d'Arthur*, *The Death of Arthur*, by Sir Thomas Malory. In the next lecture we will look at the summary of the values of the Enlightenment in what is, in one fashion, a love poem: Goethe and *Faust*.

But to Sir Thomas Malory. He was an English knight. He served with distinction in the Hundred Years' War in France, serving under the Earl of Warwick, and by the patronage of the Earl of Warwick, was elected to Parliament. But in 1459, he fell afoul of life. He and a group of fellow knights broke into a monastery, beat up the monks and robbed them. He was thrown into jail. And such were his crimes that when most of them were pardoned, he stayed on, and finally died in 1471, still in jail. But he used his time in jail as Socrates would, or as Solzhenitsyn did, to come to grips with a fundamental question. For him, it was love, and the magnificent story of King Arthur and the Knights of the Round Table.

Malory's book is a great book. It has a great theme and a theme that moves on two levels. Love, but the distinction between lust and true spiritual love, between carnal love and the love of the spirit. Moreover, it is written in noble language. It is the first lengthy work of fiction in the English language in prose, and it is a vigorous prose. It shows the foundation being laid for the English of the King James Version of the Bible. But above all, it is universal. The story of King Arthur in each generation awakens new movies, new novels, new comic books, all manner of heroes to be thought about and to be integrated into our culture and society.

But more than that, it summarizes a culture at its apex, and that is the world of the Middle Ages. We saw that Dante's *Divine Comedy* does this, and the focus of Dante is on love, the love of God that will redeem Dante. For medieval society at the spiritual level,

Christianity was the great religion of love. What is our passage? John 3:16: "For God so loved the world that he gave his only-begotten Son, that whosoever believeth in him shall not perish, but shall have everlasting life." That is love. Gothic cathedrals, as we saw when we discussed Dante, are embodiments to this idea of divine love, which transports your soul out of your self, and up to the light of God. The same way that when you stand in a Gothic cathedral you cannot look at the ground. Your eyes must go up to the light pouring through the windows. And the rose window of a Gothic cathedral is itself a symbol of God's love, as shown through the rose, the flower that is the symbol of love, and through the light pouring through.

Thomas Malory composes his great love story at the very height of the Gothic age. And even the dank prison cannot overwhelm his creative spirit as he tells the story, because, Arthur himself was an embodiment of the values of the Middle Ages, for it was not only an age of deep religious faith, but also an age of chivalry, of knights and their ladies fair. Chivalry, feudalism, they gave the essence to the Middle Ages, this notion of trust and obligation. The knight who receives his land from his king and is bound to serve that king in trust and in honor. It was an age in which honor defined a code of relations between men and between men and women. Your word was all that counted, and honor was a complex nexus, as it was in the time of the *Aeneid*, in which you had to have a reputation and a commitment to integrity, courage, and you receive this both from the outside by people recognizing that reputation, and from within. So, courage and honor.

It was an age of courtly love. When you weren't fighting wars and battles, you loved to hear minstrels sing tales of love. In fact, it was the great Frederick II, the "wonder of the world" he was called, King of Naples in southern Italy, who first composed poetry in the Italian language in the form of love songs. So, a king taking time from his duties to write about love.

The object of your love was frequently someone you could not have. It was the lady fair who was already married, and so you poured your heart out to her, this object to be worshiped from afar. Remember who guides Dante through Heaven. It's Beatrice. Has she ever been his mistress? No! He has worshiped her only from afar. So this gives it in itself a kind of a sacred character to the courtly love of the Middle Ages.

However, it wasn't always just worshiping from afar. There was a great deal of infidelity. If you could, you seduced the lady fair, and this notion of carnal love plays its role in the story of Arthur. For Arthur, the great hero who came to summarize the England of the 15th century, who, as King of England ruled over not only the whole of the British Isles, but was emperor of Europe, as well. Arthur, who with his knights of the Round Table brought an age, never to return for years to come, of justice and glory to England, a golden age, symbolized by his great palace at Camelot. All of this was captured by Sir Thomas Malory in his story of *The Death of Arthur*, borrowing very heavily upon French works. Arthur spread all over Europe, and some of the greatest songs about Arthur and tales and poetry were created in France. He lives in Spain, Italy and Germany.

Who was Arthur, in fact? He was, just like the Agamemnon of the *Iliad*, a real person. There was an Arturus who was a war leader in Britain in those dark days following the collapse of Roman rule. In fact, the *Morte d'Arthur* of Sir Thomas Malory dates the time of Arthur to around 500 A.D. And we know, from very fragmentary sources, that in 500 A.D., Roman Britain, having been deserted by the Romans, the Celtic population—the people who had been there before the Romans came, whom we might call Romano-Celtic because they still kept their Celtic language, but also spoke Latin, were being driven far to the west by the invading Anglo-Saxons, those very people we met when we talked about *Beowulf*—for one brief period, the Roman Britons rallied, and in a series of battles, stopped the tide of Anglo-Saxon conquest. This even shows some justification in the archeological record.

The legend lived on. It lived on—centered around—one great figure: Arthur. Who, at the battle of Mount Badon, won a mighty victory over the Angles and Saxons and held them up for that brief period of time.

Arthur. A mighty war leader. A duke in battle. Perhaps even having the title of king. That is a real figure, around which then grew a series of tales, kept alive by this Celtic-speaking people. And it is in the west of the British Isle, what we call Wales, that the Arthurian legend had its beginning, even as he would be born in the west of England at Tintagel, in the land of Cornwall.

So Arthur was a real person. But as with Agamemnon, around him clustered a series of marvelous events and marvelous figures, like Merlin, the magician, the wonder-worker, and the story of the Holy

Grail—it, too, an embodiment of the search of the Middle Ages for salvation, the cup and dish out of which Jesus ate and drank on the Thursday of Passover, the Holy Grail. Brought, as legend would tell it, from the Holy Land to Britain, by Joseph of Arimathaea, who himself became a wonder worker, a miracle worker, bringing that Holy Grail to England, to Britain, where it would center around the monastery at Glastonbury.

What is the tale of Arthur as Thomas Malory gives it to us? He is the son of Uther Pendragon, a mighty warrior king who is ruler over the western part of the British Isle, and conceives an infatuation for the wife of the duke of Tintagel. Igraine is her name. The tale of Arthur begins with carnal love. The duke wants her. So does Uther Pendragon. Neither one of them wants to give up this beautiful lady, so Merlin intervenes and he transports Uther Pendragon to the castle of the duke of Tintagel while the duke is away, and has Uther Pendragon assume the form of the duke of Tintagel so his wife doesn't know it's not her husband she's sleeping with. And all this time that Uther Pendragon is there, the duke of Tintagel is being killed. In fact, he is killed three hours before his wife embraces Uther Pendragon in the form of her husband. So Arthur is not a bastard, don't you see? Now, take this on faith—and having discovered this, the lady is quite willing now with her husband dead to marry Uther Pendragon.

Thus, Arthur is born. The father explains everything to all of his knights in waiting, and they, too, accept that Arthur is a real, legitimate king. When Uther Pendragon dies, Arthur is raised by wards, and grows up to be a sturdy young man, and one day they are riding to an assembly in London, and the word goes out that the next king of England will be whosoever can draw this great sword out of a mighty stone. All the nobles of England try to draw that sword out of the stone, but only this young boy, Arthur, achieves it. The great knights can't believe this. This happens at Christmastime. They say, "Let's come back later." Once again, Arthur alone can draw it out. "Well, let's come back at Easter time." Once again, Arthur draws it out and no one else can. "Let's come back at Pentecost." Once again, Arthur draws it out. Finally they agree that Arthur must be king of England.

And so, with a miracle, the king is born. With a miracle the king assumes his power and even assumes his sword. That sword is not the sword that will follow him. It is a new sword—Excalibur—that is given to him by a strange woman, in a lake far away in the west.

Excalibur—"cut steel"—will be the sword of Arthur, and with that sword and with his innate goodness he unifies first Britain and then the whole of Europe into one great kingdom. He is emperor over it, and from his capital city at Winchester, or Camelot, the knights come to settle and to serve him around their great table—round, because everyone is equal there.

He weds the beautiful Guinevere. Out of love he cherishes her. So there is the age of Camelot as it flourishes, and of all those knights who are gallant serving Arthur always in the cause of good. Riding through the world on great errands—to save maidens who are attacked by dragons, save maidens who are in boiling pots, save maidens who were imprisoned unjustly. Always treating them with justice and kindness. Of all of these, the greatest of all the knights is Lancelot. Lancelot is the perfect knight. Brave, courteous and bold. He has only one flaw: He loves Queen Guinevere. He loves the wife of his sovereign. And you know what? She loves him, too. Their love reaches out across the boundaries of marriage, Lancelot himself staying unwed to keep himself pure for his lady fair.

On one of his journeys, he is riding and he comes to a strange castle. He enters that castle. It is ruled over by King Pelleas. And in this never-never land, Lancelot asks King Pelleas, "Who are you?" and Pelleas says, "You know, I am cousin—first cousin, as a matter of fact—to Joseph of Arimathaea." "Joseph of Arimathaea, who served our Lord?" "Yes. He is my first cousin." "Oh." Well, you don't wonder that that's 450 years later, because Joseph of Arimathaea, like all of these men, lives to miraculous ages. King Pelleas says, "You know what? I would like you to sleep with my daughter, Elaine." "Oh, no. I keep myself pure for one whose name I cannot speak." "Yes, but just sleep with her. I don't care. You don't have to marry her, because the son that you will sire upon my daughter will be the perfect knight." "No. No, no. I will not do it. But thank you for the offer anyway."

King Pelleas, by his magic, transforms his daughter Elaine, to look like Guinevere, and Lancelot does not seem surprised when she appears in his bed that night. So perhaps his love is not quite as pure as we think of it. Anyway, thinking he is sleeping with Guinevere, he does, and goes away happy the next morning. And from her—Elaine—is born Galahad. He truly is the perfect knight. He is raised by nuns; and he appears at Camelot, led by nuns, and comes into the great chamber where the Round Table is—and you know, in Winchester, you can still see something that they claim is the Round Table. And there he moves towards the one seat that has never been filled: the Siege Perilous, the dangerous chair. The only person who dares to sit in there is the one who is chosen by God to find the Holy Grail, to go out on that mission and achieve it. Anyone else will be struck dead immediately. And a young boy goes and… "Don't sit there! Don't sit there!" But he sits down, and suddenly there appears just fluttering through the air, a chalice, and wings of an angel over it, and then it disappears.

But all have seen this vision of the Holy Grail, and they lift up the curtain that surrounds the Siege Perilous, and read on it, "450 years after the death of our Lord, Galahad will begin his quest for the Holy Grail."

But you are warriors and knights, and men of honor. Why leave it to a boy to achieve this great gift? So the whole of the Round Table now sets off to see if they cannot find the Holy Grail. And Arthur? Arthur, he is completely distraught. "This is the end," he says, "of the Round Table. So many of you," he says in truth, "will never come back. You will die on this lonely errand." But off they go, because they are men of honor and courage and deep faith.

And Lancelot goes with them; Galahad goes with them, carrying a shield that was originally pure white, and now bears a red cross, a red cross from the blood that flowed from the nose of Joseph of Arimathaea. He made the cross upon it. And so they go in pursuit, Lancelot and his son pursuing together the Holy Grail. Together for six months they ride on a boat, in a deep and dark and empty sea. They part again, and Lancelot continues his quest alone. He comes to a far-off place—for all of this is in a never-never world; a world that once was and never will be again; or never was and may be again— he comes to a tiny chapel in a far-off place and goes inside, and there falls asleep. And in his sleep, once again, this chalice comes to him, this plate and cup. Out of it he sees a baby arise, and he can reach out and almost touch that cup. He asks, "What is this?" And the voice answers, "It is the cup out of which our Lord, to whom you are devoted, partook that Last Supper." "Let me have it!" "No. You cannot. You are a noble knight, but you have this eternal sin, and you know what it is." He wakes up, and of course he knows what it is. It is his carnal love for Guinevere, and that will prevent him from ever seeing and holding and possessing the Holy Grail. He can only catch it from a distance, in a dream.

But Galahad. He is pure, and has kept himself for this. And with two friends, Sir Percival and Sir Bors, Galahad continues this quest. He will find the Holy Grail. It will be shown to him. And not only will he be able to hold it in his hands, but he will see the figure of Christ rise out of that chalice, his hands still bleeding, his feet still bleeding; the wound in his side still fresh. Christ himself will give him, Galahad, to partake of our Lord's own blood and flesh.

And these two, Percival and Bors, accompany Galahad far off to the East, to the city of Sarras, whence came Joseph of Arimathaea. And there, in a great shrine of gold and jewels, Galahad will put back the Holy Grail. And so content is he at having achieved this, that he is happy now to die, and he passes away. His friend Sir Percival stays with him there, and in a short time joins Galahad in death. Sir Bors, after performing many a wondrous deed against the infidel, the Turks, makes his way back to tell Arthur what has happened, and to tell Lancelot of the death of his son, but his immediate ascension into heaven for his goodness.

But in Camelot, as Arthur foresaw, all is coming to ruin. Lancelot and Guinevere have allowed their lust to overcome them. Their affair has become the open secret of the entire court. Everyone knows about it but Arthur. And he, trusting in his wife, shuts his ears to any ill-fated rumors. But the rumors circulate again and again and again, until finally, he is told by close advisors like Sir Modred, jealous and envious of Arthur and of Lancelot, "You must, you must show to the world that your Guinevere is innocent. You must figure a way to prove it, or prove to yourself what we all know: That she is false to you and an adulteress. Go out on a hunting trip. Take Lancelot and all of us with you." It is the merry month of May, when people are most vigorous in their lives. "Go out hunting, and tell Guinevere you will not be back for several days. See what happens."

Arthur feels that he must put his wife to this test. So he lets her know and they go off hunting, and no sooner does night fall than the lusty Lancelot rides back in a hot fever to Guinevere and enters into her chamber. Arthur comes back and discovers the truth. Guinevere and Lancelot go off together. They stay together a few happy moments in his castle, the Joyous Gard—the Joyous Castle—and there they enjoy their forbidden love. But Arthur, now shamed, must wage war against Lancelot. Lancelot must leave Britain and go far off to Europe, and Arthur now, without Lancelot at his side, faces rebellion and revolt, led by Sir Modred.

In a great battle, the armies of Arthur, the armies of good, clash with the armies of rebellion and evil and Sir Modred. Both Arthur and Modred are slain. As he lies dying, Arthur says, "Take my sword, Excalibur. Take it to the lake and throw it in and come back and tell me what happens." And the knight comes back and says, "I threw it in and there was nothing but waves and water." "No! You didn't do it! Do it again!" "I threw it in. Nothing but waves and water, I tell you." "You've still got it. Throw it in. Come back." "An arm of a woman came up and grabbed that sword and pulled it under." "Now I can die."

But did he die? Malory says there are many who say that Queens from the West took him away, far out to the islands, far, far in the sea, and there he still awaits a time when Britain will need him. He will come back.

Hic iacet Arthurus, Rex Quondam Rexque Futurus. "Once king, and he will be king again."

Lancelot and Guinevere, repenting of all that their carnal love has caused, become a nun and a monk. Fasting. Serving their Lord. 'Til Lancelot hears the word that Guinevere has died. He goes, takes his beloved—her corpse—and leads her in a religious procession back to Glastonbury, where, some men say, Arthur is buried. And at last lays her down there, besides the grave of the king they both loved so much.

After that, he no longer can eat or drink. He has no joy in anything, except to pray and to waste away, and to die. To be buried by those knights who once fought beside him so gallantly. So, this tale of love, this search for the Holy Grail becomes, ultimately, a story of redemption. The fact that you have sinned very, very greatly, like Lancelot and Guinevere, caused great trouble and destruction to those you loved. But God, in the teaching of the Middle Ages, can take away all of that sin. And so, they died in the peace of God.

It is a great love story. It is a great religious story. It is a book that profoundly speaks to the values of that Middle Age, so remote from us in time and in spirituality.

Lecture Twenty-Eight
Johann Wolfgang von Goethe, *Faust*, Part 1

Scope:

Goethe ranks with Shakespeare and Dante as one of the three supreme geniuses of European literature, comparable to Homer and Vergil from classical antiquity. Goethe's genius was the most far ranging of all: poet, novelist, statesman, philosopher, and natural scientist. Throughout his long and highly productive creative life, Goethe grappled with the figure of Faust, the medieval searcher for wisdom who sold his soul to the devil. The first part of *Faust* was published in 1808. In it, Dr. Faust appears like the Oedipus in Sophocles's tragedy *Oedipus the King*. Faust is man intent upon knowledge at any cost. He will explore the whole of human experience, moving beyond all ordinary constraints of morality and religion. He will become like God, "knowing good and evil." His tragic destruction of Gretchen is the triumph of supreme egotism over conscience.

Outline

I. Love—both spiritual and carnal—is the theme of *Morte d'Arthur* by Thomas Malory.

   A. *Morte d'Arthur* epitomizes the ideals of the Middle Ages. It was published after the death of Malory, in 1471. William Caxton, the first major figure in English publishing, was its editor.

   B. The theme of love is crucial to any discussion of great books and great themes. Love is a power that rules everyday affairs.
   1. Early Greek thinkers believed that the force of love brought the world into being.
   2. Dante concludes *The Divine Comedy* by referring to the love that moves the universe.
   3. In *Morte d'Arthur*, Lancelot allows his love for Guinevere to distract him from his great goal, seeking the Holy Grail. The work asks whether we sometimes pursue what is irrelevant and let slip our great missions in life. *Morte d'Arthur* also has a theme of redemption: Lancelot made mistakes but was redeemed, although

England was destroyed and King Arthur's Camelot was gone.

   4. Love is also a theme in *Faust*, by Johann Wolfgang von Goethe.

II. Goethe, who lived from 1749 to 1832, is the genius of German literature. He is seen as the embodiment of the Age of Enlightenment, as well as the Romantic Age that followed it.

   A. Goethe was well educated and fluent in Greek and Latin. He showed the love of classics that was a hallmark of the Enlightenment.

   B. Europeans of the 18th century believed that Europe was freeing itself from the shackles of the wars of religion and the Middle Ages.

   C. Enlightenment thinkers believed that the man was a rational creature, and reason was key to man's advance. The idea of progress was the hallmark of the Enlightenment.

   D. The era was an age of enlightened despots, such as Maria Theresa of Austria. A well-intentioned absolute ruler, it was believed, could give his or her subjects the greatest benefits and ensure true freedom for individuals to live their lives as they chose.

   E. The spirit of the Enlightenment is embodied in the U.S. Constitution, which is a rational document and does not mention God.

   F. Many thinkers of the Enlightenment believed that God had made the world, but men and women made their own destinies.

III. Goethe became the supreme representative of the Enlightenment.

   A. He was a notable and influential civil servant of the duke of Weimar.

   B. He was a scientist who conducted original research into the theory of color.

   C. He was traveler, who wrote his observations, for example, on Italy.

   D. He was also a poet of supreme lyrical ability, as well as a playwright.

E. He was the most admired intellectual of his day, in an era that lionized intellectuals.

IV. Throughout his life, Goethe grappled with the story of Dr. Faustus.

   A. Dr. Faustus was a real person who lived in Germany at the time of Martin Luther, probably between 1480 and 1540.

   B. Dr. Faustus had a reputation for not just wisdom but magical wisdom.

   C. A legend grew that he had sold his soul to the devil to acquire knowledge.

   D. He was portrayed in Punch-and-Judy–type shows that featured him in fights with the devil. These shows also dealt with the theme of ambition and the desire for knowledge.

V. The first part of Goethe's *Faust*, the subject of this lecture, was published in 1808.

   A. Like the biblical Book of Job, *Faust* begins in heaven with God and the devil. The devil is an erudite man of the world who pays reverence to God. God tells the devil that he has given humanity free will, which enables people to make choices. The devil questions this freedom and gains God's permission to take possession of Faust's soul if he succeeds in tempting Faust.

   B. In the next scene, we meet Faust, a professor of great repute, learned in theology, medicine, law, Greek, and Latin. He laments that all he has learned in his studies is that man knows nothing. He would give anything for true wisdom.

   C. Faust rejects the biblical concept "In the beginning was the word." For him, the act, not the word, was the beginning.

   D. Faust decides that the only act that has meaning to him is suicide, but he defers his suicide when he hears the bells of Easter.

   E. The next day, Faust and Wagner, his research assistant, are out walking and encounter a poodle. When Faust and the poodle return to Faust's study, the poodle transforms into a scholar. He announces that he is the devil and says that he can bring meaning to Faust's life.

F. Faust declares that he wants really to live. Instead of studying, he wants money and women. The devil makes the bargain for Faust's soul in return for giving the professor everything that he wants; he has Faust sign a contract in blood.

G. After a visit to a wine cellar, Faust wishes for true love with a woman who loves him in return. He has set his eye on Margaret, or Gretchen, a pure young woman. The devil encourages Faust to seduce Gretchen and plants jewels in her room. Gretchen keeps the jewels although she knows that she should not.

H. The devil gives Faust a sleeping potion for Gretchen's mother, to get her out of the way while Gretchen and Faust make love. Gretchen gives the sleeping potion to her mother, but the potion kills her.

I. Gretchen's brother returns, and the devil kills him.

J. The devil advises Faust to abandon the pregnant Gretchen.

K. While Faust and the devil are celebrating at a wild revel, Gretchen is imprisoned on charges of murdering her mother and the baby.

L. Faust wants to return to Gretchen, but the devil insists that Faust is powerless to prevent her death and has no responsibility in the matter.

M. Faust returns to Gretchen, who has become insane. The devil tells Faust that he is guilty as an accessory to the murder of Gretchen's mother, baby, and brother. He reminds Faust of the contract and that Faust will die a sinner. Faust leaves with the devil and Gretchen is executed.

Essential Reading:

Goethe, *Faust*, Part I.

Supplementary Reading:

Sharpe, *Cambridge Companion to Goethe*.

Questions to Consider:

1. Would you sign a pact with the devil?

2. Does Gretchen deserve any blame?

Lecture Twenty-Eight—Transcript
Johann Wolfgang von Goethe, *Faust*, Part 1

In our last lecture we discussed the theme of love—spiritual love and carnal love—and looked at the great book *Le Morte d'Arthur*, of Sir Thomas Malory, that great embodiment of the ideals of the Middle Ages that came out after the death of Malory in 1471. It was edited and brought to fruition by the very interesting figure of William Caxton, who was the first major figure in English publishing.

The theme of love is, I think, crucial to any discussion of great books and great themes. We have talked about how love is a power that rules our own every day affairs, and early Greek thinkers believed that the world was brought into being by the force of love. Dante concludes his magnificent *Divine Comedy* by referring to the love that moves the universe. Love has power, power in our daily lives. We learned that from Sir Thomas Malory, but perhaps we also learn—because I always think you should take these great books and ponder the great themes that they raise, but also relate them to your own life. What is the story of Lancelot and Guinevere really about? Didn't Lancelot allow his love for Guinevere, which he did not choose—we very frequently do not choose the people we love, isn't that right, we don't know why we love them—but he loved Guinevere and she loved him, but that allowed him to be distracted from what was his great goal in life, which was the Holy Grail. In our own lives, I think we should, from time to time, ponder—are we pursuing something that really doesn't matter in the long run, and may even be bad for us, and letting slip our great, unique mission in life? That's what happened to Lancelot.

With it was the theme of redemption. He made all of these bad mistakes, but he died redeemed. In the meanwhile, England had been destroyed, and Arthur's Camelot passed away.

Love is also our theme in our next great book; Goethe's *Faust; Faust* by Johann Wolfgang von Goethe is truly a great book. It takes its place right there with *The Iliad*, the *Aeneid*, the *Divine Comedy*. Goethe, like Shakespeare for the English and like Dante for the Italians, is the German set apart from all the other mighty figures in their literary history. He is truly a genius, a universal genius. Goethe, who lived between 1749 and 1832; in other words he was both the embodiment of the Age of the Enlightenment and of the Romantic Age, which came in the wake of the French Revolution. His was a long and distinguished life, such as few of us can ever hope to attain. He was very well educated. He came from reasonable circumstances, very well educated, fluent early on in Greek and Latin. He imbibed that love and admiration for the classics that was a hallmark of the Age of Enlightenment, the 18th century. The age in which Europe felt that it was freeing itself from the shackles of the wars of religion, freeing itself from the shackles of the Middle Ages in which the human mind—reason alone—should decide matters. Man was a rational creature, and by employing that reason, man and woman could always move upward. It was an age that believed in progress, that the world was better in the 18th century than it had ever been before. That there was more freedom in the 18th century than there had ever been before. It was an age of enlightened despots, like Maria Theresa of Austria or King George of England wanted to be, who believed that a well-intentioned absolute ruler could do the greatest benefits for their subjects, and ensure true freedom – that is, the freedom of the individual to live as they choose.

The Age of the Enlightenment is embodied in our Constitution, which is a rational document. It does not mention God, and for many thinkers of the Enlightenment, God had made the world, wound it up like a clock, and then stepped back from it; men and women made their own destiny.

Goethe was educated in this Age of the Enlightenment and became its supreme representative. Early on, he went into the service of the duke at Weimar, one of the many local potentates in the principalities of Germany. Germany in those days was divided, it was said, into 365 little principalities, one for each day of the year, and at Weimar, Goethe became a very notable, influential civil servant. In fact, he was really the ruler of Weimar, the duke doing about everything he told him to do. He had a very busy everyday life, looking into the economic resources of the dukedom and looking into all manner of military questions. At the same time, he was a scientist, and a scientist who was universally admired in Europe, making very original researches for the time into the theory of color. He was a traveler. And his prestige allowed him to travel in grandeur and write observations, for example, on Italy.

He was a poet, a poet of supreme lyrical ability. He was also a playwright. He came to be admired as no intellectual was in Europe of the day, and it was an age that admired intellectuals. It was the age of Montesquieu and Diderot, a very great age, and he was the supreme intellectual of the time. People came from all over, just to say that they had talked with Goethe.

All through his life, he grappled with but one theme; probably from the time he was a boy. He had seen, in the marketplaces, what we would call Punch and Judy shows—little puppets—of Doctor Faust or Doctor Faustus. Dr. Faust was a real person. He had lived in Germany at the time of Martin Luther, probably between 1480 and 1540, and he had achieved an enormous reputation as a man, not just of wisdom, but also of magical wisdom. The story grew that Faust was so smart and so knowledgeable and learned so much because he had sold his soul to the devil to acquire knowledge. So you would see, as you were walking along with your mother or father, evil roles and things, the devil come out and have a big fight with Faust there on the puppet stage. It was an engaging theme, because it was also about ambition, was it not? It was about the desire for knowledge and wisdom, and the supreme ambition of Faust had been to know everything. The English playwright of great, great ability, Marlowe, wrote a tragedy on Faust.

Goethe kept coming back to this theme, because he was a man who really wanted to know everything and seemed to have every success in life. In 1808 he brought out the first part of *Faust,* which he had long been working on, the first part of the *Tragedy* of *Faust.* We will discuss this work of genius in two lectures. Part one, the *Faust*, and then we will devote a second lecture to Part Two. The second part was not published until 1831. As with any genius, we can trace the marvelous spiritual and mental progress of Goethe.

In 1808, the first part of *Faust* was brought out, and it really begins like the *Book of Job*— in heaven, with God and the Devil walking back and forth. Now, the Devil here is not a cloven-hoofed monster, though he can be. He is a very erudite man of the world. Picture him in his knee-britches and wig, walking up and down with God, to whom he pays great reverence.

"You know, I continue to look out on the human race that you created, and they're a pitiful bunch. They're like a bunch of grasshoppers to me, hopping all around and never getting anywhere." "No, no," says God, "You misunderstand them." This was a civilized conversation between absolute good and absolute evil. "No, you misunderstand them. Men want to achieve, and as long as men and

women are striving, as long as they are trying to do something—
they'll make mistakes—but the striving is what's important. That's
why I've given them free will." "Ah, yes, free will. What does that
really amount to? Do you really give them free will?" "I do; they can
make any choice they want. Do you know Faust?" "Doctor Faustus?"
says the Devil, "Yes I do." "A very learned man." "He is." "Why
don't you go and see him? If there were one human I would want
you to get to know something about, it is Faust." "Can I do anything
I want to with Faust?" "Of course you can." "Could I have his soul if
he agreed to give it to me?" "Well, yes, if he agreed to give it to you.
He's got free will." "Thank you, so much."

Next scene, then, is Faust in his chamber. Now, he's a professor, a
professor of great repute. His father has been a very distinguished
doctor of medicine, and Faust is learned in a whole range of subjects:
theology, medicine, law, Greek and Latin; all of these he has studied.
He is in his chamber. Picture a Gothic chamber. Picture a table
scattered with scientific apparatus, like a retort and things lying
around, and a skull. There is Faust, all alone, dressed in his scholar's
garb. Once I was honored to be at the 900th anniversary of the
University of Bologna. I was representing my university, and there
were rectors, you know, presidents from universities all over Europe.
The rector of the University of Leipzig looked like a magician. He had
this big, high-pointed hat, this long flowing robe with stars on it, and
this huge necklace around him. That was their medieval garb. So that's
how Faust would have been dressed, as a wise man, and he is sitting
there, thinking to himself, and just to give you a touch of the original:

> *Habe nun, ach! Philosophie,*
> *Juristerei und Medizin,*
> *Und leider auch Theologie*
> *Durchaus studiert, mit heißem Bemühn.*
> *Da steh ich nun, ich armer Tor,*
> *Und bin so klug als wie zuvor!*
> *Heiße Magister, heiße Doktor gar*
> *Und ziehe schon an die zehen Jahr'*
> *Herauf, herab und quer und krumm*
> *Meine Schüler an der Nase herum—*
> *Sehe, daß wir nichts wissen können!*
> *Das will mir schier das Herz verbrennen*

"You know, here I am. I have studied philosophy. I have studied law. I have studied medicine. I have even studied theology. I have for ten years been a teacher. I have pulled my students around by their nose, trying to get them to learn. Pointing out that one corner and trying to get them to see the other three corners, and I'm going to tell you one thing: all I have learned is that we cannot learn anything. We don't know anything, and that is just eating me out. It's just gnawing at me. I would give anything for true wisdom."

Suddenly there's a knock on the door. "Sir!" "Oh, my gosh, it's my research assistant. What do you want, Wagner?" "Sir, I heard you in here speaking late at night. I thought you were reciting a Greek tragedy. I so want to read Greek tragedies with you." "Well, maybe I was reading a comedy." "Oh! I'd like to read comedies, too. I understand that even a preacher can learn from a comedian." "If the preacher himself is a comedian, perhaps." "Sir, please let me study more with you. I know a lot already," says Wagner, the research assistant. "I want to know everything." "Ah, don't we all. Well, we will. We will read that tragedy together, but right now, please, I have some things to do. Please excuse me." "All right, but you will be back in touch to read the Greek tragedies." "Of course I will. Of course I will. Ahh. Never can I even have five minutes of thought.

"I'm going to read the Bible. Look at this. I open the Bible. 'In the beginning was the Word.' The Word? What could a word do? How could in the beginning be the word? 'In the beginning was... '...hmmm...how about 'the deed'? No, no. Not quite. 'In the beginning was the act. In the beginning was the act.' That is what it is. 'In the beginning was the act.' But now, I know so much and yet know nothing. The only act that can give any meaning to me now is just to kill myself. That's what I'm going to do. O skull over there, speak to me. I'm going to join you soon. Look, there're Daddy's medicines and all of the bags of instruments he had. People respected my father, and he knew where he was in life and what he wanted to do and that he was doing good. I'm doing nothing. I'm going to have a drink of poison. Ah, you golden liquid. How glorious you seem to me. Soon it will all be past. Just to drink you now."

DONG! DONG! DONG! DONG! The bells begin to ring out. "*Christos anesti*! Christ is risen!" "It's Easter! It's Easter right now," says Faust. "Easter. Why do those bells...? Why does that chanting that Christ is arisen—does that mean anything to me? I'm too wise to take any of that seriously. But it does. It does. Perhaps I will put off taking this poison. I can always drink it tomorrow. I will put it off."

The next day, to clear his mind, he goes out for a walk, and he feels obligated to Wagner, the research assistant, to talk to him. They're walking along and Wagner is just talking, talking and talking. "You're so lucky to be a professor and a full professor at such a young age. How happy! You've reached your height, your heart's desire." "Yes. Yes, I have." "Look at how all the people step back and take off their hats. 'Herr Doktor! Herr Professor Doktor!' What a wonderful thing that must be!" "Oh yes, it's just great." "Herr Professor Doktor. Not only are you a great man, but your father was a great man also. He cured me." "Oh. Thank you very much." "Isn't that wonderful that people remember your dad?" "No, it isn't. He's just a typical doctor. He probably killed about as many as he cured." "You seem so angry." "Well, I'm not angry. I'm just telling you how…" "Look at those boys and girls over there frolicking. They're having such a good time. Gosh, I wish I had that kind of innocence." "Well, come on, Wagner. Let's go back. What is that creature over there, Wagner?" "That dog?" "Yes. Interesting creature isn't it, Wagner?" "I don't know. It just looks like a poodle looking for its master." "No, no, no. Look. It's coming to me. Hello, old boy. Let's take it home." "You don't want that poodle!" "Yes I do, Wagner. Bring him on with us." "All right."

Here's Faust, back in his chamber again, pondering all his problems, and suddenly that poodle begins to grow and grow and get bigger. "What's going on with that poodle?" says Faust. He's sitting there all by himself. And suddenly that poodle is no longer a poodle, but another scholar, a traveling scholar arrayed in scholarly garb.

"Who are you, sir? I do not know you." "I am the Devil." "I don't believe in the Devil." "But I am." "But the Devil is supposed to have a tail and horns." "I know, but if I'm the Devil, can't I assume any form I want?" "Well, I guess you can. What are you doing in here?" "You invited me in." "No. I said to the poodle, 'come on in, boy.'" "Well, that's me."

"What do you want with me?" "It's what you want with me. Didn't you say you wanted some meaning to your life?" "Yes." "Didn't you say you were willing to do anything to have the wisdom about life?" "Yes." "What do you want to do with life?" asks the Devil. "I want to live for a change. I don't want to study and be tied up with books.

You know, here I am in middle age, and I have never had a romantic fling, for example, and I am poor." "You want money?" "Ohhh, I want so much money!" "All right. You want girls?" "Oh, yeah. Not just girls, but lascivious girls." "Oh. Okay. What are you willing to do for that?" "I don't know." "What do you expect? Can I have your soul?" "Ha! My soul? Sure. My soul."

"You know, you didn't take the Devil seriously. He's here. Maybe you should take your soul seriously. I'm giving you the disclaimer here, don't you see? You may have a soul, and I may claim it for all eternity." "I am willing." "You are willing?" "Yes." "Then sign this document." "Document? Sure. I know you want to handle these matters in a business-like fashion. But you're the Devil!" "Look, business is business. We're making a contract here. I give you everything you want, and then I get your soul." "Done." "Un-uh. Ink won't do. Blood." "Blood?" "Yes. I know, a very expensive commodity. Your soul for blood." "All right."

"Now, let's get on. Let's get on with this new life you want to live." "All right. I'm rich! Oh, gosh. It's office hours. I forgot all about it. Oh look, there's a student out there." "Why don't you go and get ready for a night on the town, and I'll talk to the student." Suddenly he assumes the form of Faust. "Come in boy. What can I do for you?" "Oh, I need some advice on my career planning." "Sure. What do you want?" "I don't know what I want to do in life. Maybe I'd like to study philosophy." "Oh, I don't know. There's a lot of things you have to learn and a general education that really won't mean anything to you." "Yes. What would you recommend, Doctor?" "Oh, I would recommend you become a doctor, perhaps." "A doctor?" "Yes. You get to see girls in the nude, don't you know, and nobody can do a thing about it." "Sir!" "Well, you asked me what you should do." "That doesn't seem proper advice, but I'll ponder it."

"Sir, I've got your textbook here. Would you sign it?" "Sure – '*eritis sicut Deus, scientes bonum et malum*' – 'You will be like God; you will know good and evil." "Thank you, sir." "Fine. Come back any time."

"Well, now, got your students out of the way. Let's roll!" Off they go to a wine cellar, and there are students drinking, the way Faust had always wanted to do when he was being a studious undergraduate and graduate student. They start drinking, and they join Faust and the Devil. The Devil looks just like any other wandering scholar, and they begin to drink and drink, and suddenly the Devil turns their wine into fire. "AAAHHH!" They're burning. "Ah! That's what I call fun and pranks. You ever get to do that when you were just a student, Doctor?" "No. I didn't!" "Well here we are." "They're coming after us now." "We'll get out," and they ride away on a wine barrel.

"That was marvelous." "That was pretty good fun, wasn't it? Well, now, Doctor, so you've seen a little bit of the wild side of life. What would you like to do now?" "I want a girl." "You want a girl?" "Yes. I want to feel true love, deep inside me. I want a girl, a woman, really to love me, and I've found the one." "You have?" "Yes. Today I was walking the street." "I knew I shouldn't have let you out of my sight. Who'd you see?" "Oh, no, no, no. She's a wonderful, young, fair creature, and I saw her going to church. Her name is Margaret." Or the German short name is Gretchen. "Oh. I think I know the woman you mean. She's not for you. She's a really nice girl. She's got a mother she helps take care of. Her brother, I think, is off in the army. You don't want her. I thought you said you wanted a lascivious woman." "No, no, no, no. I've changed my mind. She's so beautiful." "Well, all right. If that's the one you want, I'll help you get her, but we've got to step-by-step seduce her, don't you see?" "But you said she was a good girl." "Uh, no girl is good. No man is good. Let's just check a bit."

"Tell you what. See these jewels?" "Yes." "I'm going to put them in her room, and she'll discover them. Now, you approached her on the street, right?" "I came up and tried to walk her home, and she wouldn't have anything to do with me." "Ah, but she knows you're interested, doesn't she?" "Yes." "We'll put them in there, and her immediate assumption will be that you, this 'unwanted' suitor has given them to her." Surly enough, Gretchen—Margaret—comes into her room that evening, and there are the jewels. "How in the world did these jewels get here? We are very poor people. These are magnificent. Oooh. I wonder if it could have been that man that very handsome traveling scholar, that man of the world who came up to me on the street. What should I do with the jewels?"

"Well, you know what you should do with the jewels. You should take them to your mother and tell her." "Mom will take them away from me, I know. She's very strict. I'll go next door to Auntie Martha, an old lady, don't you know? She's got a way for the world." "Auntie Martha, what do I do with these jewels?" "You keep them. You keep them." "But wouldn't that be wrong?" "Why? You didn't steal them. Keep them." See, she's already taken that first little step, not telling her mother, keeping the jewels.

Then there's a rap at the door. "Sir. May I help you?" "Yes, madam. I am a wandering scholar. I have just come from Italy to bring you some news." "Good news or bad news?" "Pretty bad. Your husband is dead." "Ah, my husband's dead!" This is to Aunt Martha. "Yes, he died. I was with him when he died. They buried him in Padua, near Saint Francis." "Did he leave me any money?" "No he didn't. In fact, he spent it all on a prostitute in Naples, but nonetheless, he said, 'Fare you well.'" "Is that all he said?" "No. He said you were the cause of his running away from home." "What?" "Yes. You hounded him all the time. You nagged him all the time. He had to go out and work all day, to bring money home for you and the kids, and they just fought and quarreled all the time, so he just ran away and took up with this prostitute in Naples, and that's that. That was his message to you." "Oh. That's so sad. May I give you supper? You're a handsome man of the world." "Thank you, Martha. May I call you that?"

Meanwhile, Faust is there with him, and Gretchen is there. Faust says, "Young lady would you accompany me out in the garden?" He begins to get to know her, and day after day he comes back and calls, and comes back and calls again, and again and again. One day they are walking in the garden, Faust and Gretchen, this beautiful, innocent young thing. They're walking along and she says, "I just don't see why you keep coming and paying visits to me. You're such a worldly man, handsome, debonair. You've seen the world." "But never have I seen anything as fair as you." She picks a little daisy, a little flower. "He loves me. He loves me not. He loves me. He loves me not. He loves me. He loves me!" "I do, and we've got to do something about it, Gretchen." "What do you mean?" "Surely, if we love each other, we want to take that next step." "Oh, I don't know." "I can't wait for marriage. I must have you now." "But my mother won't approve." "Oh, you know what I've got right here?" "I know. But my mother sits right outside the door, every night." "She's worried about you. You see this little medicine right here? It's just like a sleeping tablet. Your mom will just take a good snooze, and then we can be together," and they do, but the sleeping potion has been prepared by the Devil, and it's deadly. So now the mother dies.

Well, Gretchen didn't know it was poison, but she gave it to her mother in order to commit a sin, didn't she? So step-by-step—keeping something that wasn't hers, lying to her mother by implication, and now she's killed her mother. Now she's deep into the romance with Faust.

One night her brother is home on leave, and he comes storming down the street on a dark evening, swearing and ranting, "I can't believe. I go into a pub to have a drink and suddenly all my old friends are snickering about my sister saying that she's running around with all these guys. I don't believe it. My sister was always fair, and I'm going to prove it. I'm going home right now to see what she's doing. Now that Mom's gone, who can take care of her?"

Suddenly, as he comes down the street, he sees both Faust and the Devil coming out of the window. "Two of them! I can't stand it!" He leaps upon them with his sword, and they start slashing back and forth, and the Devil runs him through. Her brother, Valentine, has now been killed. "Let's go, Doctor! Come on!" says the Devil. Faust says, "I can't leave her alone! I can't leave her alone! She's told me she's going to have a baby." "Doctor, are you going to stay here and go to jail, or are you coming with me?" "All right, I'll come with you." So off goes Faust.

Then word comes—while Faust has been with the Devil, celebrating a wild revel on the mountains, in the Hartz Mountain region of Germany, on the Devil's Night, cavorting with all manner of devil women, the lovely Gretchen has been arrested and put into prison on charges of murdering, not only her mother, but the baby. Faust says, "I must go back and see her." "Why, Doctor? She's done for. They're going to put her to death. You'll just get in trouble." "Don't you understand? I have a responsibility to that girl." "What responsibility?" "I seduced her, and now I've abandoned her." "So what? You wanted to see life. That's what life is about. I thought you wanted to go on and see even bigger things. Don't let yourself be caught up in some little romance at the cost of your life." "I'm going back for her. I am going to do my duty; aren't you?"

Back he goes and enters the jail cell. Gretchen, with all that has happened to her has become unhinged. "Did you really kill our baby?" "Ah, the poor little thing. I didn't know what to do. I put him in the stream. I put him in the stream. He died. I didn't know what to do. Why did you leave me?" "You killed the poor, innocent baby?"

"I did. I killed my mother. I gave her that medicine that you gave me. Why did you leave me? Why weren't you here to stay with me, to take care of me?" "I'm sorry. I'll try to take care of you now." "What can you do? The jailer is coming right now. They're going to execute me now, for murder." "I'll stay with you."

Then there's the jailer, coming down, and you hear his footsteps, and the footsteps of the priest and the executioners who are coming to get you. The Devil says to Faust, "Doctor, what are you going to do?" "I'm going to stay here and explain." "Explain what? That you're an accessory to the murder of her mother? Explain that you're an accessory to the murder of the baby? That's death. Are you going to say that you killed her brother in a duel? When he was just defending her honor? That's how it will look, that you're guilty of murder. They're going to put you to death. What are you going to tell them? 'The devil made me do it'? Ha! Bye, bye, doctor, I'm out of here." "No." "Oh, and by the way, here's that document. As soon as they put you to death, I've got your soul for all eternity. Remember you signed it." "I signed it, didn't I?" "Oh yeah, and I'm collecting. You know, you're going to your death with mortal sins upon you, and you're doomed for all eternity, *Herr Doktor*, coming with me?"

"Heinrich—that is the name Gretchen knows him by—Heinrich, you won't leave me, will you? Why are you talking like that?" "Coming, Doctor?" "Heinrich, don't leave me." "Doctor?" "Here I come," and off they go, then the executioner comes for Gretchen and she dies. That is how the first part ends of our *Tragedy of Doctor Faust*.

Lecture Twenty-Nine
Johann Wolfgang von Goethe, *Faust,* Part 2

Scope:

Goethe stood at the center of two great cultural currents of modern Europe: the classicism of the 18th century and the romanticism of the 19th century. The second part of *Faust*, completed in 1831, explores the meaning of art for Goethe, the German nation, and his age. Can the art and literature of classical Greece provide the absolute model for Europe? Are the classical canons and forms absolute standards by which we measure our own cultural achievements? Is it the purpose of art to appeal to human reason? Or is it the purpose of art to appeal to our feelings and emotions, and must each new age and each people finds its own way, its own standards and criteria of beauty? The question of the role of beauty and cultural standards is one that every thoughtful person must decide on his or her own terms. We explore these themes against the backdrop of the moral growth and ultimate redemption of Dr. Faust.

Outline

I. As previously mentioned, the first part of Goethe's *Faust* was published in 1808, and the second part was published in 1831.

   A. The poem is about both love, ambition, and wisdom. In the first part of *Faust*, the professor gave his soul to gain knowledge but lost wisdom in the process. The second part of the work shows how Faust reclaims wisdom.

   B. *Faust* is ultimately about redemption. To Goethe's admirers, the conclusion of the work was a surprise, because they saw in Goethe a mind of the age of Enlightenment, unfettered by religion.

II. Goethe lived from 1749 to 1832, a period that encompassed the Enlightenment, the French Revolution, the age of Napoleon, and the revolutions that shook Europe in 1830.

   A. Goethe was educated in the values of the Enlightenment.

   1. Chief among Enlightenment values was admiration for the classical cultures of Greece and Rome. People believed that the Greeks and Romans could be emulated but not surpassed; the models were the *Iliad* and the *Aeneid*.

2. The Enlightenment was also an age of universality. Europeans believed that Europe was one unified culture and civilization. This culture moved across boundaries. France was seen as the great modern example of culture, and cultivated people, including Goethe, frequently wrote and spoke in French.

3. Thus, both the classical culture, with its models, and the contemporary world formed a unified cultural outlook.

B. These attitudes of the Enlightenment were shattered by the French Revolution and Napoleon, both of which preached doctrines of liberty and equality but brought despotism.

1. The Germans, Italians, and Spanish came to understand that they had unique cultures.

2. The finest minds of the day, including Fichte and Hegel, put forth the belief that every civilization was unique and that each people, having defined itself as a nation, should develop its culture in its own way. This belief was strongest in Germany.

C. With this new thinking came revulsion at some of the ideals of the Enlightenment, which had taught that men and women were creatures of reason.

1. From the new perspective of romanticism, men and women were creatures of impulse; the irrational plays an important role in human life. People can try to suppress their emotions under a veneer of reason, but the emotions will break free.

2. While the Enlightenment sought to control nature, romanticism celebrated nature as uncontrollable and saw it as a source of eternal renewal for humanity.

3. The Enlightenment had celebrated classical Greece and Rome, but romanticism believed that the Middle Ages, when France and Germany had come into being, had been a time of true enlightenment.

4. Christianity took on new meaning during the Romantic era. The life and the suffering of Jesus were idealized. Some people turned back to the Catholic Church as a repository of faith and wisdom.

D. Goethe abserved and absorbed the ideas of both the Enlightenment and romanticism. He is unique and stands in neither age.

III. The second part of *Faust* examines the issue of whether a unique set of values exists for each nation, and whether standards of absolute beauty exist forever, or each individual must judge beauty for himself.

    A. The second part of *Faust* opens in the wilds of nature in the spring. Faust, shattered by the death of Gretchen and his own abandonment of her, is with his comrade, the devil. At the opening of Part II of *Faust*, elves, the helpers of mankind, have pity on the man of sorrows, whether he is good or evil.

        1. In Part I, Faust draws back from suicide at Easter. It is no coincidence that Dante carries *The Divine Comedy*, his story of redemption, through Easter week. Orwell's *1984* begins the story of Winston Smith in April.

        2. The two parts of Faust are linked by spring and the renewal of the earth. At this time of year, the man of sorrows—both Christ and Everyman, whether he is good or evil—can be pitied and helped.

        3. Faust can renew himself, take charge of his life, and become responsible again. The devil asks him what he is doing, and Faust replies that he is gaining strength from nature.

    B. The devil tells Faust that they must make a living and suggests that they go to the court of the Holy Roman Emperor.

        1. Until 1806, when Napoleon abolished the Holy Roman Empire, the Holy Roman Emperors saw themselves as a direct continuation from the Emperor Augustus; their line had been renewed by the Emperor Charlemagne and had ruled over most of Europe.

        2. By the time that *Faust* was written, the Holy Roman Emperor was essentially a figurehead, who in theory, ruled over the 365 independent principalities of Germany.

        3. In *Faust*, the Holy Roman Empire is a shadow of Rome and the ancient world and is testimony to how the modern world has allowed the shadow of antiquity to overwhelm and oppress it. *Faust* is a statement that contemporary people must break that tie and create something new.

        4. When Faust and the devil arrive at the court of the Holy Roman Emperor, the devil assumes the role of court fool. The emperor has no funds, and no one is taking the government seriously.

5. The devil and Faust have an answer to this problem: Because the emperor owns everything under the ground, he can issue currency backed by theoretical buried treasure. As long as people accept the funds in transactions and as long as this method makes the economy work, it is valid.

6. The emperor puts Faust in charge of court ceremonies. The court wants to see a reenactment of classical antiquity. Faust and the devil invoke classical antiquity and the court sees that the classical world is not ideal; Paris is not as handsome as he is reputed to be, nor is Helen as fair.

C. Faust returns to his study. His former research assistant, Wagner, now a professor, has created artificial life in the form of Homunculus, a tiny man in a test tube. Another student informs Faust that his education did nothing for him and only real life has taught him anything.

D. Homunculus goes with Faust and the devil to the Mediterranean to discover the roots of classical antiquity.

1. The devil conjures up the mythological world and creates a wild night of revelry in classical antiquity.

2. Homunculus explodes; the being created without love could neither survive nor experience real emotion.

3. Faust wants to possess power and the most beautiful woman who ever lived.

4. Faust recreates a new kingdom in Sparta that is a blend of the medieval Germanic world of knights and the classical world. Faust weds Helen. Their child, Euphorion, is a blend of the world of Germany and the world of the classical past.

5. Helen and Euphorion die because an artificial culture created from this blend of classical and romantic civilizations cannot survive. This is Goethe's statement that each age and nation must set its own standards of beauty and establish its own way in art, literature, philosophy, and wisdom.

6. Faust's attempt to return to the classical past has failed.

E. Faust returns to Germany and the Holy Roman Emperor.

1. The imperial economy has collapsed, and the empire is about to be overrun.

2. Faust, aided by the devil, creates a phantom army that drives out the enemy and saves the empire.
3. As a reward, Faust wants a new kingdom, a land bordering on the sea, in which to create a new world.
4. Faust rules over a vast domain. He has drained the sea and created new land. People labor on his behalf, but they enjoy peace and prosperity because he protects them. He feels that his life has been rewarded. He realizes that he wanted power to do good things.
5. Faust hears a church bell and asks the devil to destroy the chapel where the bell is housed. The devil, with some henchmen, burns the chapel and kills the people who lived there. Faust realizes that his request has caused their deaths.
6. The devil informs Faust that his death is approaching. Faust reminds the devil that his contract states that he can live until he says that everything is perfect, which he is unwilling to do, but he sees beauty in human striving.
7. The devil claims Faust.
8. A chorus from heaven is heard, and a shower of roses (a symbol of love) appears. Gretchen is praying to Mary for the salvation of Faust's soul.
9. Faust is saved, the devil loses his prey, and Faust ascends to heaven.
10. The chorus sings, "It's a mystery, we can never understand life; ...all we can say is that the eternal feminine raises us to heaven."

Essential Reading:

Goethe, *Faust*, Part II.

Supplementary Reading:

Sharpe, *Cambridge Companion to Goethe.*

Questions to Consider:

1. How do you interpret the religious ending of *Faust*?
2. Can the character of Faust be taken in any sense as an allegory for each and every human life?

Lecture Twenty-Nine—Transcript
Johann Wolfgang von Goethe, *Faust,* Part 2

In our last lecture, we discussed the first part of Goethe's *Tragedy of Faust*, which was divided into two parts, the first published in 1808, and the second, which we discuss now, in 1831. It is truly a great book. The theme for us that we center around is love, and it is most certainly in both parts, a story about love. Goethe was a genius, and like any genius, and like any great book, it cannot be easily pigeon holed. Its theme is love, but it is also about ambition. It is about that central motif of all of our lectures, wisdom. Because Faust gave his soul to know knowledge and in the process lost wisdom, the second part is how Doctor Faust reclaimed wisdom. It was thus, ultimately, a story about redemption, and its conclusion came as a surprise to many of the admirers of Goethe who saw in him the mind of the Enlightenment, unfettered by religion.

Goethe lived from 1749 to 1832. He thus lived through the great age of the Enlightenment, through the French Revolution, through the age of Napoleon, and on down to see those revolutions that shook Europe again in 1830. He was certainly educated in the values of the Enlightenment, in that admiration for Greece and Rome. That cultural belief that said the ancients—Greek and Roman—could be emulated, but never surpassed, that the models were the *Iliad* and the *Aeneid*. We try to copy them, but we must recognize that we are all just standing on the shoulders of these giants.

It was also an age of Enlightenment, of universality, in which Europe was thought to be one unified culture and civilization—aristocrats speaking easily to each other across the boundaries and culture moving very easily across the boundaries. France was the great modern example of culture, and men like Goethe very frequently wrote and spoke in French. That was the great language of civilization. So there was the universality of knowing the classical culture, and its models and ideals, and the contemporary world that also was unified in its cultural outlook.

That was all shattered by the age of the French Revolution and Napoleon. Napoleon and the French Revolution had preached a doctrine of liberty and equality, but in fact, the armies of France carried despotism in their wake. In rebellion against Napoleon, not only armies like those of Prussia rose up, but whole peoples rose up, too. The Germans and the Italians and the Spanish in this age of repression by Napoleon came to understand that they were unique cultures. There arose a deep-seated belief, put forth by some of the finest minds of the day, like Fichte, like Hegel, that every civilization was unique in itself, and each people, having defined itself as a nation, should develop its culture in its own way.

Nowhere was this belief stronger than in Germany. With it came a revulsion against some of the ideals of the Enlightenment. The Enlightenment had taught that men and women were creatures of reason. This new age, that we can call the Romantic Age, said, "No, men and women are creatures of impulse. The irrational plays a very important role in human life. It ways that you can try to suppress emotions under a veneer of reason, but they will break out. They will erupt like a volcano. The Enlightenment had sought to control nature. A wonderful statement of the Enlightenment ideals is a garden, carefully laid out with little fountains, little carefully cut hedges and flower gardens. The Romantic Age celebrated Nature as uncontrollable, with volcanoes erupting, ominous portraits of lakes amidst wild woods, and a storm sweeping across. Nature could not be controlled by man; Nature was a source of eternal renewal for human beings. They should immerse themselves in Nature. The poet Wordsworth celebrated, "Throw away your books. Walk in a field of daffodils. That is natural beauty."

The Middle Ages is where you sought true enlightenment. The Enlightenment had celebrated the world of Greece and Rome. The Romantic Age said it has nothing to say to us. The Middle Ages were the ages of Germany and France, when they came into being. We love ruined castles. We love to sail along the Rhine and look at its wild mountains and ruined buildings rising up.

Christianity took on new meaning in the age of this revolution. There was a romantic sense of the life and suffering of Jesus, and some turned back to the Catholic Church, as the repository of faith and of wisdom. Goethe saw all of this come into being. He absorbed it all. As a genius, he stands neither in the Age of the Romantics or in the Age of the Enlightenment. He is unique unto himself.

The second part of *Faust* is a profound examination of this question of where do cultural values lie? Is there a unique set of values for each nation? Can we really find models? Are there standards of absolute beauty? If we want to deal with the theme of beauty, it's one of the most profound questions we must ask. Are there standards of beauty, as Plato says, existing forever? Or is each one of us the judge of what is beautiful? Is everything beautiful in its own way, as the song went? These profound cultural questions are worked out by Goethe, through his continuing fascination and exploration of the theme of *Faust*.

The second part of *Faust* opens out in the wilds of Nature. Faust, shattered by the experience, the death of Gretchen, his sense of having left her abandoned, is there with his old comrade, the Devil, and the Devil wants to know why Faust is just lounging around. After all, they have to make a living. The first lines of the poem, this tragedy in its second part, are a little song, singing down from Heaven, of bells.

> In the springtime, everything turns green again.
> The world becomes alive.
> And the little elves, the helpers of mankind,
> Rush to and fro
> And they [in this little chorus they are singing out] have pity
>   on the man of sorrows,
> Whether he is good or whether he is evil.
> In the spring, they have pity on the man of sorrows.
> Whether he is good or whether he is evil.

Do you remember in our first part how Faust rescued himself from suicide at Easter time? It is not a coincidence. Dante begins his *Divine Comedy* and carries the story of redemption all through the period of Easter. I don't think it is a coincidence that George Orwell, part of this great tradition, begins the story of Winston in April, for it was to be the redemption of Winston and showed how impossible that is.

So *Faust* links the two parts by the celebration of spring and the renewal of the Earth. The man of sorrows, who is Christ, but who is Everyman, and whether he is good or evil, he can be pitied and helped. So spring is a time of renewal. Faust can renew himself. He can take back charge of his life and become responsible again. He is pondering this when the Devil says, "What are you doing just lying there?" Faust says, "I am looking at Nature! I am gaining my strength back from Nature." "What is Nature?" says the Devil. "It is nothing. It's just what we make. You know, you've got mountains, you've got volcanoes..." "Don't you understand that Nature is a great force of renewal?" "No, I don't, but you can think that if you want to. Right now we've got to make a living." "How are we going to make a living?"

"Well, I've got a new scheme," says the Devil. He is never at a loss. "You know much about the Holy Roman Emperor?" "Well, nothing except he's the figurehead ruler of Germany." "Exactly, Doctor Faust. And I want to go to his court." "Why do you want to go to the court of the Holy Roman Emperor? What is the Holy Roman Emperor?"

Well, the Holy Roman Emperor in our magical time of Faust, and right down until 1806, when Napoleon abolished the Holy Roman Empire—*Das heilige Reich der Deutsche Nation*, the Holy Roman Empire, *Das heilige rumische Reich der Deutsche Nation,* the Holy Roman Empire of the German Nation—they saw themselves as the direct continuation of the Emperor Augustus. The Emperor Charlemagne renewed them when he had been crowned on Christmas Day in 800. At one time a Holy Roman Emperor, such as Charlemagne, ruled over most of Europe, but by the time of Doctor Faust and by the time of its abolishment by Napoleon finally in 1806, the Holy Roman Emperor essentially was a figurehead. In the time of Faust he ruled over, in theory, this Germany of 365 independent principalities. Some of them, such as Bavaria, were large. Some of them nothing more than an independent knight, riding around with his saddle and his horse, but each of them was independent, and owed allegiance only to the Holy Roman Emperor.

The Holy Roman Emperor was elected. It is against this backdrop, of an Emperor with no real power, that Faust and the Devil go to his court. Of course, what is the Holy Roman Empire if you step back and analyze it? It is but the shadow of Rome and of the ancient world. It is one more testimony, Goethe tells us, of how we have allowed the shadow of antiquity to overwhelm and oppress us. It no longer works, don't you see? Break that tie and create something new for yourself. That will run all the way through the second part of the *Faust*.

Faust and the Devil are there, and the Devil assumes the role of the court fool, and the Emperor comes out with his entourage, and he says, "Where's my old fool? I don't see him." "Oh, he just happened to fall down the steps and break his leg, but you've got a new fool." "Oh, we've got a new fool." "Yes, and he's got a wise man with him."

"Well, fool, we're in a terrible situation. Listen to the reports of all my advisors." And sure enough, the head of the treasury says, "We are absolutely bankrupt. We have no money whatsoever." The Ministry of Justice says, "We are in a serious crisis. No one obeys the law. They run up and down the streets, murdering and killing, and there is theft. Nobody takes government seriously."

"Oh, this is a terrible situation. What do you suppose we could do?" "What does the Minister of the Army have to say?" "Our armies will not fight. They are not paid. We cannot get justice, we cannot get soldiers, because our economy is in a ruin." "What am I going to do?" "I don't know. You have very little power to do any taxation. Well, what can I do?"

Ah, well, Faust and the fool, the Devil, have an answer. "Sire, Your Majesty, Emperor of the Holy Roman Empire, have you ever considered all the vast resources at your disposal?" "What do you mean?" "Sire, by the ancient law of your realm, you own everything that is under the ground." "Everything under the ground?" "Yes. Mineral rights, we might say, to everything that is under the ground." "I do?" "Yes, sire." "Why is that so?" "Well, long ago, when the barbarians swarmed into the Roman Empire, many people buried great treasures under the ground to keep them safe. The law was that if those treasures were ever found, and the people were dead, then they belonged to the state. Now, sire, what you can do is issue currency backed by those treasures." This is Faust and the Devil, masquerading as the fool. This is the advice they are giving.

"You mean I've got to go out and dig up all those treasures?" "No, no, no, no, no. Don't you see? Just the very fact that everybody knows treasures are in the ground ought to make your currency good, so you can print all the money you want, just on the idea that there is treasure under that ground that will back it up?" "Won't that money be worthless? Won't it be like a dollar bill in your pocket, that isn't backed by anything?" "As long as people accept it in transaction, then it's good. As long as it makes the economy work." "You mean I can pay my soldiers in that money?" "Of course you can." "You mean I can get rid of all the national debt with that?" "Of course you can." "And people will take it as long as it is backed by the government?" "Yes, they'll take it." "This is a wonderful idea! Now we're solvent once again, and you! I'm going to reward you so highly! That is tremendous economic advice." In other words, they had built an economic structure much like we have today, a service economy.

"You know, you are such a wise man, *Herr Doktor*, that I would like to put you in charge of court ceremonies, and you know what everybody at my court wants to see?" "What do they want to see?" "They would like to see a re-enactment of the beauties of classical antiquity. If you could put on a show like that, why, my admiration and devotion and rewards for you would be without end."

Faust ponders a bit, and the Devil pulls him aside and says, "Yeah, we could put on a great show." "All right. We'll put on a show." Now, at this time, when his empire, of course, is in such serious difficulty this is what the emperor is thinking about, putting on a show that will revive classical antiquity, and that's what they do.

The ladies of the court come in and the nobles of the court are there. What Faust and the Devil put on for their entertainment is a re-invoking of Classical antiquity. Suddenly, out of the mist hovers up, created by the power of the Devil, a real Classical temple. Let's say it's the Parthenon. It rises in all its beauty and majesty. Now, the Parthenon and the buildings of Classical antiquity are the models for the architecture of the Enlightenment. They cannot be surpassed, remember? But suddenly they see this reality of the Classical world, and what it was truly like. Then the architects say, "That's not a very good looking building. Those columns look a little too squat for me. That pediment's not quite correct. That's not very good." In other words, they don't want the reality of what the Classical world was.

Then suddenly there's a figure that comes, and it's a man. Who is that? He is, in reality, the handsome Paris. Remember, the man Helen fell in love with, that took her away to Troy, the handsomest man of his day? "He doesn't look very handsome to me," the men say. His legs are a little skinny; he doesn't have much of a chest. Look at those puny little arms. That's what Classical antiquity was about?"

"Ah! There is a woman." "That is Helen." "That is the woman whose face launched a thousand ships?" "Yes," and the ladies say, "She's kind of tubby. She's kind of old, isn't she? Look at the little bulge around her stomach. That's beauty in the Classical world?"

Well, of course, the economy of the empire has gone to rack and ruin in the meantime, and Faust and the Devil have to get out of there, so they head away, and they show up back at Faust's old university. They go in and Faust opens the door of his old office, but he's been away for a long time, and he didn't get a sabbatical. So there is his old research assistant. Remember Wagner? He's now the professor. "Professor, you're back! You know, I'm now in charge, but I am so glad to have you back, because I am deep in a very profound experiment." "What are you trying to do?" says Faust, and suddenly there is a knock on the door. There is a student there, but older looking. "Hi! Remember me, Professor Faust?" "Not really." "Don't you remember giving me that advice? Look, here is the textbook that you wrote in. 'You will be like God, you will know good and evil.' You don't remember that, when I came by your office hours?" "Well, yes." "You know, all my education has done nothing for me. Only real life taught me anything. I just want to say thanks for nothing."

That was kind of depressing. "What about your experiment, there, Wagner?" "I am creating human life in a test tube." "What?" You might think something like cloning. "You are creating a human life?" "Yes. And I just about got it then." He's got his bellows and he's pushing away. "And look, it's coming into life; it's coming into life; it's coming into life! There it is!" Surely enough, there is this little, tiny man, in the test tube. Humunculus, the little man, speaks! He says, "Hello Daddy!" to Wagner. That's what he says. "Hello Daddy." "Hello, puppy, I have created life!" Faust says, "This is amazing! I worry though. You have created life without any love." "Yes. There was no need to have the act of love whatsoever to create this little man, and look, that little man has a will of his own!"

"That's, that's…I want to go with you! Where are you going? It looks so interesting." "Oh, well, my friend the Devil and I are leaving for the south, for the Mediterranean, where we are going back to the roots of Classical antiquity." "I want to go!" "Don't hold me here, Daddy! Let me go with them. I want to experience life." "Well, I can't hold you back. Take that test tube with you."

So off they fly, Faust, the Devil and the little man, in his little test tube, off they fly. Faust has had enough of the dark, dank, gloomy, rainy world of Germany. Besides, the Devil, in Germany, from time to time, has to revert to a cloven-hoofed monster. He wants to go to the Mediterranean world, where they had a different concept of the Devil, so he flies down with Faust, and there they arrive. The Devil is able to conjure up the whole of the mythological world of antiquity, with its nymphs and its sirens and the god Neptune. Just as the Devil was able to create a Devil's Night in the dark Hartz Mountains of Germany in our first act, now he creates a wild night of revelry in the Mediterranean Classical mythological world. The little man is right there with them, flying around, singing along in his little test tube, and he gets a ride on the back of the nymphs, these beautiful, luscious, lascivious creatures that are going to take him out into the ocean.

In the very midst of all this joy, the little man explodes! His little test tube blows up. "Good bye, Daddy!" For you see, created without love, he could not survive. He could not experience real emotion, since he had not been created with it, Goethe tells us. "So think about cloning. Think about whether you can remove that act of love," Goethe would say to us today.

But Faust, Faust goes ever deeper into the world of Classical antiquity, accompanied by his friend the Devil, who seems to be able to make everything happen. "What would you like to do? Haven't you sold your soul for knowledge? That hasn't proven to be very much good. In fact, your student has come by and said you never really taught him anything useful. But what is more important than knowledge is power. Power! I wanted love. That didn't work out. Gretchen was a real disappointment to me. Knowledge? I want power. I want to be a ruler. I want to possess something. So why not be a ruler and possess the most beautiful woman who has ever lived? Not fool around with little Gretchens, but go back to Helen, because I didn't think she was that unattractive, and I want to have the most beautiful woman who ever lived."

The Devil creates this for Faust. There in Sparta, where once Menelaus had ruled and Helen had been his wife, Faust recreates, through the help of the Devil, a new kingdom, a kingdom that is a blend of the Germanic medieval world of the knights, that we met in *The Death of Arthur*, and in the Classical world, but it's not a complete invention. After all, in the 14th century, Germanic knights and French knights ruled kingdoms in Greece. They had come there from the Holy Land, as part of the Crusades. They had carved out for themselves kingdoms in Turkey and in Syria and in Greece, and he kingdom of the Moraea, the kingdom around Sparta, was just such a Teutonic medieval kingdom.

So it's reality. There is Faust, as the knight, and he weds Helen. For a while they are so happy. He has rescued her from danger. They live in their great palace, and they have a child, Euphorion. He is a blend of the world of Germany and of the Classical past, of Faust and the beautiful Helen. They go out one day with their little son, Euphorion, on a picnic. He begins to dance and flit around and feel his youth and his lovely looks. Jumping around he is just gorgeous to look upon, the perfect mixture of Romantic and Classical.

He finally takes such a high flight that his father and mother say, "Be careful! Be careful, child!" His mother tries to go and get him and save him, but they perish. He falls and is broken. Because, you see, culture created out of this mixture of the Romantic and the Classical cannot live. It is artificial. It is not reality. Each nation, Goethe has finally decided each age, must set its own standards of beauty, must find its own way to art, to literature, to philosophy and to wisdom. So the attempt to go back to the Classical past has failed for Faust.

He must go back, once again, to Germany, and once again he goes to the Holy Roman Emperor. The Holy Roman Emperor is now in even more desperate straits. His economy has collapsed. He can't put his army into the field, and he's about to be overrun. So Faust, aided by the Devil, creates a phantom army for him, and that phantom army drives his enemy from the field. Once again the Roman Emperor is saved. To reward Faust, he says, "I will give you what you want. What do you want now?" And Faust says, "What I want is a new kingdom, something that I can create entirely fresh, not like the old classical Sparta; nothing like that, but something that I can create entirely fresh. Give me land that borders on the sea. Let me drain the sea. Let me create a new world. Let me bring people there to live, and to farm that land for me.

Faust, as our work begins to draw to its close, is ruler over a vast domain. Years have passed. He's over 100 years of age. He looks out from his palace, over land filled with homes and people working so hard. The sea has been drained away, like Holland, and a new land has been created. "It is so beautiful," says Faust, "They all labor on my behalf, but they gain prosperity and peace because I protect them. What a beautiful vista it is. Now I feel my life has been rewarded. Now I see why I wanted power. To do these good things."

"Oh, what is that ding-dong, ding-dong. Every time I get to a good point, as when I was going to kill myself in the first act, there is a ding-dong. There's a bell ringing again, a church bell. I said I didn't want any church bells. There's that little chapel. I thought I told my subordinates that that little chapel was to be removed, and those old people. There are two old people who live there. They are nice, kindly old people, but they still cling to that private property. That was the one piece of land I couldn't buy, and they've got that little chapel. Now that just blocks my vision, and it irritates me. I thought I told you to take care of that business."

Surely enough, the Devil, with a couple of henchmen, run off and take care of that business. The next thing Faust sees is a fire, and that little farm has been burned. "What did you do to those old people?" says Faust. "The Devil said to kill them. Burn down their place. You said, 'take care of it.'" "I didn't mean kill them!" "Well, you said, 'Take care of it.' I didn't know how to do it if they didn't want to sell, so we killed them and burned down the place, and now it's yours. Look, I even got them to sign the deed before I killed them." "Oh, what a terrible thing!"

"Yeah, and you know what old fellow? I think the time's getting near. You've lived an awfully long time." "No, no, no, no. Look at the contract. The contract says that I can live until I say everything is perfect. And I'm not going to say that yet. Oh, all right."

With Faust looking out over this beautiful landscape, seeing these people hard at work, he says, "You know, the very fact that humans keep striving every day, the fact that they work on and on and on, no matter what happens, they come back. They breathe for freedom. They live for freedom. They keep striving. Just to look out on people living in freedom and striving every day, every day beginning again, why, it's such a beautiful scene, I would like to say *'verweile doch! du bist so schön!'*—'stay for a moment, you are so beautiful.'"

"I've got you now," says the Devil. "You said it's perfect. Now, you're coming with me!" "I don't want to come." "You're coming with me! You're going to your grave." And sure enough, the lemurs are already there, digging a grave, and Faust is in the hands of the Devil, when suddenly a chorus appears in Heaven. The sky opens up, and a shower of roses—remember the rose is a sign of love, remember the rose coming through the Gothic cathedral's rose window—a shower of roses comes down. Our eyes go up to Heaven, and there, kneeling, is a woman, a penitent, who has been saved from her own sin. She was once called Margaret or Gretchen, and she is praying to Mary, "Save the soul of Faust. Save his soul." Suddenly a voice booms out, "He is saved. Give him here!" The Devil loses his prey, and Faust is raised up into Heaven. The chorus sings out: "It's a mystery. We will never understand life. The whole of the universe is a mystery. All we can say is, *'das ewige Weibliche zieht uns heran'*—'The eternal feminine raises us up to Heaven. We are saved by the eternal feminine, the eternal love.'"

Lecture Thirty
Henry David Thoreau, *Walden*

Scope:

Every thoughtful person must come to terms with nature, with the natural world around us. Is nature a source of wonder and revitalization for the soul, or is nature the servant of humans to be conquered and exploited? Are we one with nature or above it? The classical vision brings nature under control, order out of chaos. The Romantic reveres nature, untrammeled and untouched. Thoreau, the most American of thinkers, is an unabashed Romantic. *Walden* is the journal of his recovery of self-meaning and independence by his return to nature. It began significantly on July 4, 1845. Thoreau studies the life of nature with intense sympathy. Out of this comes a deeper understanding of the meaning of his own life. *Walden* is a profoundly individual story. I have found my own way, Thoreau says to us. Now you must find your way.

Outline

I. The previous lecture completed the discussion of Goethe's *Faust*, a magnificent epic poem in two parts.

   A. The theme of the first part of *Faust* was love, a romantic love that can destroy. Faust seduced and abandoned Gretchen, who caused the death of her mother and child.

   B. In the second part of *Faust*, the professor followed his ambition to its limits but was redeemed by divine love through the Virgin Mary and Gretchen herself, praying for him.

II. This course has examined several epic poems: the *Iliad*, *Gilgamesh*, *Beowulf*, the *Aeneid*, and *The Divine Comedy*. The epic has been the vehicle for some of the noblest ideas in literature.

   A. Malory's *Morte d'Arthur* is an epic; although it is not written in poetry, it deals with epic material in magisterial prose.

   B. Like *The Divine Comedy*, *Faust*, and the *Aeneid*, *Morte d'Arthur* is a story of redemption. Contemporary society does not allow people to forget their mistakes, nor does it seem to allow redemption, although the concept of redemption lies at the center of Christianity and Islam, and redemption is also central to the *Bhagavad Gita*.

C. Epic poetry has been a source of great inspiration, as have philosophers, or searchers after truth, such as Socrates, Jesus, and Confucius. Socrates believed that epic poets were not philosophers, because they could convey great ideas but could not analyze them.

III. Thoreau spoke out against conformity in the United States at a time when Americans thought they were moving forward to becoming the greatest nation in the world.

   A. Melville, a contemporary of Thoreau, said, "We are the bearers of the ark of liberty to the entire world."

   B. The Declaration of Independence had enshrined the values of life, liberty, and the pursuit of happiness and had taken democracy to much of North America. The United States was becoming a leading industrial power, and Americans believed in progress and democracy.

IV. Henry David Thoreau was an eccentric.

   A. Thoreau went to Harvard, where he studied Greek, Latin, and natural and moral philosophy. He taught for a while, but realized that as a teacher, he never had an opportunity to learn. He then tried writing, but no one wanted to publish his material.

   B. On July 4, 1845, when he was 28 years old, Thoreau celebrated his independence by going out to Walden Pond near Concord.

   C. Thoreau considered himself a transcendentalist, as were several of his friends in Concord, including Emerson and the Alcotts. To transcendentalists, ideas were most important. This belief was similar to Socrates's belief that ideas shaped everything—a philosophy opposed to that of most Americans, who believed in practical, empirical information.

   D. Thoreau considered himself a mystic, that is, someone who is cut off from the factual reality of the world.

V. Although Thoreau read and took seriously German philosophy, particularly Kant, and knew Plato, he wanted, above all, to think for himself.

   A. He wished to cut himself off, as much as possible, from contemporary life and give his eccentricity full rein. He was not a hermit, however; people visited him, and he was a genial host.

B. Thoreau believed that material possessions are fetters that bind us.

C. Thoreau recognized that if he was going to achieve fulfillment, that is, develop his inner self, or soul, he would have to be selfish.

D. Thoreau found he needed little to live. He discovered that all that was necessary was some kind of covering and something to eat, which he could produce himself. Although he was not a skilled craftsman, he built a small cabin, and grew his own food.

E. In so doing, he discovered how much fulfillment he could get from independence. His time was truly his own. The *Bhagavad Gita*, one of Thoreau's favorite books, teaches that to do someone else's work is slavery, but to do one's own work is freedom.

F. Thoreau would sometimes spend an entire day baking bread and watching it in the oven—or watching the grass—and contemplating. He found himself in a world filled with information. He believed that some people turned information into knowledge, but almost no one took time to contemplate and turn knowledge into wisdom.

VI. For contemporary Americans, *Walden* is a magnificent examination of nature.

    A. During the Enlightenment, people believed that they should control nature. During the Romantic age, people saw nature as an overwhelming force that gave renewal. People of the 21st century believe that nature should be controlled. Contemporary Americans isolate nature in national parks.

        1. Thoreau wanted to subordinate himself to nature so that he could understand it; the routine of life on Walden Pond, where he stayed for two years, held profound meaning for him.

        2. Thoreau was a self-trained natural philosopher who immersed himself in nature out of a belief that nature is sacred and that humanity is a part of it.

B. Thoreau developed reservations about eating meat and fish. He found that he could obtain everything he needed to eat from his garden.

C. Thoreau's friends were concerned that he was not getting on with the work of his life, but he believed that learning to know *himself* was indeed the work of his life.

D. When spring came to Walden Pond, Thoreau saw it as he had never seen it before. He saw the world coming alive. He found in the renewal of spring the same mystic sense of redemption of the great epic poets.

    1. In *The Divine Comedy*, Dante begins his journey to save his soul at Easter.

    2. Faust was rescued from suicide by spring and Easter.

    3. Spring was also the time of year when Athenians put on tragedies, which were focused on redeeming oneself through understanding suffering, and gaining wisdom from the lives of others.

    4. Thoreau believed that spring was a mystical time and that God, inside him, was renewing the world.

    5. Thoreau believed that God was more present in trees coming back to life than in cathedrals built by man.

    6. Thoreau announced that he forgave everyone. He believed that brooding over wrongs done to him allowed others to control him.

    7. He believed that in spring, the time of renewal, all debts should be forgiven.

VII. Thoreau asked difficult questions that reveal his eccentricity.

A. He asked, for example, how many letters are truly worth the postage. He wondered how many letters transform a person's life and are good for the soul. His solution was to stop reading mail.

B. Thoreau did not read newspapers. His friends were concerned that he was not being a responsible citizen and was not staying informed. Thoreau believed that newspapers contain a rehash of past events, with names and locations changed. By reading newspapers, people destroy their ability to commune with themselves. So many impurities enter the self from the outside world that the individual can never break free and loses forever the chance to save his soul.

VIII. After two years, Thoreau left Walden Pond; he had other paths to follow.

    A. As individuals, we do not have to stay at the same thing or have the same ideals for all our lives. We should not be afraid to contradict ourselves. Thoreau stated that he had only started to explore himself and that he could continue to do so wherever he was.

    B. Thoreau believed that the beauty of nature could not be surpassed by a work of art in a museum.

    C. The *Bhagavad Gita* points out that the sun is the morning star and that every morning is new, allowing the individual to begin again. The idea that the sun is a morning star concludes *Walden.*

IX. Thoreau believed that American democracy was not perfect. Slavery was a stain on all of America. Boston merchants, for example, depended too much on trade with the South to truly want to abolish slavery. The soul of the South was too corrupt to rid itself of slavery.

    A. Thoreau decided that he would not pay taxes to support a country that supported slavery. He believed that in a country with true freedom, people should have the freedom not to pay taxes.

    B. Thoreau greatly admired John Brown. His essay on Brown states that Brown was a man of conscience who had come to understand that slavery was a great wrong and could be abolished only through bloodshed and civil war. If you want to be a person of the world, Thoreau said, do it the way that John Brown did: Fight and die for something with true meaning—freedom.

X. Thoreau's legacy is to encourage people to love nature, because in nature, the individual can find a way to truth.

Essential Reading:

Thoreau, *Walden.*

Supplementary Reading:

Thoreau, *Political Writings.*

Questions to Consider:

1. Where might you find your own Walden?

2. Contrary to Thoreau, it might be argued that all human progress is based on the conquest of nature. What do you think? We might start by asking what we mean by *progress*. That is what Thoreau challenges us to do.

Lecture Thirty—Transcript
Henry David Thoreau, *Walden*

In our last lecture, we completed our discussion of Goethe's *Faust*, that magnificent epic poem in two parts. The first part had as its theme love: Romantic love, love that can destroy. Faust seduced and then abandoned Gretchen, and she caused the death of her own mother and her own child. In the second part we saw Faust redeemed in the end, after following his ambition to the absolute limits. He was redeemed, not by himself—for he died having ordered a murder, did he not—but through the divine love of God, through the Virgin Mary and then through Gretchen herself praying for him.

We have examined, in the course of this set of lectures, a series of epic poems—*The Iliad, Gilgamesh, Beowulf,* the *Aeneid,* Dante's *Divine Comedy*—and the epic has been the vehicle for some of the noblest ideas in literature. Sir Thomas Malory's *Le Morte D'Arthur* is an epic, not in poetry, but dealing with epic material in its magisterial prose, it too conveys an epic. And like Dante's *Divine Comedy* or the *Faust* of Goethe or the *Aeneid*, it is a story of redemption.

Redemption. We live in a society in which people are not allowed to forget mistakes. Not even the most powerful politician in the world can avoid something they did when they were 21 years of age. It will always come back. Of course, with our inexhaustible supply of news media, it can always be resurrected and there to haunt that person. And who is courageous enough to say, "Yes, I did that. I was a different person then. Now I have changed." So, it is a society that cannot accept the notion of redemption, even though redemption lies at the very center of Christianity, of Islam, or, as we saw, of the Bhagavad Gita. Redemption. Remember? You can be the greatest sinner in the world, but if you come to see that God is truth, you will be saved the Bhagavad Gita tells us.

Epic poetry has been the source of great inspiration, as has the philosopher, the searcher after the truth—Socrates, Jesus, or Confucius. Now, Socrates believed that epic poems and the epic poet were not true philosophers, in the sense that they could convey great ideas—they got all inspired, as Homer did—but they could not then sit down and analyze them. He was always going around to the poets of his day, like Sophocles, whom he particularly disliked, and asked them to explain some particularly truth-sounding poetry that they had produced on the stage at Athens. That, of course, made Socrates disliked. Socrates liked to call himself a "gadfly."

The subject of today's lecture, the lecture that we're on right now, Henry David Thoreau, was another such "gadfly" and searcher after the truth. Socrates, of course, made himself so unpopular that he was put to death. And you know, looking at these figures like Socrates and Thoreau in terms of our own society, or Solzhenitsyn who was just such a gadfly and made himself disliked, not only in the Soviet Union, but in the United States—I mean, that took a certain amount of ability, Socrates would have admired that—we would call such people—we might say they had a "chip upon their shoulder," wouldn't we? Why else would they go around saying things weren't perfect? Everybody knew the Athenian democracy was perfect; everybody knew that the Soviet Union was perfect; and everybody knew that the United States was perfect. And here you have these figures going around saying, "Well it's not! And I'm telling you this for your own good, and not only for your good, but for the good of my soul. That is my mission in life. To go around and tell you that you have mistakes, because I know I have mistakes. And, by helping you understand your mistakes, I can deal with my own mistakes. I can redeem myself." So you get in big trouble doing that.

Henry David Thoreau spoke out against conformity in the United States in an age in which Americans thought they were moving ever forward to being the greatest nation in the world, in the same way that we do today, and quite rightly, because, after all, America had established itself with its Declaration of Independence—life, liberty and the pursuit of happiness. It had then established a constitution, which, by 1845, when Thoreau would go out to Walden Pond, had taken this democracy over a good part of the continent. "Bidding fair to have the whole of the continent under democracy, we are," a contemporary of Thoreau said—Herman Melville—"the bearer of the ark of liberty to the entire world."

We were becoming a leading industrial power. Why, American factories were turning out goods in huge quantities. Our cities were beginning to bloom and blossom and become enormous cities, like New York or Boston. Railroads were making their way across the country, bringing people ever faster to places. Bringing the mail ever faster. The same way today that we just communicate ever faster and faster, and became ever easier—to use today's language, to "stay connected." That is what people wanted to do, to "stay connected." There were newspapers, and they got to your doorstep very fast now. You could read news of the entire world and be an informed citizen to make decisions in this democracy the same way you can today. I mean, you can wake up in the middle of the night, at 2 A.M., not able to sleep, and you can turn on the news, and find out what's going on. Inform yourself and make these decisions.

So the world of Thoreau was much like our own in terms of its belief in progress and in democracy. And all of this did not suit this one man, who was eccentric. Now, to say about somebody in a job that they're eccentric is not a letter of recommendation. John Stuart Mill, of course, said that the whole purpose of individual liberty was to defend eccentricity. But eccentrics have chips on their shoulders and they are gadflies. Thoreau was just such an eccentric. He had gone to Harvard. He came from a perfectly respectable family—no reason to think he would turn out like this. He did perfectly well at Harvard. He would have studied Greek and Latin in the original, studied natural philosophies, a certain amount of science; studied moral philosophy. But then he did not go out and get a good job. He taught for a short while, but he realized that "if you spend all your time teaching people, you never learn anything." That's what he said. I didn't say that, but he said that. You never learn anything. So he stopped doing that.

He had tried to write a little bit, but nobody ever wanted to publish it, and he got no money for it. I mean—he was a failure. And like a failure, well, maybe he developed a chip on his shoulder.

So at the age of 28, on July 4th, 1845, when his countrymen were celebrating their independence, he celebrated his independence by going out to Walden Pond, near Concord. In Concord there were a circle of people who knew him and liked him and respected his eccentric ways. People like Ralph Waldo Emerson and the Alcotts. He would consider himself, like Emerson and the Alcotts, a Transcendentalist. That is to say, he believed that ideas were most important. Thus, he joins Socrates in the belief that ideas shape everything. This was very different from most of his countrymen who believed in practical, empirical information.

He also called himself a mystic. A mystic is someone who, by his very nature or her very nature, is cut off from the factual reality of the world. He read and took seriously German philosophy, particularly Kant. He knew Plato well; but he above all thought for himself, and that is what he wanted to do when he went out to Walden Pond, to cut himself off as much as possible from contemporary life. He did not become a hermit. People came and visited him, and he was perfectly genial as a host. But he wanted to disconnect and to give his eccentricity full rein.

He understood—as Socrates did, who cared nothing for material possessions—that our material possessions are the fetters, the chains that bind us. He is, Thoreau, a very selfish person. He did not want to be bound by any concerns. In the same way, Socrates was very selfish. Remember? Towards the end of his life when he is in prison, and his friends say, "You have got to escape or go into exile, Socrates, because who will take care of your children?" He said, "I don't care. I don't care." So, Thoreau was selfish, and he realized, if you are going to achieve fulfillment; if you are going to develop your inner self, your soul, then you must be selfish.

So, he set out to decide how little you really need to live—and it is amazingly little, if you will just think about it. All you need is some kind of covering and something to eat. You can produce all of that yourself. So, even though he was by no means a skilled craftsman, he built himself a little cabin, and it suited him. Most people would think it was a terrible-looking structure, but it suited him. It kept the wind and the rain out most of the time. There he could fix his meager little meals. All it took was a garden, and it was amazing how much nourishment you could get just from potatoes or beans.

More than that, how much fulfillment there was in taking care of yourself. Being dependent on no one. Because then your time was truly your own, you were not rushing back and forth to be somewhere at eight o'clock in order to fill your job. You were not looking at the clock constantly because you were doing somebody else's work. Remember that from the *Bhagavad Gita,* because now, as we come to the end of our lectures, we want to bring these together. The *Bhagavad Gita* says to do someone else's work is slavery. To do your own is freedom. Do you know what book Thoreau liked best? The *Bhagavad Gita.* He read the Indian classics. In fact, he said, "I had a copy of the *Iliad* on my table there at Walden Pond, and from time-to-time I would look at a page of it, but in fact mostly I was spoken to by works from the other civilizations. Do we know," he said, "you who study Greek and Latin, that the Vatican could be filled up with a whole set of holy books from

Persia, from the Islamic world, from India and from China. Look what I've read."

So he labored at his own task. He would lie for a whole day, just baking bread and watching it bake there in the oven. Or some days he would just lie all day and watch the grass and contemplate and meditate. He found himself in a world that was surrounded and filled with information. Some people took the trouble to turn that into knowledge, but almost nobody took the time to contemplate and to meditate—that led to wisdom. That is what Thoreau wanted to do.

For us, *Walden* is a magnificent examination of the theme of nature. We all should come to grips with nature. We saw that in the Age of Enlightenment where men and women thought that they should control nature. In the Romantic Age that Goethe lived to see, nature was an overwhelming force that gave you renewal. Well, our society here in the early 21st century has made its decision. We control nature, and nature is to be bent to our will. You can't think anything else when you drive the highways of America, and you look along the side and you see one McDonald's followed by a Wendy's, followed by a Burger King, followed by car dealerships, followed by an Applebee's, and so on. All that wonderful, fruitful land, covered over with asphalt and fast food places. We control nature.

Yes, we have National Parks like Yellowstone in which we have carefully cut off and isolated nature, where you go and there are officers to let you in and officers to control you at every step of the way. Officers to make sure that you have a permit to walk into the back woods. And that's all good, no doubt. But our idea is that we control nature.

Thoreau wanted to be controlled *by* nature, to subordinate himself to nature so he would understand it. So the routine of the crops came to mean something to him, and the routine of nature there on the Pond where he stayed for two years watching and recording. "I'm a natural philosopher to boot," he said. "I'm a mystic, a transcendentalist, and a natural philosopher to boot." He was a scientist, pretty much self-trained. But in that little microcosm of the universe that was Walden Pond, there he studied nature. Have you ever looked at the ice in the winter? It changes. It gets deeper and then sometimes it gets shallower. It makes noises. Strange, strange noises, if you will attune your ear. So he studied the depth of ice in Walden Pond; thought about the elements that made its color different from the ice you might cut further in Concord or in Boston; noticed the patterns of birds and how they migrated; looked at the stars over and over again, just to wonder about them.

So he immersed himself in nature out of the belief that nature is sacred and we are all part of nature. So he began to have reservations about eating animals. You could get all the nourishment you wanted from vegetables. At first he fished, and that seemed to him to be part of nature because herons came and caught fish. But taking an animal! Have you ever gutted a pig? First you kill that creature, and it is just dirty. The whole work is dirty. So he said, "I'm not going to eat any more meat." And finally he came to feel that perhaps he wouldn't eat any more fish either. They, too, were part of nature, and why was he preying upon them when he could get everything he wanted from his potatoes and his beans and a salad?

So, he took a real commitment to be part of nature. Seldom reading. Pondering a lot. Friends coming to see him from time to time, just to see that he hadn't totally lost his mind, because it was so bizarre what he was doing out there and not getting along with the work of his life, as though finding himself were not the true work of his life. People always asked that of Socrates: "You ought to be getting on with the work of your life, or at least participating in politics, which is the work of an Athenian citizen," and Socrates could never make most of them understand that learning yourself should be the work of your life.

Spring came to Walden Pond and Thoreau saw spring as he had never seen it before. The world becoming alive, the plants springing up out of the dead earth, and he found in the renewal of spring that same mystic sense of redemption that we have found in our great epic poets. Remember, where does Dante begin his journey to save his soul? At Eastertime. What brought Faust back from suicide? Spring and Easter. When did the Greeks, the Athenians, put on their tragedies that are all about your redeeming yourself to understanding the suffering and learning wisdom from what happened to others? In the spring.

Thoreau understood that this is a mystical time. Once again, if you are living your everyday life, Thoreau would say—with a chip on his shoulder, not me, but Thoreau would say—"You're dismissing the whole of spring and all of nature." All spring might mean is that the roads are going to get slushy, and then, well, you've got some flowers outside, maybe, if you plant them and carefully nurture them.

But it is just one more part of your year, isn't that right, because it all runs together. Not for Thoreau.

God, inside him, was renewing the whole world. Thus, he writes in *Walden Pond*, having gone through each season there at the pond, he says, "You know, on a bright spring day, it became absolutely clear to me, why doesn't the jailer go into his prison and say, 'Everybody is released. You are all redeemed.' And why doesn't a minister say to his congregation on that bright blue day in spring, 'Everybody, just go away. Just go away. You don't need to be in a building. God is far more present in these trees coming back to life than he is in all the cathedrals ever built by man. God is more alive in these birds and their singing in the spring and celebrating the spring than in all the hymns, all the books ever composed by men and women.' And the teacher ought to say, 'Go away, students. Be free.'"

Thoreau said, "You know, I have, on this spring day, forgiven everybody who ever did anything wrong to me. Why should I allow them to continue to control me? Because that's what they're doing by constantly thinking about the wrong they have done to me, petty or great. Then they continue to control me, and I am no longer free. So you are all forgiven, and I just wish everybody, everywhere, could be free like that and say, in spring, 'All debts are forgiven.'"

Why, yes, why didn't the creditor go to you and say, "I have forgiven you your debts." Again, when Thoreau tried to explain this to his friends, they couldn't grasp it. They might even have said, "Well, someone has pissed on your wick. You're really losing all your ardor for life if you can't hate people." "No! It's because I have all this ardor for life that I want to live it," Thoreau said. "I want to live because I have this ardor for life."

In the course of spring, in the course of thinking, he asked questions that are still very much—or should be very much—on our mind. But that makes it clear how eccentric he was—because it sounded just as eccentric to his friends as it will to you—but he asked the question, "How many letters have you gotten in your life that were worth the postage?" Think about it. How many letters have you gotten that really transformed what matters in your life? Oh, you might have gotten some letters that you thought were good at the time, offering you a job that just increased your servitude. You might have gotten a letter that gave you opportunities in the Far West that just increased your servitude. How many letters have you got that were really good? Good for your soul? Maybe one or two in a lifetime?

Well, just stop getting mail. It takes away even a few minutes of your time. But you today—and again, this would be Thoreau speaking—how long do you sit every day at your e-mail? Because now not only do you have letters coming in, though they are fewer, but you have the telephone jangling, the fax, all of these intruding on you. That e-mail—that has become sacred. No one dares to say, "I did not look at your e-mail. I don't look at mine. I've got 1500 e-mails blocked up there, and I'm not going to look at a one. I haven't looked at one since March 24th." Now they would think you were completely irresponsible. But if you held a position, you'd have to be crazy, you'd had suffered a nervous breakdown. Truly, someone had pissed on your wick. You have lost all your ardor for life, if you are not going through all those e-mails. Isn't that true? Yes or no? How about you? Yes. You know it's true. All right.

Thoreau would say, "Just throw that computer away. You're not writing any better or communicating anything that is important with it." "Well, that's pretty drastic," you might say, and I don't think anyone will follow this goal of throwing away their computer, because we must be connected. We are, of course, connected every day through the news, and Thoreau never read a newspaper. His friends said, "How can you be a responsible citizen and not read the newspaper to keep informed?" Thoreau said, "You know what? If you read a newspaper from 25 years ago, just change a few names, and it is saying exactly what is true today." He picked up a newspaper that one of his friends was so diligently studying, "Look, here's some news about what's happening in Spain. Just change a name here and here, and the prime minister or the king of Spain, and it's exactly the same." Interestingly enough, the other day I was reading Winston Churchill's book on the world crisis, the end of World War I, and he had an appendix there; he had sent a memorandum to the Prime Minister about Iraq. "We are trying to nation-build in Iraq. It's not going well. There may be a civil war there. British troops are being killed every day, and the British taxpayer is getting very upset at this huge expenditure." Well, I just ask you if there is truth in what Thoreau says.

So newspapers and keeping up with the news is one more way in which you destroy your ability to commune with yourself, because sooner or later, it's just like eating so much meat. You'll get so much impurity in yourself from the outside world that you can never break free of it, and you have thus lost forever that chance to save your own soul, Thoreau said.

After two years, he was done at Walden Pond. "I had other paths to trod." And that, too, is an important lesson for you. You don't have to stay at the same thing or the same idea all the rest of your life. People might say, to him, as they did, "You're contradicting yourself. You know, you said you were going out there, and now you're leaving it?" Well, all right. Never be afraid to contradict yourself. Never be afraid to say, "I've learned enough" or "I'm never going to learn anything in this idea, and I'm going on to something new."

"So I had other worlds to look at," said Thoreau. And you know what? I could go out to the Far West. Why I could sail all the way to Hawaii. I could go to the land of the Antipodes, off to Australia, but why? I have the most uncharted world in the universe inside me. I have only begun to explore myself. So wherever I am, I can explore myself, and that's what I should be doing, instead of spending—he would say to you—hours in an airport somewhere to go off to look at some museum somewhere, when all of it is within me. The beauty of nature can never be surpassed by any work of art that you're going to find in a museum. And you know what? If you do want to read, think of that Indian classic. Think of the *Bhagavad Gita* and the *Vedas*, which point out to you that every morning is new and fresh. Every morning you can begin again. And do you know what? The Sun is a morning star."

That's how he ends *Walden*. Think about it. The Sun that lights the whole world is a creature of the morning. Every day, you can start your life anew. Oh, you won't. You're just looking through your notes there and pondering. But every day is new and fresh if you will seize that chance.

Like Socrates, however, Thoreau, as a person of conscience, as one who said, "Yes, I'm eccentric, because I march to a different drummer." Every time you say somebody is out of step, what they're really doing is marching to their own drummer. And I'm going to tell you, as Socrates did, that your democracy is not perfect. In fact, it has on it a terrible stain, and it's called slavery. But you know, you merchants in Boston whose contributions to the campaign of legislators send them to Washington, you make too much money out of trade with the South to want to get rid of slavery. You

Southerners, you've become so corrupted in your soul that you'll never get rid of slavery. "We're now fighting a war with Mexico," he said in 1846, "that has as its only goal to spread slavery. I'm not going to pay taxes."

Well, everybody should pay taxes. Taxes go to all kinds of good things. "I'm not going to," and so he was thrown in jail. One of his friends came and bailed him out. But that's all right, if they wanted to bail him out, they could do that. It didn't hurt him. It didn't hurt his soul. Because, he said, "If we have true freedom, then we ought to be free enough for the state to say, 'there are ten people in the state of Massachusetts who aren't going to pay their taxes.' Leave them alone. I don't care. Let's respect freedom in that way."

But he found one man he could admire: John Brown. In 1859, when John Brown seized that arsenal at Harper's Ferry, when he was taken prisoner, tried and hanged very quickly—there were no nine or ten year delays with John Brown; he was taken prisoner in October and in December he was hanged—all those wealthy, high-browed good-meaning people in New England who had supported him with money suddenly washed their hands and burned their files and wanted no one to know they had ever had anything to do with John Brown. Not Thoreau. He wrote an essay on John Brown. John Brown is a man of conscience. John Brown, who had come to understand from his own internal searching that slavery was such a great wrong it could only be removed by bloodshed and civil war. "There," said Thoreau, "is a man worth following. If you want to be part of the world, then do it the way John Brown did. Fight and die for something that truly means freedom." That was Thoreau's legacy—to love nature, because in nature you find a way to your own truth.

Lecture Thirty-One
Gibbon, *Decline and Fall of the Roman Empire*

Scope:

If we are concerned with the meaning of our own lives, we must ponder deeply the meaning of history, for our personal lives are but a microcosm of the larger story of history. In these terms, we must address two primary questions: Do we study history simply to learn about past events, or do we learn history to apply its lessons to our own day? Second, is history nothing but a series of random encounters, leading nowhere, or is history a story that moves forward, even in fits and starts, toward a better world for the human race? Most academic historians today would scorn both questions. We take them very seriously. Edward Gibbon's *Decline and Fall of the Roman Empire* is the greatest history written in the English language. In the Teaching Company course *A History of Freedom*, we explored Gibbon in the context of the ideas of freedom in the American Revolution. Here, we look at him and his history as a statement of "a philosophical historian," who searches the past for laws to guide us in the future.

Outline

I. The previous two lectures, on the second part of Goethe's *Faust* and on Thoreau's *Walden*, explored the themes of the ideal of beauty and the ideal of nature. Do absolute standards for beauty exist? Can we say, as Socrates does, that in heaven, there exists perfection of beauty and that everything on earth is a reflection of it? Are there absolute standards, which are based on the ideal of beauty, by which we can judge works of art? Can we teach these ideal values to students?

   A. The democracy of Athens would have answered in the affirmative to these questions. The Athenians believed that Greek temples could achieve perfection. The Athenian democracy set out to build the Parthenon and make it perfection.

   B. The contemporary United States would answer in the negative to these questions. Americans do not believe in absolute standards. Americans accept ugliness that would have appalled an Athenian.

C. Thoreau brings to our mind the concept of nature. For Thoreau, nature is the great source of renewal for the thoughtful individual. A truly thoughtful society should do all that is possible to preserve that beauty and engage itself with a natural rhythm that is part of that beauty.

II. History, the past, is another topic that every thoughtful individual must consider. What is our relationship with the past, and does it have any meaning for us today?

    A. The *Iliad* is about preserving the past. It tells the Greeks of 800 B.C. about their great past and its warriors.

    B. Confucius believed that one of his most important tasks was to teach his students about antiquity.

    C. Our era is essentially ahistorical. Many historical works and biographies are published, but we lack a criterion for studying and relating ourselves to the past that the age of Enlightenment, the era of the founders of our country, called a *philosophical view of history*. In this view, history is a means of understanding the present and looking into the future.

        1. The founders of the United States were influenced by the past. When they wrote the Declaration of Independence and the Constitution, they studied classical antiquity for models of how republican and democratic governments had worked in the past.

        2. They believed that history was a tool and that no society was immune to the process of historical decay. They also believed that all nations would eventually pass away.

    D. The Romans of the 2nd century A.D. believed that Rome was eternal, as the emperors told them. For individuals in the Enlightenment—including Goethe, the Founding Fathers, and Gibbon—the story of how and why the Roman Empire had passed away was of compelling importance.

III. Edward Gibbon's *Decline and Fall of the Roman Empire* is the most influential historical work written in English.

    A. It ranks—along with the works of Thucydides, Herodotus, Livy, and Tacitus—as one of the five greatest histories ever composed.

    B. *The Decline and Fall of the Roman Empire* was published between 1776 and 1789, the time of the Declaration of

Independence, the War of Independence, and the Constitution of the United States.

    C. For part of the time between 1776 and 1789, Gibbon was a member of Parliament. He later said that his time in Parliament was a school of civic virtue and patriotism, the first qualities that a historian needs.

IV. *The Decline and Fall* is a long, sad commentary on the history of a nation that gave up political liberty to become a superpower.

    A. Under the republican constitution that the Founding Fathers admired and Gibbon describes, Rome enjoyed a balance between the senate and the people, with a strong executive commander-in-chief.

        1. Rome rose from a tiny city-state to master of its world.

        2. By the 1st century B.C., Rome's multicultural and diverse empire resulted in tremendous affluence.

        3. This affluence corrupted every aspect of the republican political system; elections were openly bought and sold, and political factions were so strong that the Roman senate was gridlocked.

        4. Finally, the Roman people lost confidence in their government and in the republican way of life. They wanted peace and order.

        5. The Roman people gave up their political liberty and transferred all real power to a military dictator, their emperor. The first emperor was Julius Caesar, who was followed by the great statesman Augustus. Caesar and Augustus created a new order that brought peace and prosperity to their world.

        6. The Roman Empire reached its apex in the 2nd century A.D. It stretched from the North Sea to the Sahara and from Scotland to Iraq. The inhabitants were joined in common allegiance to Rome.

    B. Gibbon begins his story of the decline and fall of the Roman Empire in the 2nd century A.D., in the age of the Antonines.

V. Gibbon was born in England to a family of wealth and standing.

    A. He went to Oxford for a short time but found it uninspiring. His conversion to Roman Catholicism while at Oxford led his father to send him to a private tutor, a minister, in Lausanne, Switzerland. There, Gibbon converted nominally to Protestantism, learned Greek and Latin, developed a love for history, and became fluent in French.

B. He returned to England and served briefly in the Hampshire Militia. He believed that this experience was not insignificant for a historian of the Roman Empire, because he learned about military tactics.

C. Gibbon then traveled in Europe. He had decided that he wanted to make a name for himself by writing a history and began to search for a theme. He became engrossed by the concept of liberty and considered writing about the Florentine republic or the cantons of Switzerland.

D. In Rome in October 1764, sitting on the Capitoline Hill looking out over the Forum, which had become a cow pasture, Gibbon pondered the downfall of Rome. He decided that his topic would be the decline of the Roman Empire: why the grandeur of the empire "collapsed before barbarism and superstition and why Christian monks and German barbarians came to rule Rome."

E. He had a broad vision that the culture of the Roman Empire was as important as its political history.

    1. His treatments of the Middle East and Muhammad are superb and fair-minded.

    2. His treatment of Christianity as a historical phenomenon got him into trouble.

F. *The Decline and Fall of the Roman Empire* shows broad vision, a superb knowledge of sources, and magnificent use of the English language.

G. Gibbon's work describes the death of the ancient world and the birth of modern Europe. The Franks, the Germanic tribes, and the Angles and Saxons had all taken the place of the Romans. After centuries, these new people "restored a manly spirit of freedom and laid the foundation for the progress of our own age."

H. Gibbon was convinced that history is a story of progress and that one of the greatest signs of progress was America.

    1. In Parliamentary debates about the American Revolution, Gibbon said nothing.

    2. Because Lord North offered Gibbon a sinecure to sit on the board of trade, Gibbon always voted on North's side.

3. In letters, however, Gibbon clearly indicated that England was making a grievous mistake. In the pages of his history, he made oblique comparisons between the fall of Rome and what he perceived to be the decline and fall of the British Empire.

I. The first volume of *The Decline and Fall of the Roman Empire* appeared in 1776, became a runaway bestseller, and was immediately recognized as a masterpiece. Gibbon became independently wealthy.

J. When the government of Lord North collapsed, Gibbon retired to Lausanne, Switzerland, to write the final volumes of his work.

K. Gibbon also wrote a charming autobiography, in which he said that as an individual reaches the end of life, he can take consolation in going to heaven, or in his children, or in knowing that he set out to do something great and did it.

VI. Gibbon's history still speaks to us today, because Gibbon saw eternal lessons in the fate of Rome.

   A. The Roman Empire was the only superpower in history until the United States.

      1. A superpower is defined as a nation that is absolutely dominant, militarily, politically, economically, and culturally.

      2. Like Rome, our culture is derivative. Greek culture provided the common cultural cement of the Roman Empire. European civilization provides this for the United States.

   B. Gibbon shows us that Rome collapsed because of its involvement in the Middle East and its failure to solve the problems there.

      1. In the 3rd century A.D., Iran experienced a tremendous revival of fundamentalist religion.

      2. Eight hundred years earlier, the prophet Zarathustra had proclaimed his religion centered on the Lord of Truth, who was in constant struggle with the lie. This religion was one of ethical righteousness in which a person would go to paradise if he chose the Lord of Truth, fought for the Lord of Truth with fire and sword, and spread his religion.

3. The Iranians swept into the borders of the Roman Empire, and Rome never recovered from the devastation of the 3rd century A.D.

4. The Middle East had come to absorb all the attention of the Romans. Rome had been involved in nation-building for three centuries in the Middle East and had poured vast wealth into the region. However, it also kept large numbers of troops there, which alienated the population.

5. The civil war, expenses, and loss of manpower were a constant drain on the Roman Empire. In addition, the Romans were distracted and underestimated the potential danger in Central Europe, including the growing power of Germanic barbarians along the Danube and the Rhine Rivers. In the 3rd century A.D., these northern barbarians crashed through the Roman frontiers.

6. The failure of the Romans to solve the problems of the Middle East resulted in military, political, and economic.

7. Roman politics was disrupted because the constant war with the Iranians led to the collapse of the ordered government of the 1st and 2nd centuries A.D.

8. Rome emerged as a bureaucratic, totalitarian state that was incapable of solving the problems of the Middle East.

9. Gibbon speaks with profound relevance to us in the 21st century.

Essential Reading:

Gibbon, *The Decline and Fall of the Roman Empire.*

Supplementary Reading:

Gibbon, *Memoirs of My Life and Writings.*

Questions to Consider:

1. How would you say the American experience in the Middle East confirms or contradicts Gibbon's view that similar circumstances will always produce similar events?

2. In weighing objectively the impact of Christianity on the Roman Empire, Gibbon points out the deleterious effect on national unity of the orthodox Christian persecution of heretics. What, if anything, in the Christian religion justifies the persecution of heretics?

Lecture Thirty-One—Transcript
Gibbon, *Decline and Fall of the Roman Empire*

In our last two lectures, on the second part of *Faust* by Goethe and on *Walden* by Henry David Thoreau, we have explored two themes that I believe every thoughtful individual must come to terms with, the ideal of beauty and the ideal of nature. Are there absolute standards for beauty? Can we step back, as Socrates said, and say that in heaven there exists perfection of beauty? And that all else on Earth is but a reflection of it? Then, are there absolute standards based upon that ideal of beauty by which we judge works of art? Can we then teach these ideal values to students? The answer of the Athenian democracy was, "Yes." They believed that the Greek temple could achieve perfection within the limits it set for itself, and Athenian democracy set out to build the Parthenon and to make it perfection.

We, as a democracy, say, "No." We do not believe that there are absolute standards, and we accept ugliness that would have appalled an Athenian. Highways of American cities, as we mentioned in our last lecture, are an enduring testimony to our acceptance of ugliness.

Thoreau brings to our mind the concept of nature. For Thoreau, as I believe it should be, nature is the great source of renewal, for the thoughtful individual, and a society that is a truly thoughtful society will do all possible to preserve not just that natural beauty, but to engage itself with a natural rhythm that is part of that beauty.

A third topic that every individual must deal with is history, the past. What is our relationship to the past, and does it have any meaning for us today? The great work that we began with, *the Iliad*, is all about preserving the past. It is telling the Greeks of 800 B.C. about their great past and about warriors such as Agamemnon and Achilles, the past. Confucius believed that it was one of his most important tasks to teach his students about antiquity.

Our own age—you can ponder this with me—is essentially, in my view, "ahistorical." A lot of history works are published. A lot of biographies are published. But we lack that criterion for studying the past and relating ourselves to the past, which the Age of Enlightenment, the age of the founders of our country called a "philosophical view of history." That means that history is viewed as a means for understanding the present and looking into the future.

The founders of our country were profoundly influenced by the past. They studied Classical antiquity as they forged the Declaration of Independence and as they forged the Constitution, to provide models of how republican and democratic governments had worked in the past. They believed that history was a tool, that no society was immune to the process of historical decay. Every nation would pass away. Now, when I ask students that, only two or three will raise their hands out of a class of 400, if I say, "Will America ever pass away?" Will, one day, some professor be standing to a group of students far, far away in another galaxy talking about the Americans? Perhaps devoting two whole lectures to them. At the end, some student will come up and say, "Are the Americans going to be on the test? Are they really that important?" But, no one would accept that; no one of my class admits that. The Romans of the 2nd century A.D. believed that they were eternal; that is what the Emperors told them. We are eternal. *Aeternitas*. It is a symbol of Rome. "The Roman Empire will never pass away." But of course, it did.

For the Age of Enlightenment, for the 18th century, for figures such as Goethe, for the founders of our own country, and for Edward Gibbon, the story of how and why the grandeur of the Roman Empire passed away was of compelling importance. Edward Gibbon wrote the greatest single work of history ever composed in English. I would suggest to you that it ranks right along with Thucydides, Herodotus, Livy, and Gibbon's own great model, Tacitus, as one of the five greatest histories ever composed. His *History of the Decline and Fall of the Roman Empire*, significantly enough, was composed and published between 1776 and 1789, the very period in which the American Declaration of Independence, the War of Independence and the Constitution were being forged. Gibbon, for part of that period, sat as a Member of Parliament, and, as he said, "I watched every issue of the day, all of them centering around the great question, the independence of the American colonies. My time in Parliament," Gibbon said, "was a school of civic virtue, of patriotism, the first quality a historian needs."

As with the founders of our country, indeed, even with the Tories who were fighting against them, the central theme was liberty. Gibbon's great history is a long and sad commentary on the history of a nation that gave up political liberty to be a superpower, for that is what the Romans did. Under their republican constitution, which our founders so admired, and which Gibbon described in brilliant sentences, under that republican constitution with a balance between the senate and the people, with a strong executive commander-in-chief, the Romans rose from being a tiny city-state by the Tiber River to be masters of their world. By the 1st century B.C., they were absolute masters of their world.

That empire that they had won, that multicultural, diverse empire poured enormous affluence and wealth into Rome, and it corrupted every aspect of their republican political system, so that elections were openly bought and sold for vast campaign contributions. Political factions became so strong, and the infighting became so great that the senate was brought to gridlock. Tiny problems in the Middle East, which could have been solved with rapidity and with benefit for all, were allowed to drag on and on with constant changes in policy until, finally, the Roman people lost all confidence in their government, in their republican way of life. They, like the provincials they ruled over, wanted just peace and order, so they gave up their political liberty and transferred all real power to a military dictator. Oh, we call him an "emperor," but he was, and remained throughout the course of the Roman Empire, a military dictator.

The first of these was the greatest man who ever lived. We met him—Julius Caesar. Is there anyone like that on our horizon? Then, the greatest statesman who ever lived, Augustus, followed him. Between the two of them, they created a new order that brought peace and prosperity to their world. This reached its apex in the 2nd century A.D., when the Roman Empire spanned the North Sea all the way to the Sahara, and from the moors of Scotland out to the Tigris and Euphrates River valleys of Iraq. Joined together in common allegiance to Rome, with the individual citizen guaranteed rights, peace and prosperity unequalled again until the 20th century, which is where Gibbon begins his discussion of *The Decline and Fall of the Roman Empire*, the Roman Empire in the age of the Antonines.

He came to his work from a very well off childhood. He was born to a father who had a lot of money, and a grandfather who had made that money in the cloth and wool business. He had gone to Oxford for a short time, but he had found Oxford most uninspiring. He said, "I went the first day to my tutor and we read a little bit of Terence. He listened quietly, came back the next day, but I wasn't very well prepared. He listened quietly; said nothing came back the third day. I was very badly prepared, said nothing, smiled as I left. Missed the fourth day and wrote him a little note. He thanked me politely. Missed the fifth day and didn't write him anything. He didn't care. So I never came back."

Instead, he spent his time rummaging around in the bookstores of Oxford. In fact, he said, "If I had spent my time among the monks of Oxford, steeped in port the way they were, I never would have written *The Decline and Fall of the Roman Empire*."

Like Winston Churchill, or like Polybius, he was not an academic historian. What he did do as a youth, rummaging there in the bookstores of Oxford, was to meet a Catholic, at a time when Catholics were not allowed to go to Oxford, where there were heavy civil disabilities for being a Catholic. He converted and went home on spring break and said, "Dad, guess what I've done! I've become a Catholic!" His father was outraged, and shipped him off to Switzerland, put him under the tutelage of a Protestant minister with a very unclean wife. "Slovenly" is the way Gibbon described her. She set a very dirty table for him, but the minister brought him back into shape, and he converted, nominally, back to Protestantism and the Church of England. Mainly, though, he learned Greek and Latin really well this time around, developed a great love for history and learned French so well that you would have thought him French after that.

Then he came back to England and served for a brief time in the Hampshire militia. At the time it was thought that the French were going to invade England, and he said, "You know, those few months in the Hampshire militia were not insignificant to the historian of the Roman Empire, because I learned about military tactics and what it was like to be a soldier.

Then he traveled in Europe. He had already decided that he wanted to make a great name for himself by writing a history, so he searched for a theme. He was engrossed by the concept of liberty and thought about writing a history of the Florentine Republic, spurred on by Machiavelli. He thought about writing a history of the brave little cantons of Switzerland.

But in Rome in October of 1764, Gibbon was sitting on Capitoline Hill, where the great temple of Jupiter, Optimus Maximus, the guardian of the Roman Republic and Empire, had once been. He was sitting on the steps of what was now the Church of San Maria in Aracoeli, looking out over the Forum. The Forum in those days was called the Cow Pasture, because it was nothing but a grown-over field with a few columns poking up. There, where Cicero had once been, cows and sheep pastured, and a few people lived in torn-down, crumbling ruins. He was pondering why had all the grandeur of Rome passed away when these monks came down the steps, barefoot, their hoods over their faces, chanting their evening prayers. Gibbon decided right then, "I would write a great history: *The Decline and Fall of the Roman Empire*, about why the grandeur of that great nation collapsed before—and these are his words— barbarism and superstition, about why Christian monks and German barbarians came to rule Rome."

That became his task. He began to prepare himself by wide and voluminous reading, and I'll tell you this right now, you can sit down with Gibbon and read him and learn as many facts that are as accurate about the Roman Empire as you can read in a book published right now. He went beyond many of the historians of the next century, the 19th century, in the careful use he made of archeological evidence, the use of coins, the use of art, and in his broad vision of the culture of the Empire, as being just as important as the political history, in his broad vision of what the Roman Empire was. His treatment of the Middle East, his treatment of Muhammad is superb and very, very fair-minded. In fact, to many of his critics, it was much more fair minded than his treatment of Christianity, which got him into big hot water. He made a lot of people mad at him about his treatment of Christianity, because he professed just to go through and look at it as a historical phenomenon and asked whether these miracles really occurred, then write this.

He had a broad vision, superb knowledge of the sources, and he had a magnificent English style. Oh! If you want to learn English prose the way it should be written, read Gibbon. I'll tell you, someone who did was Winston Churchill. Churchill believed that most Great Books were wasted on young people, and probably if you read too many books, it was a bad thing. So he read a few books, very, very carefully. When he was a lieutenant in India, he had his mother send him a complete set of Gibbon. "There," he said, "I learned to write. There, I gained that mastery of the English language that would stand me in such good stead when I was in Parliament."

There he learned those rolling phrases that would rally a nation that would never surrender and never give up. I want to read you just a bit of Gibbon because I think it is a monument of English prose. Let's just see how he begins his work, because it is not without interest and relevance for us today.

> In the second century of the Christian era, the Empire of Rome comprehended the fairest part of the Earth and the most civilized portion of mankind. The frontiers of that extensive monarchy were guarded by ancient renown and disciplined valor.

Notice his use of commas. Notice his use of adjective—"ancient renown," "disciplined valor." You can hear Churchill speaking, "the gentle but powerful"—ah, what a contrast there!

> The gentle but powerful influence of laws and manners had gradually cemented the union of the provinces. Their peaceful inhabitants enjoyed and abused the advantages of wealth and luxury. The image of a free constitution was preserved with decent reverence. The Roman Senate appeared to possess the sovereign authority and devolved on the Emperors all the executive powers of government.

Ah! That had been part of the mastery of Augustus, to leave the old constitution standing as a façade, while gathering all real power into his hands, because people, as Gibbon understood, want prosperity and peace, and they care nothing about liberty, as long as they have jobs and are prosperous; or, as the emperors understood, "bread and circuses," plenty to eat, good incomes, and good entertainment. Put it in today's words, lots of affluence and cable TV. That was all people wanted, and the emperors gave it to them.

> During a happy period, from A.D. 98 to 180, of more than fourscore years, the public administration was conducted by the virtue and abilities—Gibbon will never use one word where two can be got in; three even better—of Nerva, Trajan, Hadrian and the two Antonines. It is the design of this and of the two succeeding chapters to describe the prosperous condition of their empire, and afterwards, from the death of Marcus Antonius, to deduce the most important circumstances of its decline and fall. A revolution, which will ever be remembered and is still felt by the nations of the Earth.

That first paragraph not only told you what he's going to write about, but he has left you with a profound sense of how important this historical event is, for it was the death of the ancient world and the birth of modern Europe. The great nations of Gibbon's own day—England, the land of the Angles and Saxons; France, Frankreich, the land of the Franks; and Germany—these had all been born in the collapse of the Roman Empire. And these great Teutonic nations, Franks, other Germanic tribes, the Angles and Saxons, had all taken the place of the Romans.

Gibbon will refer to how this race of giants, as he called the Teutons, burst upon the scene and pulled down the small pygmies that the Romans had become. After a series of centuries, he says—these are his words, not mine—"restored a manly spirit of freedom and laid the foundation for the progress of our own age." Gibbon was convinced that history is a story of progress. There will be fits and starts, but ultimately we in the age of Enlightenment; the age of the 18th century, had moved far beyond in terms of our technology. Do you know one of the greatest signs he saw of progress was America? He said, "You know, if there ever were another barbarian flood to break out upon us, from some nations we no longer take seriously, why, the progress of Europe would continue in America, already peopled with Europeans, where the language and literature and culture of Europe continues to flourish." Because it was interesting that during all the debates on the American Revolution, Gibbon never said a word. "The example of both the good orators and the bad ones prevented me, but I was an attentive listener," he said. "However, you have to live, now, do you not?" That's why I like Gibbon so much. A short, portly man, balding early. He liked good port, liked to buy books, liked to live well.

Writing French very well, he was given the chance by the government of Lord North, the Prime Minister during the Revolution, to write a paper that would justify British policy to Europe, and it needed to be written in French, the language of diplomacy. He wrote a masterful example of it, and it did well. It did. It conveyed the English position extremely well. Then he was offered a sinecure to sit on the Board of Trade, which never met, but paid a handsome salary. When called upon to vote, he always voted on the side of Lord North, but in his letters, he made it clear that England was making a grievous mistake. From time to time, obliquely, in the pages of his history, he will say what England really needs to be done. As the Roman Empire is in its great period of decline in the 5th century, Gibbon says if only the Emperors had had the sense to establish provincial assemblies in each one of their provinces, allowed the provincials to elect their representatives to those provincial assemblies, given them complete control over their internal affairs, including their taxation, why the Roman Empire would have endured forever, supported by the loyal arms of free men.

Well, that's what England really should do, but is there anything wrong with his voting for Lord North? Absolutely not, because it gave him the quality of port, the quality of roast beef, to write these immortal pages. In 1776, the first volume came out, and it was a runaway best seller. "I awoke to find myself famous," Gibbon said. "My book was on every coffee table and in almost every toilet in England." It was a masterpiece, and immediately recognized as such. It went through a series of official editions, and there were a number of pirated editions. Gibbon now became independently wealthy.

When Lord North's government collapsed and he lost his position on the Board of Trade, he retired to Lausanne, Switzerland, and there wrote his final volumes, finishing on a June night. He took a walk around his villa, looked out over the calm sea and said, with considerable regret, "I had taken leave of a friend that had been with me all those years, that wonderful story of *The Decline and Fall of the Roman Empire*. I could also say that I had made myself famous, and that's what I set out to do."

He did make himself famous. He would go on to write an *Autobiography*, which is one of the most charming and interesting autobiographies in English. In it he refers to why he decided to write *The History of The Decline and Fall of the Roman Empire*, and he ends up with some message, maybe, for all of us. "As you reach the end of your life—and that will come, even to you—as you reach the end of your life, you can perhaps take, if you are an enthusiast, as he called them, some consolation in going to heaven, if you believe that. Or if you don't, you can say, 'Well, at least I've got these children, and they'll carry on', if they are really worthwhile. Or you can say, 'I set out to do something really great and I did it,' and believe me, that's the best feeling in the world."

His history still speaks to us today because Gibbon saw in the decline and fall of the Roman Empire, eternal lessons. I want to draw one of those lessons for us right now.

I believe that the Roman Empire, this vast, militarily powerful and prosperous nation, was the only superpower in history until the United States. I want to define "superpower" for you carefully. It is a nation that is absolutely dominant militarily, politically, economically, and culturally, which Rome was, in its world, and we are now. As with Rome, our culture is derivative. Rome was the bearer of Greek civilization. The Roman Emperors were all bilingual, speaking Greek as well as Latin. Greek was the official language of the Empire, along with Latin, and the Roman Emperors believed that Greek culture—the values of Plato, the literature of Sophocles—provided the common cultural cement of their Empire. It was a tolerant and multicultural Empire in which Romans built temples to the gods of Egypt, to the gods of the Celts. You could plead your case in court in Celtic or in Syriac. The Roman Emperors also believed there must be a common culture, and they found that in Greece.

We are the bearers of European culture. Now, many nations have added to the richness of America, but the language we speak is European, the alphabet we write in is European, and the basis of our whole school system is European. Our very ideals are European. So we are the bearers of European civilization, and like the Romans, we are one of only two superpowers that have ever existed. In the pages of Gibbon we find why Rome declined and fell. It fell because of its involvement in the Middle East and its failure to solve the problem of the Middle East. Gibbon describes the Middle East in the time of the 3rd century A.D., when Iran, the great eastern power that was the only possible counterbalance to Rome underwent a tremendous religious revival, of religious fundamentalism. Eight hundred years before, the prophet Zarathustra had proclaimed his religion, centered around the Lord of Truth, in constant struggle with the lie. The same way that Muhammad would later proclaim God to be the Lord of Truth, in constant struggle with the lie. Zarathustra proclaimed a religion of ethical righteousness, in which you made your decision. If you chose the Lord of Truth and fought for the Lord of Truth and spread his religion by fire and sword, you went to Paradise. If you lied and said the Lord of Truth was not, then you passed into eternal hell.

Revitalized by that grand, powerful religious fundamentalism, the Iranians swept out of the desert lands, and into the borders of the Roman Empire. So much so that a Roman Emperor was taken captive, carried off to Iran, flayed alive, and his skin hung up in the temple of the Lord of Truth, Ahura Mazda. From that devastation of the 3rd century A.D., Rome would never recover. Oh, there would be fits and starts back, but Rome was broken from that moment. The Middle East had come to absorb all the attention of the Romans. Going all the way back to the annexation of Judaea, Rome had found itself involved for three centuries in trying to "nation-build" in the Middle East; in pouring vast amounts of wealth into the Middle East; keeping large numbers of troops there that only alienated the people of the Middle East. So that civil war, expenses, and the loss of manpower were a constant drain upon the Romans.

But more than that, it distracted them from other dangers, and above all, a focus upon the Middle East made the Romans underestimate the dangers in Central Europe. The same area that today we would call Poland and [former] Soviet Union and the eastern part of Germany. They underestimated the growing power of the Germanic barbarians along their Danube and Rhine River frontiers. In coordination, then, with Iran, those northern barbarians would crash through the Roman frontiers in the 3rd century, ravaging and plundering; so the failure of the Romans to solve the problem of the Middle East, once they had become involved there, provided the military, the political and the economic source of their collapse.

It even completely disrupted the politics of Rome, because the constant war with the East, with the Iranians, led to the collapse of the ordered government of the age of the 1st and 2nd centuries A.D. Rome would emerge from this a bureaucratic, totalitarian state, still incapable of solving the problem of the Middle East, so in the pages of Gibbon we read the story of one more empire that found its graveyard in the Middle East. Gibbon speaks with very profound relevance to us as Americans in this 21st century.

Lecture Thirty-Two
Lord Acton, *The History of Freedom*

Scope:

Lord Acton believed that history was the story of the march of liberty. It is a message of supreme importance to us today, citizens of a superpower, engaged in bringing democracy to the world. Acton never wrote his planned history of liberty. But in numerous essays and unpublished notes, he left behind a legacy of historical thought. Acton taught that thinking historically was more important than knowledge of historical facts. His was a "liberal" vision of history, as John Stuart Mill had a liberal vision of political thought and Winston Churchill, a liberal vision of political action. Acton was deeply religious. He defined liberty as "the reign of conscience." True liberty would be achieved when every individual is free to follow the dictates of his or her individual conscience. Classical antiquity, the Middle Ages, the Renaissance and Reformation, the age of Enlightenment, and our modern age have each contributed to the march of liberty.

Outline

I. The previous lecture began the discussion of the theme of history. Is the past meaningful? Does the past tell us anything about the present or the future? Is there a point to history, or is it a random collision of events?

   A. The question of whether history has a purpose lies behind the first known historical work composed. In his histories of the Persian war, Herodotus attempted to discover what was permanent behind all the passing empires.

   B. Gibbon also explored the reasons that empires passed away. He was a philosophical historian, one who sought laws of history, which would—like laws of science—apply forever. Gibbon also believed that the historian had a duty to pass moral judgment.

   C. Historians today dispute the claims of Gibbon. They do not believe that history is a guide to the present or the future, and they would say that the historian must be careful about passing historical judgments, because no universal set of values exists. This coincides with the ideas of Machiavelli, who says that nations are not bound by any moral strictures and that a nation exists only to serve itself. This view became the realpolitik of Europe in the 19th and 20th centuries.

II. Lord Acton stood out boldly against the idea that morality can be separated from history.

    A. Acton is a great spokesperson for moral judgment in history, laws in history, and the idea that history has a grand theme.

    B. Acton believed that the theme of the progress of history is liberty. In this belief, he agrees with the tradition of historians going back to Herodotus.

III. Lord Acton had an unusual upbringing.

    A. He was born in 1834 to a distinguished family of English and continental aristocrats. Acton was a baronet, the lowest level of English nobility.

    B. Acton's family was Roman Catholic, which in early 19th-century England still carried some liabilities, including ineligibility to attend Oxford or Cambridge.

    C. The grandfather of Lord Acton had lived most of his life in Europe and had served at the court of the king of Naples.

    D. Denied admission to Cambridge because of his Catholicism, Acton was sent by his family to study in Germany under the Catholic theologian and priest Johann Ignaz von Doellinger, who was a historian of the church. Acton, like Gibbon, never received a university degree.

    E. Under Doellinger, Acton developed a sense for 19th-century progressive history, which focused on the use of documents.

IV. After his return to England, Acton sought to use his skills as a journalist to take an active role in the reform of the Catholic church, a movement in which Doellinger was involved. The purpose of this movement was to bring the Catholic Church into the 19th century.

    A. Although Acton was a devout Catholic who accepted the doctrine of the church, he believed that the church had to be brought into agreement with the liberal currents sweeping Europe.

B. Acton believed that instead of supporting autocratic governments, the Catholic Church should support democratic governments and accept scientific thought. He saw no contradiction between the truth of God and the truth of science.

C. At that time, the Catholic Church was becoming more reactionary, fearing the loss of political authority over the Papal States and the temporal power of the pope.

D. Acton had already developed a central theme in his life, the idea of the educated conscience, which was the most important guarantee of individual freedom. He called liberty the reign of conscience and said that true freedom would exist in the world when every individual was free to exercise his or her conscience.

E. Acton believed that papal infallibility stood in opposition to the idea of freedom of conscience, because people were not allowed to question the pope's actions. Through his study of history, he learned that papal infallibility contradicted the teachings of the church. Church councils had historically played a powerful role in setting doctrine.

F. Acton took an active part in the debate on papal infallibility, traveling to Rome when the ecumenical council was called to debate the question.

G. Acton was absolutely defeated. He saw that high officials who had opposed the doctrine denied their consciences and went along with the majority.

H. Acton was almost excommunicated. He remained a Roman Catholic but subsequently played no role in the church. He believed that the church had lost its chance to support progressive governments around the world.

V. The second great disappointment for Lord Acton was the defeat of the Confederacy.

A. Acton was one of the first people in England to recognize that the United States had a great political literature in the *Federalist Papers*, and he compared the Declaration of Independence and the Constitution to the writings of Plato.

B. Acton wrote learned articles for the British government explaining what the American Constitution was about and why the idea of states' rights was so important.

    1. At that time, the British believed that American democracy had the same flaws as the Athenian democracy and that it was a radical democracy with no check on the will of the people.

    2. Acton argued that states' rights served as a balance in America and resulted in a check on a centralized, radical democracy.

    3. Acton believed that a radical democracy is imperialist abroad and despotic at home. In the Athenian democracy, the conscience of the individual was subordinated to the will of the majority. For Acton, the Athenian democracy was immoral and amoral.

C. In 1861, the Civil War began in the United States. Although the British government did not approve of slavery, it favored the Confederacy and hoped that the defeat of the Union would lead to further dissolution of the United States.

D. Acton wrote papers for Gladstone and the British government, delineating the issues of the Civil War. His research showed that the finest Confederates, including Robert E. Lee, were morally opposed to slavery and that Southern states would eventually end slavery. Acton saw a risk in the intervention of the federal government, which might destroy states' rights on the pretense of ending slavery.

E. With the defeat of the Confederacy at the Battle of Gettysburg, Acton again lost.

F. He believed that the United States had had a chance to become a beacon to the world but would instead become a despotic democracy without any regard for the rights of individuals, that it would control all aspects of the lives of its citizens, and that it would become fiscally irresponsible in its expansion.

G. Acton admired Robert E. Lee. He wrote to Lee and asked him his feelings about the war. Lee replied that he had seen in states' rights the only hope for avoiding the course of every democracy, including that of Athens. He believed that these democracies had destroyed the rights of the individual in the name of the majority.

VI. The defeat of the Confederacy was also the defeat of the federal idea. Acton believed that federalism, not centralization, was the hope for a guardian of liberty.

    A. Acton saw that the United States was no longer a federal republic but a unified country.

    B. Federalism was also being discredited in Europe. Germany and Italy united, not as confederations of semiautonomous states, but as centralized nations.

VII. Since the time of his studies with Doellinger, Acton had planned to write a *History of Liberty.*

    A. This work would describe the history of liberty from its earliest days to the present. It would be based on the concept that ideas make history and that historical thinking is more important than historical knowledge.

    B. *The History of Liberty* would apply the lessons of history to Acton's time. Acton believed that learning from the examples of the past was the greatest way to shape one's conscience. Great events, individuals, and economic and social forces—all of these are shaped by ideas. He believed that the greatest of these ideas is liberty.

    C. Acton began to compile a library, which ultimately included 70,000 volumes.

    D. He took notes on slips of paper, wrote down his own ideas, penned aphorisms about liberty, corresponded with other historians, engaged in debates in English historical journals about such questions as moral judgment in history, and gave lectures based on his work. But he never actually wrote the book.

    E. Acton finally explained to two people why he never wrote this great work.

        1. To Mary Gladstone, he explained that no one agreed with him about what liberty truly is and about the importance of moral judgment.

        2. To Doellinger, he indicated that Doellinger did not agree with his idea of moral judgment. Acton believed that there could be no separation between public morality and private morality. A statesman should be judged by the same moral code used to judge an ordinary citizen. Murder is murder, whether committed by the state or by a criminal. Acton said that much of history is the justification of the actions of such murderers as Alexander the Great.

F. Acton wrote to Bishop Creighton: "All power tends to corrupt and absolute power corrupts absolutely. Very few great men are good men."

G. Acton's financial situation degenerated. Gladstone intervened, and Andrew Carnegie bought Acton's library but allowed him to use it for the rest of his life.

H. Acton was a man of great moral courage, fortitude, and purity.

I. Acton's *History of Liberty* was falsely derided as "the greatest book never written."

VIII. In fact, Acton's ideas, as evidenced by his notes and occasional papers, still speak with compelling immediacy.

A. Acton understood the dangers of nationalism and socialism.

B. Acton was not a conservative, but his legacy has been usurped by conservatism. He believed that conservatism was about not educating the conscience.

C. Acton admired Gladstone and his ideal of democratic liberty. He supported Gladstone's idea of beginning a welfare state. Acton, Gladstone, and Churchill all believed that there must be basic welfare for all citizens if a democracy is to flourish.

D. Acton believed that uncontrolled capitalism was a force of evil. For Acton, the idea of a free-market economy is a form of determinism, and he hated all forms of determinism.

E. Acton believed that racism was evil because it denied the ability of conscience to redeem the individual.

F. Nationalism, Acton thought, was a primitive idea that represented the worst kind of racism. He believed that nationalism, which most people thought to be progress, would lead to ethnic cleansing.

G. According to Acton, socialism would help nationalism along. He saw socialism as determinism that reduces people to economic objects. The notion that ideas are products of economic and social forces destroys the conscience of mankind.

H. Acton believed that dismissing the idea of federalism was wrong. Federalism was a way to bring various units together, while maintaining their uniqueness and resisting the soulless destructive power of a centralized, bureaucratic government.

I. Acton distinguished between British liberals, such as Gladstone—who believed in God, conscience, and the individual—and liberals of the continent, such as Cavour, who believed not in the individual but in the state. These European liberals argued that the state should intervene in every aspect of human life.

J. It is perhaps no coincidence that the National Socialist Party brought Europe to ruin, but federalism delivered Europe.

K. In 1948 in Zurich, Winston Churchill said that Europe would rise from the ruins and that France and Germany would lead Europe into a federal nation, a United States of Europe.

L. In his aphorisms, unpublished works, and essays, Acton left a compelling legacy of the importance of history, our duty to do what is right and just in the present, and a vision of how a better future can be created.

Essential Reading:

Fears, ed. *Selected Writings of Lord Acton*, vol. I, pp. ix–xxvii and 5–85; 216–279; 409–458.

Supplementary Reading:

Fears, ed., *Selected Writings of Lord Acton*, vols. II and III.

Questions to Consider:

1. How do you reconcile the fact that Acton was both a great lover of liberty and a supporter of the Confederacy?

2. Acton distinguished between the British liberal, who believed in limited government, and the continental liberal, who believed in big government. Gladstone, for Acton, represented the British ideal liberal. The Italian statesman Cavour represented the ideal continental liberal. Can the two ideals be reconciled?

Lecture Thirty-Two—Transcript
Lord Acton, *The History of Freedom*

In our last lecture, we began our discussion of the theme of history. My view is that every thoughtful individual must come to grips with how they regard the past. Is the past meaningful for them? Does the past tell us anything about the present? Does it tell us anything about the future? Is there a point to history or is it simply a random collision of events? Is it "a tale told by an idiot, full of sound and fury, signifying nothing," or does it have a purpose?

Of course that idea of "is there a purpose to history?" lies behind the first work of history ever truly composed, Herodotus and his histories of the Persian War. What he wants, he says, is to discover what is permanent behind all the passing away of empires. That, too, was the goal of Edward Gibbon. That is why he was a "philosophical historian," one who sought the laws of history, laws that would operate forever, just like the laws of physics. So what we learn from the Roman Empire we can apply to the American superpower of today. That is the great meaning of Gibbon.

Gibbon was also aware that a historian has the duty to pass moral judgement. He says history would not be worth studying unless historians took upon themselves to judge evil that had been done in the past and tell the future about it, and to judge good things and tell the future about it. So that if you do an evil deed—even if you get away with it—later generations will know you were a very, very bad person. So let's not gloss over the evil of Tiberius, let us say.

Now, historians today would dispute both of these claims. In fact, I would say almost all academic historians would say that history is not a guide to the present or to the future. Almost all of them would say the historian must be very careful about passing historical judgments, because—and here we come back to one of our central themes—by whose values is the historian going to judge? There is no universal set of values. Hence, the historian cannot dare pass judgment. This of course is to allow, say, Josef Stalin to be judged simply on the basis of expediency. That of course, is why Machiavelli is so important. Because he set the standard that there is a profound difference between the behavior of an ordinary person and the behavior of a statesman, a leader. That nations, in fact, are not bound by any kind of moral strictures. A nation exists only to serve itself. A statesman, the leader of that nation, may have to do many deeds that would end the ordinary person on the gallows, and that became the policy of *realpolitik*, as practiced in Europe in the 19th and 20th centuries. Whatsoever serves the purpose of the state is right.

Lord Acton, the subject of this lecture, stood out boldly in the 19th century against the idea that we can separate morality from history. He was the great spokesperson for moral judgement in history, for laws of history, and for the ideal that there is a grand theme to history. For him the grand theme of the progress of history was liberty, and he follows in the great tradition of historians, going right back to Herodotus, Thucydides, Polybius, Livy, Tacitus, Saint Augustine and his *City of God*, and Edward Gibbon, who told the story of liberty as the central theme of history.

Acton, like Gibbon, had a very unusual education. He was born in 1834, and he was English. But, he was Catholic at a time when Catholics—as we mentioned in our last lecture—still suffered numerous disabilities, including being not allowed to attend Oxford and Cambridge. Moreover, his background was not that of an ordinary English aristocrat. He was a baronet. That's the lowest level of English nobility. But his grandfather had lived almost all of his life in Europe. In fact, John Acton, the grandfather, had become a very prominent figure—a statesman, really—at the court of the King of Naples. In Naples today there is still a Via Acton. He served the Bourbon kings of Naples, and Acton, on both sides was descended not only from English aristocracy but also from European aristocracy.

The wife he married was also a European aristocrat. So Acton grew up speaking, very naturally, not just English, but French and German and Italian. When it got time for him to go to university, he was turned down at Cambridge, because he was Catholic. So he was sent by his family to study in Germany, in Munich, to study with a very well known Catholic theologian and priest, Ignaz Doellinger, who was a superb historian of the Church. There Acton learned about history. So, like Gibbon, he never had a university degree. He read Plutarch and the classics, but above all, under Doellinger he developed a keen sense for 19th century progressive history, which focused upon the use of documents. So he had a historical training in the use of original documents far superior to anything he would have received at Oxford or Cambridge.

But that's not what he wanted to do. He did not want to be a historian, in his twenties. He wanted to take a very active role in the reform of the Catholic Church. A movement that Doellinger, his mentor and life-long close friend, was very involved in. The purpose was to bring the Catholic Church into the 19th century, and Acton throughout his life remained a very profound Catholic. As Gibbon was a very happy skeptic about all things religious, Acton said, "I am conscious of never having doubted any single doctrine of the Church." So he accepted all Church doctrine, he said.

But the Church had to be brought into the 19th century, and had to be brought into agreement with the liberal currents that were sweeping Europe. So when Acton returned to England, he began to write and even found a series of journals, magazines that talked about how the Church had to be made liberal; that the Church, instead of supporting autocratic governments, should support governments that were democratic; that the Church should agree with all elements of science; and that there ultimately could be no contradiction, Acton said, between the truth of God and the truth of science. This at a moment when the Church was becoming ever-more reactionary, in worry about the political currents that were going to sweep away the Papal States, the temporal power of the Pope. And, as part of that reactionary movement, as Acton understood it, was this strong current of thought that wanted to proclaim the infallibility of the Pope, the fact that when the Pope spoke on matters of doctrine, he was infallible. He could not be questioned.

By his twenties, Acton had already developed the central theme of his life, which was the idea of conscience, that the most important guarantee of freedom is that every individual has an educated conscience. He called liberty, "the reign of conscience." He said that true freedom will exist in a world when every individual is free to exercise that conscience and that conscience has been educated in a free fashion. And Papal infallibility was the exact opposite of that, wasn't it? If the Pope is infallible, you cannot question it. So it left no room for conscience. Acton, through his study of history said, "This is absolutely contrary to the teachings of the Church. In fact, if you go back and look at Church history, there has been a very powerful role played by Church councils that set the doctrine." Instead of then just sitting back and writing newspaper articles, Acton got into the fray. Like Socrates, or like Jesus, he came out and got deeply involved.

When the ecumenical council was called in Rome to debate this question of Papal infallibility, Acton went to Rome. He had a number of contacts through his family to high Church officials, and he fought as hard as he could. He was absolutely defeated, and he saw all these bishops and high churchmen who had said that they opposed Papal infallibility, when it came right down, went along with the crowd. In other words, they denied their conscience and did what was expedient. Acton was almost excommunicated from the Church. Finally he was not excommunicated, but for him, he would remain a believing Catholic, but he could play no role in the Church, and the Church would go on its own way, being left behind by the 19th century, and losing the chance for Catholicism to become the supporter of progressive governments all over the world.

A second great disappointment occurred to him in the 1860s—the ecumenical council coming to its culmination in 1870. That was the loss of the Confederacy. Now this is going to surprise some of you, since Acton was a great believer in liberty. He loved the United States, and, in fact, was one of the first Englishmen to realize that America had a political literature as great as anything that Greece had ever composed, in the *Federalist Papers*. He thought that the Declaration of Independence and the Constitution and the *Federalist Papers* were works worthy of comparing with Plato, and he wrote very learned, excellent articles for the British government, including Gladstone—William Gladstone, the great liberal Prime Minister with whom he became ever closer—explaining what the American Constitution was about and why states' rights was so important to the American Constitution. Because in Britain, people tended to assume that America was a democracy, and exhibited all the worst characteristics of the Athenian democracy. It was a radical democracy with no check upon the will of the people. Acton said, "No. That is wrong. It is a balanced constitution, and the supreme balance to it are the rights of the states. It is, indeed, a confederation of states, and in the power of the states will always lie a check upon a centralized, radical democracy. For a centralized, radical democracy will be imperialistic abroad and despotic at home."

Acton had no love whatsoever for the Athenian democracy. He thought it a monstrous government, in which the conscience of the individual was completely subordinated to the will of the majority. What had they done to Socrates because he spoke his conscience? They had put him to death. The Athenian democracy represented what happened when the will of the majority was all-powerful. In fact, Acton would say, "You can assassinate a king. You can even throw out a government. But you cannot do anything against the majority. It is all-powerful. It is immoral. It is immoral and it is amoral every time we see it in history. It will always sink, ultimately, to the lowest common denominator."

In 1861, the Civil War broke out. And as you will know, the British, at the upper level, the government, was very favorably disposed toward the Confederacy. It was only the question of slavery that was a real sticking point. But the British government was very favorably disposed towards the Confederacy, and, in point of fact, of course, hoped that the defeat of the Union would lead to the breaking up further of the United States. Acton wrote papers again for Gladstone and for the British Government, including Lord Palmerston that focused on what the Civil War was really about. He called it "the American Revolution." It was, in his eyes, the second American Revolution.

He went through and carefully gathered large numbers of newspaper clippings and other material that showed that the finest Confederates, like Robert E. Lee, were opposed to slavery. They believed slavery to be a great moral wrong, and that the Southern states would end slavery in their own time. But the far greater danger was for the federal government to intervene and destroy the rights of the states under the pretence of getting rid of slavery. This was the argument that Acton made.

But the defeat at Gettysburg pushed all that aside. It became absolutely impossible for the British government to recognize the Confederacy. Acton had lost again. He wrote to a friend, "I weep more for what was lost at Appomattox than for what was won at Waterloo. I believe that the United States had the chance to be the beacon to the world, and now it will become a despotic democracy, without any real regard for the rights of individuals, controlling every aspect of the individual's life, peering into any and every corner of that individual's life, fiscally irresponsible, running up huge budget debts, and expanding as far as it can to become a great superpower."

He enormously admired Robert E. Lee. His wife, at his urging, wrote to Mrs. Lee and asked for a photograph of Robert E. Lee. Mrs. Lee sent it to Mrs. Acton. That gave Acton the encouragement to write to Lee and said, "What do you think about the war? Could I have your feelings about it?" And this is what Lee wrote back: That he had seen in states' rights the only hope of preventing the United States from going the course of every democracy in history, including that of

Athens—to destroy the rights of the individual in the name of the great majority. That is why he had fought, and they corresponded back and forth, Acton and Robert E. Lee.

But this was the second great disappointment for Acton. First the Vatican Council destroyed his hope that the Church would become a great force for liberalism, and then the defeat of the Confederacy. Of course, here we disagree with him, but for Acton, that, too, prevented the United States ever from becoming a great force for liberty.

It was also the defeat of the Federal idea, and he had a very deep conviction that federalism, not centralization, was the great guardian of liberty. He saw that the United States was no longer a federal republic, but was instead a unified country. At the same time, all over Europe, federalism was being discredited. Italy and Germany both, in 1870 would be united, not as a confederation of semi-autonomous states, but as absolute republics and monarchies. So federalism was discredited. The Church was no longer a force for liberty.

But there was still his history, and he had planned since his studies with Doellinger to write a great *History of Liberty*, the sweep of liberty from its earliest days all the way up to the present. It would be a history of liberty based upon his ideal that ideas make history and that historical thinking is far more important than historical knowledge. History is not about trivia questions, it is not about knowing the Presidents of the United States in order; it is about applying the lessons of history to your own day. That is why historical thinking is important, and it is the greatest way to shape your conscience, to learn from the examples of the past. Ideas make history. Great events, great individuals, economic and social forces, all of these are shaped by ideas. And the greatest of these ideas is liberty.

So he began to compile a great library that ultimately ran to 70,000 volumes. He would sit down every day—he, being an aristocrat and having money, did not have to worry about a job—and take notes on slips of paper, little note cards, what he was learning from the books and then his own ideas, forging many of them into aphorisms about liberty, corresponding with a wide range of historians, engaging in debates in the English historical journals over questions like moral judgement in history, but never sitting down and writing a book. His friends, and there were many in academic circles, and his friends in government circles would always ask, "Why don't you sit down and write?" His old teacher, Doellinger, would prod him and say,

"Sooner or later, my son, you must stop doing research and begin writing. All you're doing is piling up boxes full of note cards. When will you begin to tell the story of liberty?"

Well, he did, in two lectures given in 1877, carry the course of liberty from "Liberty in Antiquity" and "Liberty and Christianity." But beyond that, having gone through his papers as I have, there is hardly a page that can be called a consecutive history of liberty. He finally explained to two people to whom he was closest—one was Mary Gladstone, the daughter of the great Gladstone— he said, "Nobody agrees with me. Nobody agrees with me about what liberty truly is, and about the importance of moral judgement. So perhaps you're right, and your father is right. All I can really do is take notes and put them in books on little slips of paper."

To his old teacher, Doellinger, he said, "You don't agree with my idea of historical judgement, do you? Time and time again you've come back with this answer, that a statesman must do things that are immoral if his country is to survive. That it is was necessary for Elizabeth to order the execution of Mary, Queen of Scots. But I tell you, my old teacher, that that was murder, and for a statesman to order murder, to carry out covert operations, to lie to his country, these all ought to have the same punishment as if an ordinary person does it. But I'll tell you what: First comes the assassin with his dagger, and then comes the historian with a sponge to wipe it all out. So we write biographies of figures like Alexander the Great, who were nothing but murderers on a huge scale. And yet we try to justify it that they brought better things to the world. Well, you don't agree with me, and certainly most historians don't agree with me. Look at the big fight I got into with Bishop Creighton, when I wrote a review of his book, bringing this out. He wrote me a letter saying, 'How dare you criticize my book on the grounds that I, a bishop, do not have a sense of morality!' And I wrote him back and said, 'All power tends to corrupt, and absolute power corrupts absolutely. Very few great men are good men.' So that is why I don't write. I feel no stimulation from others and none who share my views and ideas."

So today you can still go to Cambridge University. You see the 70,000 volumes that are kept in one enormous room. In his last years he became less well off, and he was going to have to sell his library. Once again, Gladstone, that great democratic leader, intervened, and Andrew Carnegie, the wealthy American industrialist, bought that library without ever telling Acton, and allowed Acton to use it to the end of his life. And so, the volumes are still there, and you take out these yellow slips of paper right where Acton had put them, and you go through his note cards.

But I'm going to tell you one thing: Having gone through the note cards and papers of many leading people, that Acton is the only one—having read all his correspondence, all his letters with his wife, his children, and all his note cards—that I admired more when I ended than when I began. He was a man of great moral courage, fortitude and purity.

I brought together his writings in three volumes, because, although he never wrote that book, and his friends would say, "Acton's working on the greatest book never written." better, I say, just to edit one pipe row than to spend your life thinking about a book." Well, not really. Because long after all those histories written by academics and literary men are just on library shelves, Acton's ideas, spoken on these note cards and a few occasional papers, still have profound significance, not just for the 20th century, but for our own 21st century, for Acton understood the dangers of nationalism, as well as of socialism.

He was not a conservative. His legacy has been usurped by conservatives. They have written biographies about him. They have named societies after him. He said conservatism—in one of his note cards—is the reign of sin. Conservatism is all about not educating your conscience so you can put up with all the bad things of the past. He admired Gladstone, and he admired Gladstone's ideal of democratic liberty. Acton said, "What good is it to have voters able to cast their ballot, when they don't have enough to eat? When their children don't have education at their disposal? When the streets are filthy and they live in hovels?" He followed Gladstone's idea of beginning a welfare state. That is why Winston Churchill was never a conservative. He was always, in his heart, a liberal, just like Acton and Gladstone, whom he so admired. They all believed that there must be a basic welfare for all citizens in order for democracy to flourish.

Acton thought that the free market economy had some good things about it; but capitalism, uncontrolled, was nothing but a force of evil. He would have said the idea of a free market economy in which you simply believe that the market is going to make everything right is one more form of determinism, and there was nothing he hated more than determinism in history. He had a list of bad people, and it included Marx, the economic determinist. They included various racists, like Gobineau. Racism was an evil thing, because it said however you were born determined how you were going to behave. That was wrong.

Conscience was all about your ability to redeem yourself, and the uniqueness of every individual. He also had some exotics down there, he said, like Nietzsche and Kierkegaard. He didn't quite know what to make of them.

But he was a true Gladstonian liberal, and to him nationalism represented the worst possible kind of racism, and the most primitive possible idea: That you are a member of a nation just because you were born there and speak the language. He said that nationalism, which in the 19th century was seen as the great force of progress, that is why nations like Germany and Italy were being united. The idea was to bring every Italian, everyone who spoke Italian as their mother tongue under one government, every German, everyone who spoke German as their mother tongue under one government—that was the force of the future, people said.

Acton stood up and said, "No! It is a primitive idea and it will lead to the destruction of entire peoples just because they don't fit in within your borders." In other words, it will lead to "ethnic cleansing," and rampant nationalism will bring Europe to the brink of ruin. The thing that will help it along is socialism. That, too, is nothing but determinism, and, carried to its limits, it reduces men and women to nothing but economic objects by saying that everything is geared toward the economy, that all ideas about the products of economic and social forces is to destroy the conscience in mankind. He would have said *1984* shows you exactly what happens when the conscience of individuals is destroyed in the name of economics as all-important.

He said, you are wrong to dismiss the idea of federalism. Ultimately, federalism is the means for various units to be brought together to keep what is special about them, and to resist the soul-less, destructive power of a centralized bureaucratic government. He distinguished sharply between the liberals of England like Gladstone, who believed ultimately in God and in conscience and in the individual, and liberals of the Continent, like Cavour, on whom he wrote a very, very suggestive essay. Because the liberals of Europe believed not really in individuals, when you got down to it, but to the state. They believed that the state should intervene in every aspect of human life.

So, the state, nationalism, socialism—these were the great dangers, Acton said. What would bring Europe, indeed, to ruin but a crackpot party called the National Socialists. And what would deliver Europe out of the ruins? Federalism.

Winston Churchill, who knew and thought very highly of Acton, stood in Zurich not long after the war, in 1948, and he said, "You are going to think me mad. But I tell you, Europe will arise from its ruins, led by France and Germany, into a federal nation; a United States of Europe."

He never wrote the great book, but Acton—in his aphorisms in his unpublished works, brought together in the volume by me, and in his essays—left a most compelling legacy of the importance of history, and the duty of every one of us to sit down and ask, "What does history tell us about what is right and just now in our present, and how we can create a better future?"

Lecture Thirty-Three
Cicero, *On Moral Duties* (*De Officiis*)

Scope:

In the Teaching Company course *Famous Romans*, I called Cicero my favorite Roman. In this course, we rank him with Gandhi and Churchill as models of the whole person, a person shaped by the great books, a person of thought and action, who lived and died for his ideals. His book *On Moral Duties* is one of the most influential works on education ever written. It directly contradicts the view that might makes right. Cicero also contradicts what seems to be the lesson of the world. He tells us that, in spite of appearances, an immoral act can never be expedient.

Outline

I.   The next three lectures discuss three men who wrote great books. Each of these men made history, and each of them lived a life that can serve as a model to us. Our theme is education and the path we can take to foster what is best for ourselves and others.

II. In 44 B.C., on the Ides of March, Julius Caesar was assassinated. His assassins, Brutus and Cassius, as well as most of the conspirators, fled Rome.

    A. Rome was in the hands of Marc Antony, who was underestimated. Many considered him to be a drunkard and a gambler, but he had gathered all Caesar's power.

    B. Much of the Roman senate was cowed by Antony's ruthless exercise of power.

    C. One elderly man, who could have enjoyed a quiet retirement, spoke out for the free republic and for liberty, knowing that doing so might cost him his life. That man was Marcus Tullius Cicero.

        1. In a series of ringing orations, Cicero attacked the character, policy, and intentions of Marc Antony. These powerful orations are called the *Philippics.*

        2. Cicero's attempt failed. Antony joined forces with Caesar's nephew, who was later known as Augustus, and together, they eliminated all opposition. Cicero was included on the list of those proscribed and was struck dead in 43 B.C.

D. In the last part of his life, beginning in 46 B.C., Cicero refused the high government position that Caesar offered him, opting for retirement. During his retirement, he embarked on a search for truth so that he could base his politics on what was morally good in his effort to preserve freedom in Rome.

III. In searching for truth, Cicero wrote *De Officiis*, or *On Moral Duties*, which Frederick the Great of Prussia called the best book on morality and ethics ever written.

A. Cicero wrote *De Officiis* to educate his son, who was spending his "junior year abroad," studying philosophy in Athens. At that time, philosophy was not an arid academic discipline. It was the crowning accomplishment of a general education. Students who could afford the expense went to Athens to study under one of the great philosophers.

B. Cicero wrote *De Officiis* in the form of a letter to his son to enable the young man to learn from Cicero's experience.

IV. During Cicero's career as an attorney, he demonstrated that a person could be successful and wealthy, as well as a man of integrity. He took difficult and dangerous cases, defending the poor and those in political trouble.

A. Cicero realized that the highest calling was public service. He set out to prove that he could be an honest and successful politician.

B. He held high political office and was consul of Rome.

C. In 63 B.C., a faction, led by Catiline, sought to destroy the constitution. Cicero took a firm stand, although others warned him that he was following a dangerous course. Cicero put the salvation of his country, its constitution, and its liberty before his own needs. He broke up the conspiracy and took responsibility for having the conspirators put to death.

D. For a brief while, Cicero was exiled, but he was brought back.

E. When Caesar triumphed, Cicero took a stand against Caesar. Cicero believed that Caesar had enormous ability but that he sought to destroy the liberty of Rome for the sake of his own ambition.

V. Cicero tried all his life to follow the moral course. He believed that all morality was founded on the idea of natural law.

A. Natural law is the belief that God exists and is revealed in the reason of nature. The entire universe is a place of reason, and the entire universe reveals the hand of God.

B. Like Plato, Cicero believed that God had established a set of absolute values, including wisdom, justice, courage, and moderation. These values exist even if they are denied in everyday life. An individual can be good as well as successful. No dichotomy exists between morality and expediency. An immoral act, such as lying or cheating, can never be helpful. No separation exists between the private and public selves. The highest possible calling for an individual is public duty.

C. Wisdom is found in knowing the truth, understanding absolute values, and knowing how to apply these values to one's life.

    1. At the beginning, the individual needs facts and information, but later in life, he can weave these facts into a broader set of knowledge.

    2. Knowledge is worthless unless it is used to find and apply in life what is good. In the search for wisdom, the individual must avoid becoming a pedant, studying the insignificant, or retiring from the world to become a scholar.

    3. Wisdom consists of knowing how to apply the good to life.

D. Justice is the single most important quality that a person can possess. Each individual's life should be guided by justice.

    1. Justice consists of never doing harm to anyone else— either to another's person or property. The essence of justice is founded in respect for private property.

    2. One great fault is passive injustice, which is to stand by and allow another person to be wronged. Passive injustice occurs when we remain silent because of our own needs or through preoccupation.

    3. Justice can even be extended to those who have wronged someone else by avoiding excessive retribution. Except for those who have committed the most heinous crimes, such as parricide, even the guilty deserve an attorney's best effort.

4. Part of justice is generosity, but an individual should never give more than he or she can afford. We should not ruin ourselves by giving, and we should give with a sense that our generosity will truly help.
   5. Morality is built on keeping one's word, or *fides*. The Romans believed that the empire was built on integrity. However, the individual must be practical. At times, keeping one's word is wrong.

E. Courage is essential to living a life of justice. An individual must have the courage to stand up for what is right. Wisdom is essential to courage. The individual must have the wisdom to know what he should defend. Bravery in the service of evil is savagery.

F. Moderation is the fourth quality of goodness. Nothing should be pushed so far that it becomes a wrong. Moderation is a guide for living life and letting the individual know what is right.

G. In selecting a career, an individual must know, in terms of moderation, his or her capabilities.
   1. Sometimes people enter an occupation because they inherit it, because of connections, or on a whim. Each person should step back and ask what career he or she is best suited for before making a decision.
   2. The highest calling is public service. Those who would pursue a career in public service must be certain they possess the qualities for leadership of the nation. A good leader is not vindictive and does not enter public service for self-interest, self-aggrandizement, or partisanship. Public service should be a noble and pure undertaking. The public servant must always act with moderation.

H. How do we put these theoretical underpinnings into practice?
   1. We must recognize that immoral acts are never expedient.
   2. The essence of justice is keeping one's word.
   3. Active and passive injustice are both wrong.
   4. Cicero suggests as a model Marcus Atilius Regulus, a Roman senator who was taken prisoner by the Carthaginians. Regulus was sent back to Rome with a proposal for a prisoner exchange, but it was against Roman policy to release prisoners. Although Regulus

was threatened with torture and death if he was unable to arrange the exchange, he urged the senate to vote against the Carthaginian terms. Regulus then returned to Carthage, where he was tortured to death.

VI. The advice in *De Officiis* did not work for Cicero's son, who was a drunkard, sold his services to Augustus, and lent his name to the new order of Augustus. Although Cicero's son did not follow the advice given in *De Officiis*, Cicero left future generations this enduring statement of moral justice.

Essential Reading:

Cicero, *On Moral Duties* (*On Moral Obligation* or *On Responsibility*).

Supplementary Reading:

Everitt, *Cicero: The Life and Times of Rome's Greatest Politician.*

Questions to Consider:

1. Contrast Machiavelli and Cicero in their concepts of success. Do you believe that there is never a dichotomy between morality and expediency?

2. Can you give practical examples of Cicero's view of the relationship between the cardinal virtues and, thus, all morality?

Lecture Thirty-Three—Transcript
Cicero, *On Moral Duties* (*De Officiis*)

We come now to the concluding four lectures in our course on great books—*Books That Have Made History: Books That Can Change Your Life*—and I want to examine in these next three lectures three great individuals, each of whom wrote a great book, each of whom made history and each of whom lived lives that I think can be patterns to each one of us.

So our theme is education. Our theme is: How do we bring out of ourselves—for that is the root meaning of "education," to lead out of yourself—how do we bring out of ourselves what is best? What is best for ourselves? What is best for others? And, how do we judge what is best? After all, so many of us go through life following false paths, and then at the end say, "Why did we do it?" To begin, I want us to turn our minds back to the year 44 B.C., to Rome. In that same year, as we saw in our study of *Julius Caesar*, the play by Shakespeare, great Caesar has been assassinated, on March 15th, 44 B.C., on the Ides of March. His assassins, Brutus and Cassius, and most of the conspirators have had to flee Rome, and Rome is now, in the summer of 44 B.C., in the hands of Marc Antony, much underestimated by the conspirators, regarded as a drunkard and a gambler. He is, in fact, a gambler, and he has played his cards very coolly, and has gathered all of Caesar's power into his own hands. Much of the Senate is really afraid, is cowed, by the power of Antony and his ruthless exercise of this power.

But one elderly man steps forward. He could live out in quiet retirement, honored and respected, but he steps out one more time to speak out for the free republic, to speak out for liberty, knowing that it will very well cost him his life. That man is Marcus Tullius Cicero. Born in 106 B.C., he has, in the year 63 B.C. held the great office of Consul at Rome, and boldly, and in a determined fashion, put down the threat of civil war at Rome. Now, in 44 B.C., he steps forward again, and in a series of ringing orations attacks the character, the policy and the intentions of Marc Antony. *The Philippics*, they are called, these powerful orations. And, he will fail.

Marc Antony will join forces with Caesar's nephew, the man history will know as Augustus, and together they will eliminate all possible opposition to them. They will draw up a list of those who are proscribed, whose names have been written down on this list, and among them is Marcus Tullius Cicero. In 43 B.C., he will be struck dead, offering his neck forward as the policemen prepare to execute him, saying, "Strike here and strike hard." In these dangerous last months of his life, starting already in 46 B.C., when Caesar is still alive—Caesar in absolute power, Caesar having offered to Cicero a high post in the new government, wanting to lend the name of Cicero to his new order—Cicero has begun to live very dangerously. He has told Caesar "No," and he has gone into retirement, waiting for events.

In that retirement he has turned himself toward the search for truth once again, to philosophy, to the search for what is morally good, so that he can base his politics on what is morally good in his effort to save freedom at Rome. In the course of this searching for truth, he writes, and in his writing he composes what has been called "the best book on morality and ethics ever written or that could ever be written." That was what Frederick the Great of Prussia called it. It is his work *De Officiis*, his work *On Moral Duties*, on obligation, on responsibility.

He wrote it to educate his son, Marcus Tullius Cicero, who at that very time is a college student studying in Athens, having a junior year abroad, where he is studying philosophy. And philosophy was not an arid, academic discipline. It was looked upon as the crown of your general education, after you had studied literature, after you had studied how to speak well. Then you crowned it all by a year or two or three studying philosophy. And, if you could, as young Cicero could, through his father's wealth, you went to Athens and studied under one of the great philosophers. Maybe you visited two or three different universities, learning various schools of philosophical thought, such as the Stoics, with their emphasis on duty, or the Epicureans, with their emphasis upon pleasure—the good life should be one that is pleasant for you—or the Cynics, who said you can trust nothing—no knowledge can be absolute.

And to his son at this critical age in his life, a son who already had some problems—he drank much too much, and Cicero, who was a very indulgent father, he never disciplined his son, and, in fact, gave him a living allowance that in today's currency would probably translate out to about $40,000 a year, so his son could live in some luxury—Cicero wrote this work. He dedicates it to his son and puts it in the form of a letter.

"My dear son, I want you to make the best of your time in college. I know that you are studying under very fine professors. But I want to lend a bit of help, taking from my own life lessons and hoping that you will learn from what I have done in life—the mistakes that I have made, the good things I have done—and be able to fit a pattern for your life, so at the end of your years you can say, 'I did well. I did well.'"

"And what do I mean by 'doing well,' my son? I mean that you live a life that gives back to your country, gives back to your family, gives back to your fellow-citizens. You have had many great advantages. My father worked hard for me and enabled me to study, enabled me to go to Rome to study, and then enabled me to go to Greece. But I have worked very hard, as well. I have worked for my country; I have worked for my family. I made a career as an attorney, and I started out as an attorney to prove that you can be both a successful and wealthy attorney as well as an honest attorney. I took it upon myself from the very beginning of my legal career to take difficult cases, cases that were dangerous, to stand up for poor people, as well as people in political trouble, and to argue their cases with all my might, no matter how dangerous, no matter how much ill-will I incurred. And, I made a success of it."

"And having made a success financially and in the legal profession, I realized that the highest calling is public service, and I went into politics. And there again I set out to prove that you can be an honest as well as a successful politician. I reached the highest level of public trust. I held the great office of Consul, Commander-in-Chief of Rome, the chief executive office. And in my year of the Consulship, in 63 B.C., an evil faction of men, led by Catiline, sought to destroy our constitution, and I took the firmest possible stand."

"Others said, 'You must equivocate. There are many wealthy and influential men on their side, including Caesar, already a rising politician. If you try to stop them too drastically, you will be destroyed.' But I put the salvation of my country and its constitution and its liberty first. I stepped up. I broke that conspiracy; and then, on my own authority, I had those men put to death. Yes, I took the responsibility and, for a brief while, I was exiled. But the people will ultimately make the right decision, if they have the truth, and I was brought back."

"And when great Caesar triumphed, I stood up against him. He was a man with enormous ability, but he was evil because he wanted to destroy the liberty of Rome for the sake of his own ambition."

"So I have tried, in my life, to follow the moral course. What is that moral course? What are your moral obligations? All morality, my son, is founded upon the idea of natural law. The belief that there is God, and God is revealed in the reason of nature, that the universe is a place of reason. And the whole of the universe—the course of the stars, the course of the seasons—all reveal the hand of God. God has set up, as Plato tells you in his great work *The Republic*, a set of absolute values, and those absolute values have been defined when you read *The Republic* of Plato. They are: wisdom, justices, courage and moderation. Believe me, my son, those values, those virtues, exist even if the whole world says they do not." I wish there were a stronger word than "virtues." In Latin it does convey the notion of power; but virtues are not some weak, milksop idea. Cardinal virtues—the English use that term. We first have to ponder what "cardinal" means, and then we have to ponder what "virtue" means.

"The virtues are goodness. They are what is good, and what you should do. That is what we mean by wisdom, justice, courage and moderation. And now, my son, I want to go on and step by step define these for you, because no idea is worthwhile unless you can prove it, and this is what I want to prove to you. This is what I think is most important for you to understand at this critical age of your life. One: That you can be good, as well as successful. That means that you must understand that there is never a dichotomy between morality and expediency. An immoral act, a bad act, can never be helpful to you. It can never be helpful for you to do an injustice. It can never be helpful for you to tell a lie. It can never be helpful for you to cheat someone. That is where Caesar and so many tyrants have gone wrong. They thought that in the need to help their country as they said, they needed to do unjust acts. That is absolutely wrong, because the next important point to understand is that you can never separate what you are as a private person from what you are as a public person. And I tell you again, my son, the highest calling is public duty."

What then is justice? What is wisdom? What is courage? What is moderation? And then, how do you apply them? Because this is a practical book for you, a work of how to live your life.

"Wisdom. Wisdom is knowing the truth, and wisdom is the understanding of these values that God has set for all time. Wisdom is knowing how to apply these virtues to your individual life. At the beginning you will need information. You will need lots of facts.

Then, as you go into college, you'll begin to weave these facts into a broader set of knowledge. But none of that is useful unless you go on to use that knowledge to find the good and then to apply the good."

"In your search for wisdom, be wary of becoming a pedant. Be wary of studying things that really don't amount to anything much—science. It can be interesting to learn astronomy and the course of the stars, but why study the course of the stars if you don't know what is in your own soul, first? So avoid studying things that are insignificant. Avoid just becoming a scholar, retiring from the world to search for truth. That truth is of no point unless you go back into the world. So wisdom is knowing how to apply the good to your life."

"Justice, my son—and I say this as an attorney—is the most important single quality to possess. You should guide your life by justice. And what is justice? Justice is never doing harm to someone else, either in their person or in their property. Never doing harm to someone else. It is, in a sense, 'Do unto others as you would have them do unto you.' And the very essence of justice is founded in the belief and respect for private property."

"Now, my son. Justice. Applying it in the world. What is one of the great faults we make? One of the great faults we make is passive injustice. We all recognize when a Caesar goes out and harms his county. When a Caesar goes out and takes lives. We all recognize it when someone cheats openly, when someone robs you openly. And that's wrong. But no less wrong is to stand by and allow someone else to be wronged. We do this sometimes because we believe it's in our own self-interest—don't step up. Here's a person being wronged by their company, let us say—if we want to move up into the 21st century—somebody who is being fired because they stood up and said the company's policy, let's say, of polluting the air was wrong and they told the press about it. Now they're being fired on trumped up charges of embezzlement. You know the person is not an embezzler. You should stand up and say, 'This is wrong.' But you don't, because you say, 'I've got a family to feed. I've got my own needs to take care of.' Well, that is a form of wrong just as great as openly harming someone. Or sometimes we're just preoccupied. 'I've got too many things to do. I couldn't do a good job of standing up for what is right.' That, too, is wrong."

"And what you become when you do that, my son, is a hypocrite. Nothing is worse than a hypocrite, because a hypocrite, you see, claims to be doing what is just, when they are doing what is wrong. Hypocrisy. It is one of the greatest of wrongs. So avoid passive as well as active injustice."

"And, my son, justice can be extended to everyone. Even those who have wronged us require justice. And justice towards those who have wronged you is not to be excessive in your retribution. As an attorney you will extend justice to those you know to be evil, because every client who comes to you, even those who are guilty, deserve your very best effort. Only the most heinous kinds of crimes, say a patricide, killing your father—there you must say, 'You are so evil I will have nothing to do with you.' But the ordinary thief, even the ordinary murderer, who kills in a fit of anger, deserves your best efforts."

"As always, son, I want to be practical, and give you a practical set of guidelines. Part of justice is generosity, giving away money and your gifts. And there's a practical guide to generosity, as well. You should never give more than you are able to give. Never ruin yourself being a donor to your university. You should be willing to give the money in an order of merit, starting out with your family and ending up with those who are outside of your family circle. You should give it with the sense of 'Will it truly help?' And that brings us to our next aspect of morality."

"Morality is keeping your word. *Fides*. That is a noble Latin word. The Romans believed that their very empire is built upon always keeping their word. Trust. A reputation based on the fact that you always do what you're going to say you should do. So keep your word. Tell the truth. But once again we must be practical. And there are times when keeping your word is wrong. Let's say that you have promised your son a new chariot. And yet that son keeps getting drunk all the time, and you know if you give him that new chariot it's dangerous. So if you have to, say, 'It is in your own best interest that I break this promise.' Remember Apollo and how he gave his son a chariot and that son drove it too close and it crashed into the Earth? He should have broken that promise. Or what about Agamemnon, when we read the *Iliad*? Do you remember how he had vowed to the gods the most beautiful thing born in one year, if that would make the winds blow properly so he could sail to Troy? And the gods, through the soothsayer, said, 'That is your daughter, Iphigenia.' He should have broken that promise, even to the gods."

"That brings us, then, to the question of courage, because courage is essential to your living a life of justice. You must be willing to stand up for what is right. It is no good whatsoever, Marcus, to know what is just, to have that wisdom, and then be afraid to put it into practice. And I will say this about myself: I have never been afraid to stand up. It has cost me a great deal, but I have never been afraid to stand up, and that is what I want you to remember. Stand up for what is right. But understand as well, that wisdom is essential to courage. That is to say, you should know what is right to stand up for, because being simply brave in the service of an evil is just brutality. It is savagery. So you need wisdom to know what is absolutely just, and when you have that knowledge, then you stand up and fight for it, as I will always do for what I know to be right: the freedom of our country."

"And the fourth of those qualities of goodness that are set up as an absolute standard by God is moderation. Nothing should be pushed so far that it in itself becomes a wrong. Moderation, my son, is the guide to live your life by. Moderation allows you to know what is right for you. And I want to come now to your choice of a profession, the thing that will guide your whole life. These choices you are making right now as a college student. The first step is to understand, in terms of moderation, what you are capable of. Where do your traits lie? Sometimes people enter an occupation because of inheritance. You might say, 'My father was an attorney, therefore I should be an attorney.' Sometimes they do it because of connections in life. Sometimes they do it on a whim. But step back and say, 'I want to be an athlete. Am I really a man capable of being an athlete? Do I have the physique? Do I desire the training? No.' Step back and say, 'What am I best suited for?' Then make your decision."

"But the highest calling is always public service. Ask yourself, 'Do I have the qualities that make a good leader for my nation, for this great free republic.' Understand what are the qualities of being a good leader. Public service means not being vindictive. What a big mistake it is to be elected and then say, 'I'm going to go out and punish and pick upon everybody who has stood in my way.' And do not go into public service for self-interest, thinking you're going to make a lot of money out of it, or for self-aggrandizement, or for partisanship, to reward your friends. Public service should be a pure and noble undertaking. And so done, it is the finest thing you can do with your life."

"So weigh carefully your qualities. Weigh carefully this quality of moderation that should guide how you live. There's a time to tell jokes and not to tell jokes. There's a time to show off your learning and a time not to. Always act in a moderate fashion."

"Now, my son, having understood what we might call the theoretical underpinnings of your life, how do we put this into practice? How do we put into practice these qualities of wisdom, justice, courage and moderation? And how do I prove to you, my boy, that an immoral act can never be expedient?"

To step back for a moment, how many of you believe that? That an immoral act can never be expedient? How many times as we go through life, as did Cicero, do we encounter a situation in which, you know, it is absolutely in our own best interests to lie? "Officer, I really wasn't going 80 miles an hour in this 40 mile an hour zone." Or, from a student's point of view, "My computer broke. That is why I was unable to finish this paper." Or, from an older point of view, "My computer broke and that's why I don't have this report ready." Or, "It's his fault the report is not ready, not mine." It is very difficult to see that an immoral act cannot sometimes be expedient.

Cicero puts it in terms that are very much like our own day. He says, "What, for example, if you have to sell a house, and you know that house is filled with rats and termites, but it is crucial for you to sell that house." Or, what if you know your house—to jump to our own day—is built upon a nuclear waste dumpsite, and your children are turning green and their hair is all falling out? But you put out a sign and this nice couple comes up and says, "We'd like to buy that house. It has all the qualities we want and it is such a good price." And they say, "Are there any problems with the house? Because we want to move in so fast that we don't think we need an inspector or anything, we'll just take your word for it." Now, how foolish would such a person be in today's society? And they would have been just as foolish in the 1st century B.C., but they're going to take your word for it.

Or what if you have a car that the transmission is just about to fall out, but you need to get rid of that car. Maybe you've lost your job and that three or four thousand dollars will be the difference between feeding your family or not? Isn't your first duty to your family? Let's say a teenager comes up and says, "I really want that car! Wow! That's a hot-looking car, and I want it right now, and I've got the cash." Do you tell that person, "The transmission is about to fall out?" Well, you tell me. You would be a fool by today's standards not to do so. If that person were foolish enough to take that used car or to buy that house without getting it inspected, they just deserve what they got. It's called *caveat emptor*—"let the buyer beware." And isn't that a good Latin term anyway?

Well, Cicero says that is absolutely wrong. And he would tell you that a society that assumed that if you were a big enough fool not to get an inspection, you deserve to be taken, that society has serious moral problems. The very need to have an inspection is a statement that you cannot take somebody's word. Don't we go back to say the very essence of justice is keeping your word? So Cicero says you should say, "It's a great house but it sits right on top of nuclear waste, and if you buy it, your children are going to get sick."

Now, that's passive injustice, to sit by and do that. What about the Roman who had a big villa in Sicily and he wanted to get rid of it, and he invited one of his friends down and all of these fishermen—it was on the seacoast—kept coming out and catching all these fish. And the senator said, "I love this place because not only is it a beautiful place, but I get a huge income from these fishermen. A commission." "I want to buy it." "Oh, no. I can't sell it." "Oh, please!" So he buys it. First day, he goes out there in his new home, no fishermen are there. Second day, third day. He finally goes down to the wharf, and the fishermen say, "We never catch any fish out there. It's got something to do with the currents. But you know, your old friend, he paid us to go out there one day, take a lot of fish with us and act like we were catching them." That's active injustice. That's salting it. But both are equally wrong, my son.

"I want you, my boy, as I bring this to a conclusion, to think about the patterns of the past, about the great men of the past. You take as your model Marcus Atilius Regulus, the Roman senator who was taken captive by the Carthaginians during our war with them, was sent back to Rome with a message for the Senate that if the Senate would let loose the Carthaginian prisoners who were being held, the Carthaginians would exchange prisoners. But you remember it was our Roman way never to exchange prisoners. But to give Regulus an incentive, the Carthaginians told him, 'If you come back without having worked this deal to release these hostages, we will torture you to death.' Regulus went to the Senate, gave them the Carthaginian terms, and then said, 'You must vote against it. You must say, No.

We must never negotiate with an enemy while in the field.' Then he said, 'Now, I am glad you voted against it. I am going back to the Carthaginians.' And even the Senate said, 'We release you from your oath. You came home on service to the state. Now you can stay. Think of your family. Think of your country that needs you.' And Regulus said, 'No. I have given my word. And on that word, on that honesty, the whole of our moral structure rests.' And so Regulus, my son, went back and was tortured to death. That, my son, is the stern old Roman way."

Well, it didn't quite work with the son. Cicero's son grew up to be a drunkard. Continued right on that path. Sold his services to Augustus and lent his name to the new order of Augustus. So you can't always make your children come out the right way. But Cicero left us with this enduring statement of moral justice.

Lecture Thirty-Four
Gandhi, *An Autobiography*

Scope:

To many, including Winston Churchill, the British Empire was a great force for good. To an unprepossessing Indian lawyer, the British Empire, which saw itself as the bastion of liberty, was evil, for it rested on a lie. It denied to many of its subjects the very equality that was the essence of freedom. But no less evil for Mohandas Gandhi would be the use of force to overthrow it and gain independence for India. Drawing on the traditions of Indian thought and reading the *Bhagavad Gita* daily, Gandhi made his own path. Strong in the truth, he used moral power to bring a great power to its knees. His autobiography eschews many of the traditional elements in a life story. Gandhi focuses on his entire life as a search for truth, teaching us that there are many roads to wisdom and many ways to fight the battles of life.

Outline

I.   The previous lecture discussed Cicero's *De Officiis*, or *On Moral Duties*.

   A.   The theme of *De Officiis* is that the basis of all morality and good actions is doing what is true and just and right; no dichotomy exists between doing what is good for oneself and doing what is right, because the individual can never profit from doing wrong.

   B.   This great book changed history. Through the Middle Ages, the Renaissance, and the Enlightenment, Cicero was the most influential intellectual figure from Greece or Rome. *De Officiis* was held up as the epitome of what a pagan could achieve in ethical thought, and Cicero was regarded as a pagan Christian.

   C.   Machiavelli wrote *The Prince* in an attempt to refute Cicero. Machiavelli wanted to show that it is often expedient to do evil.

   D.   To his own generation, Cicero was considered a failure. He had defended the free republic and had been killed. The free republic was never restored, and Augustus established a military dictatorship that was far more efficient than Caesar had achieved. That new order brought peace and prosperity to a world that had been badly governed.

E. Theodor Mommsen, the most influential Roman historian of the modern era, also viewed Cicero as a failure and a detriment to his country. He believed that Cicero had delayed the progress of the new order of Caesar and Augustus. He viewed Cicero's writings as journalism of the worst sort, because they were not serious philosophical treatises; instead, they attempted to make philosophy comprehensible to ordinary people.

F. Cicero was a success because he was true to himself.

G. The last three lectures in this course offer the following lessons: Be true to yourself, do what you know to be right, and never give up.

II. In 1893, a 24-year-old barrister, Gandhi, was representing an Indian company in South Africa. Although he had a first-class train ticket, he was not allowed to remain in the first-class seating compartment and was thrown off the train. A stagecoach driver also refused to let him sit with the other passengers. This was Gandhi's introduction to the morality of the British Empire and its legal system.

A. The British raj was theoretically based on liberty and equality for all subjects. In reality, one standard of liberty and equality existed for white subjects and another standard existed for those of color. Even science, as taught in many universities, proclaimed the superiority of the white race.

B. Gandhi decided to take on the scientific establishment, the legal system, and the power of the British Empire. Armed only with his belief in the truth and his concept of *satyagraha*, "steadfastness in truth," Gandhi took on the empire and led his nation to independence.

C. Gandhi's life is an example of what one individual can achieve if he or she believes in the truth.

III. The story of Gandhi's life is captured in An Autobiography: The Story of My Experiments with the Truth.

A. Gandhi's autobiography was published in two installments, in 1925 and 1927. It is written in Gujarati, an Indian language, because Gandhi believed that the culture of India was his culture.

B. The subtitle of Gandhi's autobiography conveys his understanding that we are always making our way toward the truth.

C. Gandhi had a profound belief in God. He was greatly affected by the *Bhagavad Gita* and believed that God is truth, but more important, he believed that truth is God and should be worshipped. Truth is in God, and God will progressively reveal wisdom to the searcher for truth.

D. In his *Autobiography*, Gandhi does not hesitate to point out his mistakes

E. Gandhi was born in 1869. He begins his *Autobiography* by describing his family and the caste to which they belonged. Gandhi later struggled against the caste system of India.

   1. Gandhi's formal schooling had little impact on him. He believed that the teacher should be the textbook, and the teacher and the teacher's moral qualities should be what the student retains.

   2. At the age of 13, Gandhi was married to a younger girl. At age 35, Gandhi took a vow of celibacy and saw his wife as a creature of pure love.

   3. After finishing high school and passing his examinations, it was decided that he should become an attorney.

   4. In England, Gandhi gradually began to understand how unique his native country was. He met English people who were interested in mystical religions and encouraged him to read the *Bhagavad Gita* in English, and it became a part of him. The *Bhagavad Gita* celebrates God as truth and teaches us to follow the path that God has laid out for us. It also says that doing the work of someone else is slavery, but doing the work of God is true liberation. The philosophy of the *Bhagavad Gita* began to shape Gandhi's thinking.

   5. Gandhi passed his examinations at the age of 21. He found that becoming a barrister was easy. He had to attend 12 dinners, study outline notes, and pass the examinations.

F. Gandhi returned to India, obtained a job, and left his wife at home while he went to South Africa.

    1. In South Africa, Gandhi realized that God was telling him not to be afraid, to stand up and recognize the injustice around him as injustice to God, and to put an end to injustice.

    2. Gandhi began to teach his fellow Indians that they should not let anyone treat them unjustly, that they should not harm anyone, that they should stand fast in the truth, and that they should struggle for their rights.

    3. Gandhi came to the idea of *ahimsa*, "nonviolence." This was not a passive idea. Great moral courage is needed to be nonviolent.

    4. Gandhi began working with Indians in South Africa. He not only fought for their legal rights but also began a movement for education.

G. First in South Africa, then in India, Gandhi opened commune schools and began to educate his students in *ahimsa* and *satyagraha*.

    1. The teachers in Gandhi's schools were parents. Gandhi believed that parents should be the source of education for their children.

    2. At one point, an untouchable family came to the commune. The members of Gandhi's ashram believed that the untouchables would pollute the commune's well. Gandhi asked the meaning of his teachings, because he taught that all people were equal in the sight of God. Other commune members said that they believed in equality but did not want the untouchable family there. When Gandhi threatened to leave and return to practicing law, the members of the commune agreed to let the untouchables stay.

IV. Gandhi then moved to an even larger sphere—he stood up to the British Empire itself.

    A. Gandhi had begun to understand that his God-given mission was to help establish an independent India in which Muslims, Hindus, and Christians could live together in unity. This nation would be an India for the Indians.

B. Gandhi abandoned European clothes and wore simple Indian dress. He took up spinning.

    1. Indians had been required to buy cloth made in Britain. The cotton was grown in India, but it was shipped to England and made into cloth, then shipped back to India. Gandhi held mass demonstrations in which European-style clothes and cloth brought from England were burned.

    2. The spinning wheel became a symbol of liberation—the wheel of life and a sign of God, with no beginning and no end.

C. The British had a monopoly on salt. Gandhi believed that the tax on salt was unjust; it supported oppression.

    1. Gandhi said that Indians should not pay the tax on salt; they could obtain salt by marching to the sea.

    2. The English could beat the Indians but could not stop them. Gandhi, also called the *Mahatma*, or "great-souled one," taught his followers to do nothing violent but to keep coming back.

D. World opinion began to focus on Gandhi.

    1. Indians—Muslim as well as Hindu—saw in the figure of Gandhi the symbol of their struggle for liberation and enlightenment. They began to recognize that England and Europe were not the only sources of culture and that India had its own set of ideas that were foreign to the West.

    2. Gandhi believed that the culture of England was based on war, struggle, and violence and that capitalism is a form of violence, because it steals from the poor to benefit the rich. Capitalism carries within itself the seeds of its own destruction. For Gandhi, the Indian way was the way of God, truth, and nonviolence.

E. Gandhi was imprisoned many times. He found in prison new sources of strength.

    1. He read *Unto This Last*, by John Ruskin, which taught him three crucial lessons. First, the good of all is encompassed in the good of one individual. Harm to one individual is harm to everyone. Second, every form of work has its own dignity. A barber is as worthy of respect as an attorney. Third, the noblest form of work is to farm and make something with your own hands.

2. Tolstoy's *The Kingdom of God Is within You* opened a new world to Gandhi. According to Tolstoy, Jesus was not God but taught that everyone has a God within himself. A similar teaching also appears in the *Bhagavad Gita.*

3. Gandhi's readings showed that unfamiliar books, in addition to great books, can touch the soul.

F. Gandhi used self-imposed hunger strikes to protest British actions or the actions of his followers when they refused to follow his path of truth and nonviolence. When Gandhi went on a hunger strike, the British raj feared that he might die and would give in.

G. Gandhi thus harmed no one in his fight for the truth.

H. Gandhi's moral authority played a decisive role in Britain's decision to give India its freedom and in the decision of many Indians to form political parties that could achieve freedom under a constitutional government.

1. Gandhi was bitterly disappointed in 1947 when India gained its independence but allowed itself to be divided into a largely Muslim Pakistan and a largely Hindu India.

2. Gandhi believed that this partition contradicted his teaching that God had fashioned many roads to truth and that all religions teach the same fundamental values.

I. When civil war broke out over disputed territory and thousands were killed, the elderly Gandhi walked from village to village trying to bring people together.

J. The moral authority of Gandhi had become a threat. Radicals who wanted a truly separate Hindu India set out to assassinate Gandhi, and he was shot.

K. With his last word, "Ram," Gandhi invoked the name of God. The *Bhagavad Gita* says, "He who dies with my name upon his lips is freed forever from the cycle of life and joins me in bliss."

Essential Reading:

Gandhi, *An Autobiography: The Story of My Experiments with the Truth.*

Supplementary Reading:

Brown, *Gandhi: Prisoner of Hope.*

Questions to Consider:

1. Expound on your understanding of Gandhi's ideal that "it is more important to believe that truth is God than that God is truth."

2. What would Gandhi have said to Dietrich Bonhoeffer regarding the plot to assassinate Hitler?

Lecture Thirty-Four—Transcript
Gandhi, *An Autobiography*

In our last lecture, we discussed Cicero and his work on moral duties. *De Officiis* is the Latin title. It is normally translated as *On Moral Duties*. It can be called "*On Obligations*," it can be called "*On Responsibility*," for its theme is that the basis of all morality and good action is doing what is true and just and right—that is your responsibility. There will be no ultimate dichotomy between doing what is best for you and doing what is right, because you can never profit for doing wrong. It is a great book, and it is a book that certainly changed history. It is one of the most influential ethical works ever written. Cicero would go on to be, for the Middle Ages, for the Renaissance, right on down through the Enlightenment, the most influential single intellectual figure from Greece and Rome. His Latin was the model that was used in schools in the Middle Ages and Renaissance, when all educated people wrote in Latin. And the work *On Moral Duties* was held up as the epitome of what a pagan could achieve in terms of ethical thought. Indeed, he was regarded as a "pagan Christian," so much like the teaching of Christianity was his own teaching on ethics.

How powerful was the view of Cicero can be seen from the fact that, as I believe, Machiavelli wrote his *The Prince*, which we have discussed, in a determined effort to refute Cicero. To show that it is absolute nonsense to say that a good act is always expedient. Very frequently it is expedient to do evil, and you ought to get this foolish notion of always doing right out of your mind. You must do what is best for you, and that will frequently be to lie, to cheat, to kill, to be cruel, to be stingy.

It's a question of how Cicero, if he would step back, would view all that has been written about him in subsequent generations, because to his own generation, Cicero was a failure. After all, he stood up for the free republic, and got himself killed, did he not? I mean, to get killed by policemen is a sign of failure. Then, the free republic was never restored. Augustus would go on and establish a military dictatorship, far more efficient than Caesar had ever achieved, and that new order of Augustus would bring peace and prosperity to a world that had been very badly governed by the free republic of Rome. Therefore, the most influential Roman historian of the 19th century, the great Theodore Mommsen, viewed Cicero as a total failure and a real detriment to his country who delayed the progress of the new order of Caesar and Augustus, and despised the writings of Cicero. He called them "journalism of the worst sort" because they weren't serious philosophical treatises. They were an attempt to make philosophy comprehensible by ordinary people.

Cicero would come back and say to you, "I was a success because I was true to myself." And that is our theme in all of these three great figures we're going to look at now: Be true to yourself. Do what you know to be right, and never give up.

To see that in a very different world, let us turn our minds back to the winter, in the South Africa of 1893. On a train going towards Pretoria is a young, 24-year-old, recently qualified English barrister—lawyer—Mohandas Gandhi. He is riding in the first-class compartment. He is on company business. He represents an Indian company there in South Africa, which is responsible for a number of Indian migrant workers. He has his first-class ticket. He is riding along. Suddenly the conductor appears in the railroad carriage and says, "What are you doing here?" with a racial slur. "What are you doing here?" And Gandhi says, "I am going to Pretoria." "Not in this compartment, you're not." "Why not? I have my ticket." "I don't care about your ticket. This is a first-class compartment, and only white people may sit in this first-class compartment. So you get out of here. Right now!" "But I have a first-class ticket." "You're going to sit in a third-class compartment." "But I paid for a first-class ticket." "I do not care." "Sir, I am an attorney." "You cannot be an attorney. There are no colored attorneys in South Africa." "Well, sir, since you call me colored, and since I have a letter here from the Queen stating that I am a fully-qualified barrister, there must be at least one colored attorney in South Africa." "Don't you get smart with me! You're going out... Alright. You're either going out of this train or at the next stop we're throwing you out!" "I will not leave this train."

Next stop, a policeman comes and says, "You're going out of this train." And he is summarily thrown off of the train and his luggage is thrown after him. And off puffs the train. There he is sitting on the railroad side—cold night, high in the mountains of South Africa—and so outraged that he won't even go and get his luggage, which is now in the possession of the police, so he can get his overcoat out.

Next train comes. He gets in the compartment he is assigned to, and then goes on. At the little town where he has to stop, there is a stagecoach that will take him the final stage of the journey. He starts to get in the stagecoach. Once again has a first-class ticket, for the stagecoach. The driver looks down and says, "You can't sit inside with the white people!" "But sir, I have a ticket." "I don't care. You're going to sit …I don't know where. You're going to sit on the floor board here." "I am not going to sit on the floor board of a stagecoach if I have a first-class ticket." "Oh yes you are. …Alright, I'll tell you what I'll let you do. You can sit up here beside the driver, the other driver, and I'll sit inside to relieve him later."

And the time comes to relieve the driver and the chief gets on top and says, "You're going to get down on the running board now." And Gandhi says, "No." So the chief begins to beat him on the ears and pound on him. Gandhi is a very frail little man; he never weighed much more than 100 pounds. And this is an enormous stagecoach driver, and he's pounding on him, and pounding him. And then he starts to drag him and throw him on the ground, and Gandhi just holds on to the edge of the stage, until finally the passengers themselves are outraged, and say, "Let him sit inside with us!" "No, I'm not going to let him sit inside, but I will let him sit on the floorboard, rather than throwing him away."

And so, Gandhi is introduced to the customs of the British Empire and its legal system. The British *raj* at the height of its imperial power, that Empire on which the sun never sets, that Empire that stretches from the Cape to Cairo, that stretches from the Antipodes of Australia to the pine forests and tundra of Canada, and which is based upon the ideal of liberty and equality for all the subjects of the Queen.

Now, Gandhi could have gone on, practiced law, made a lot of money—because it was possible for Indian barristers not only to make a lot of money, but even to win the title of "Sir"; there were plenty of examples of them—to be a loyal subject of the British Empire, and to say, "Well, that's just how things work. There is one standard of liberty and equality for the white Englishmen and subjects of the Queen, and another for her colored subjects—to use the word that was used in those days—but let's just play the game. Let's just get by and not worry about whether this is absolutely right or absolutely wrong; besides, you cannot change matters. How can you change matters in the greatest empire in the world in an age of virulent racism? This was an age in which Cecile Rhodes set up the Rhodes scholarship for Anglo-Saxons, on the belief that they were the superior race, and in which 'science' as taught in many universities proclaimed the superiority of the white race. So how can you take on science? How can you take on the legal system, and how can you take on the power of the British Empire? Just go along with it and make a successful life for yourself. After all, you have a family to take care of."

And yet, this frail little man, Mohandas Gandhi, armed only with his belief in the truth, his concept of *satyagraha*—steadfastness in the truth—would take on that great empire and lead his nation, India, to independence, and leave us with one of the most profound examples of what one individual can achieve if they believe in the truth.

The story of his experiments with the truth is captured in his autobiography, published in two installments, in 1925 and 1927. Written in, not English, but his Indian language of Gujarati, part of his testimony that Indian culture was his culture, and that is what he should embrace: *The Story of My Experiments With the Truth*. Because Gandhi was a person who understood that we are always, in the course of our life, making our way towards the truth. He had a profound belief in God. He believed, as the *Bhagavad Gita*—so influential for him—said, that God is truth, and that it is most important to understand that truth itself is God, and that is more important than saying that God is truth. Truth is the thing that we worship, and truth is in God, and God will progressively reveal to the searcher for truth wisdom. But you're going to get it wrong a lot of times. And so Gandhi said, "I made a lot of mistakes." And he points them out, all through his story of his *Experiments With The Truth*. "I made mistakes that were Himalayan in size—that big—but I kept on."

He was born in 1869. He starts off in his autobiography very mundanely telling about his family, the caste that they belonged to. And, of course, his whole adult life would be a struggle against caste, to give to the untouchables—those that lay outside of the caste—their rights. Telling about his caste, about his father and parents, and about his early schooling. "Schooling made very little impact upon me," he said. "I never really learned much from books. In fact, I can remember almost nothing of the books that my teachers assigned. For me, the teacher ought to be the textbook, and it ought to be the teacher and the moral quality of the teacher that you carry away. So I never learned much from regular schools. I followed the will of my parents and married when I was 13. My wife was younger. That is the custom in India," he said. "I think it is wrong, but I must tell you I went along with it, and I was a lustful little 13-year-old, I have got to tell you that. In fact, when my father died a few years later, I was so lustful I was in bed with my wife, and I didn't leave to go and hear his dying words. So that was one of my Himalayan mistakes. But I have tried to overcome it," he said.

"At the age of 35, I took a vow of absolute celibacy, and from that time onward I would see my wife not as a creature of lust, but as a creature of true love. And so, we would no longer sleep together from that time." So, a vow of total celibacy; but that was in the future.

When he finished high school and passed his examinations, the discussion was what was going to become of him. And particularly, his uncles wanted somebody who would make a lot of money, and the way to do that was to become an attorney. So they were going to send him to England. Now, some of the caste members were opposed to this idea. But he was sent off at the age of 18 to England, thinking at that time that the British were the greatest people in the world. He wanted to be British, so he bought there in Bombay a full outfit of white pith helmet, white suit, white shoes, and arrived in London in November, with everybody laughing and pointing at him as he strolled down the streets of London in his white outfit. Well, he couldn't be shamed like that, so he ran off and went right into a London clothier and bought a tuxedo and a tall, stovepipe hat and now looked even more ridiculous walking around the streets of London in a tailor-made tuxedo and a stovepipe hat.

Maybe, as he began to think, England wasn't his country. He tried the experiment with eating meat. After all, the English ruled the world, and one of the reasons—Indians believed—that England, such a small little country, the size of Colorado but ruled the world, was that they ate meat. Meat must have made them big and strong. So he tried eating meat. He said, "I woke up with the image of a little goat bleating inside me – baaa, baaa, baaa. So I joined the vegetarian society, and went to restaurants there in London where I could at least get vegetarian meals, and gradually I began to come to my understanding of how special my native country was. But you know what led me there? It was not anything I had gotten in schools, but Englishmen themselves. And there, in the vegetarian restaurants, I met a number of Englishmen who were deemed eccentric by their fellow countrymen because they wouldn't eat meat, and were interested in mystical religions. They seized upon me, as an Indian, and they said, "We want you to introduce us to the *Bhagavad Gita* and teach it to us in Sanskrit." And he said, "I don't know Sanskrit. I passed an exam on it in school, but I barely know the alphabet. School exams mean nothing. And I don't know the *Bhagavad Gita*." "Well we will read it together."

"And so, in an English translation, I was introduced to the mystic beauty of *The Song of God*, and it has become such a part of me that I read it every day. I read it while I brush my teeth every day—he brushed his teeth for twenty minutes a day, so it's not for two minutes that we talk about—I read it while I brush my teeth. That *Song of God* that celebrates God as Truth, and tells us to follow the path that God has laid out for us. To do the work of someone else is slavery. To do the work of God is true liberation. And that began to shape my thinking and my commitment in life."

"Now, I would not disappoint my family. I went on and took my examinations, and passed at the age of twenty-one. It was amazing how easy it was to become a barrister. All you had to do was to go to twelve dinners—although I never quite understood how going to the dinners at law school, how that helped you become an attorney—and then you had to study this little set of outline notes that everybody could buy. 95 percent of the people passed the exams, so it took me a couple of weeks of actual study to pass them, and then I sailed back to India. There in India I got my job and went to South Africa." Leaving, again, his wife at home for quite a while.

But in South Africa, having been thrown off the train and having been beaten up by the stagecoach driver, Gandhi said, "I realized what God was telling me: Not to be afraid, and to stand up and to see all of this injustice as being injustice done to God. God was telling me to put an end to this injustice, and so I began approaching the English legal system. I sent off letter after letter in the service of these poor, mistreated migrant workers, who were forced to live in the filthiest of hovels, who received very poor salary, who had no real legal rights, who were forced to step off the sidewalk even if a white person walked by. I began to write, and I began to look at the law. I said, 'According to a decree of Her Majesty, all of her subjects have equal rights. And that decree—much like our Declaration of Independence—conflicts absolutely with the laws in South Africa about segregation, and surely a decree of Her Majesty takes prior place.' So that is how I began."

"Then I began to try to teach my fellow Indians. 'You will suffer injustice today. Do not let anyone treat you unjustly. Do not harm anyone, but with all your might stand fast in the truth, and with every means that is nonviolent, struggle for your rights.'"

"And thus I came to the idea of *ahimsa*, which is nonviolence. It is not a weak, passive idea. It takes the greatest moral courage not to use violence. Anyone can strike out at someone. To be struck and to stand there—to turn the other cheek—and then to go on and say, 'I am going to teach you in a nonviolent fashion not to strike me,' that is true courage.

"But I knew we were right; and thus I was steadfast in the truth." So he began his work there in South Africa with the Indians, that he would carry on later to India itself. But it was a process not just of fighting for their rights legally; it was of education. And first in South Africa, and then after his return to India, he opened up schools—really communes, where Indians would come and bring their children, holding everything in common. Gandhi began to try to educate a new generation to *ahimsa*, to nonviolence, and to *satyagraha*, to steadfastness in the truth. That, too, was part of his experiments with the truth. They had no professional teachers. Every one of the parents taught. Gandhi said that your parents ought to be the real source of education for you.

"The greatest possible mistake we make is in turning our children over to professional educators. We should educate them ourselves. Now, I knew almost nothing about Indian history. I knew no Sanskrit. In fact, my knowledge of my own language, Gujarati, was very poor in terms of grammar. But I set about learning these and learning them with the students, and I never tried to fool the students. They said, 'Gandhi, you don't know this!' And I would say, 'Yes, that's true. I don't know this. But maybe we can learn it together.'"

"And then in India, one day an untouchable family showed up. You know the untouchables? They are those without a caste. They are given the most menial of tasks. In fact, there was one set of untouchables that could not even be seen on the street by high-caste Hindus. They had to do all of their work, which was cleaning garbage, in the dark of night. One of these untouchables showed up, and the members of my *ashrom*—that is what it was called; my commune—said, 'We cannot take them in. They will pollute the well.' And I said, 'What is the meaning of all I have been teaching you? What have been all of our experiments with the truth if we do not believe that all are equal in the sight of God.' 'Yes, they are equal in the sight of God. We just don't want them here.' 'Then I will leave and go back to practicing law.'"

He had already developed such a moral authority that this was unthinkable. "No, Gandhi Gee. No, sir Gandhi. We will let them stay. We will learn from them." And so they did, and so that first great barrier was broken.

Now Gandhi began to move to a bigger world, to take on the British Empire itself, because he had come to understand that his mission, given to him by God, was to have an independent India, in which Muslims and Hindus and Christians all lived together in unity—an India for Indians. So he abandoned his European clothes and took to wearing just the simple Indian dress. He took up spinning, and the wheel became one of the symbols of their liberation, because Indians were required to buy cloth made in Britain. They grew the cotton, but it was then shipped to England, made into cloth in the mills of England and then shipped back. That was a major factor in the economy of England, and he said, "We can do without those clothes."

He led mass demonstrations in which European-style clothes, and the cloth brought from England was burned. He himself showed the way of how to weave your own cloth, to spin it. And the wheel itself was a symbol of liberation. It was a wheel of life from which the truth could ultimately liberate you, and the wheel that was the sign of God—no beginning and no end.

So with these ideas he took on the British Empire. Salt—the British government received a huge sum of money from its monopoly on salt. You cannot buy salt without paying that tax. But that tax, Gandhi said, is unjust. It goes to support this fabric of oppression. And believe me, the English oppression is not all light-handed. Why, when Indians stood up for their rights at a place called Amritsar in India, they were mowed down by machine-gun fire. The English officer who led them being killed, then passed a decree that if Indians came down the street and a European approached them, they were to get down on their knees or they could be beaten, and that

English officer, though lightly punished by the government, received standing ovations by Members of Parliament.

So that is the English government for you. "We will not pay that tax on salt." "Where will we get our salt, Gandhi Gee?" —or, as he was already being called, the Mahatma, the great-souled one. "We will march to the sea." "But they will stop us." "No. They will beat us, but that will not stop us. They beat us. We nurse our wounded. We tell them, 'You will not stop us, but we will not harm you.' And then we will just keep marching."

"Go into the mines where you are being mistreated. They will beat you if you stand up against them, but let them beat you. Do nothing violent to them, but just keep coming back."

And world opinion—opinion in England—began to focus on this one frail little man. And Indians—Muslims as well as Hindus as well as Christians—saw in this figure the symbol of their struggle for liberation and enlightenment, the idea that England and Europe were not the only source of culture and ideas, that India had its own fundamental set of ideas that were foreign to the West.

"Your culture," Gandhi said to the English, "is based upon violence. It is based upon war and struggle. Capitalism itself is a form of violence. It literally robs from the poor in order to make the wealthier richer. It is a system that has in itself the seeds of its destruction. We do not want to import it. Our Indian way is the way of God and truth and of nonviolence."

Gandhi then found in prison—for he was thrown into jail again and again—new sources of strength. And not just in the literature of India, but John Ruskind's work, *Unto This Last*. A work that is never read today, but in which Gandhi found truth so gripping he could not put it down during an entire night—that the good of all is encompassed in the good of one individual. So if you harm one individual, if you let injustice, either active or passive, be done to one individual, you have harmed everyone. And, two, that every form of work has its own dignity. The barber is just as much worthy of your respect as is the attorney.

Finally, perhaps the noblest form of work, though, is to farm and to make something with your own hands. So do not be ashamed, Indians, of farming. Do not be ashamed of artisans. Do not think that you have to adopt the European way of ever-greater progress and ever-greater wealth. Be yourselves. Then Leo Tolstoy's *The Kingdom of God is Within You*. Gandhi says in his *Experiments With The Truth* that that opened a whole new world for him. Now, today, *The Kingdom of God Is Within You* by Tolstoy is looked upon by literary critics as part of his old age and dotage. That is to say, he had written his great novels *War and Peace*—that's what you ought to read—*Anna Karenina*, and in his old age he suddenly got religion, and said that Jesus was a very great man, but he was not God. What he taught was that every one of you has God inside yourself.

Gandhi said, "I had read that in the *Bhagavad Gita,* but somehow seen that this Russian, who had achieved such success with his literature and then went back to the simple life, wanted to sell all of his possessions and just follow Christ, Christ's lesson to sell all you have and give it to the poor, that gave it new meaning to me."

So it is not always those books, which are on a reading list of great books, but strange, out-of-the-way books that you find that can touch you, as they did Gandhi.

In prison and then in his self-imposed hunger strikes—for if the British did not do what he thought was right, or if his own followers quarreled and refused to follow the path of truth and non-violence he would start starving himself to death, and he meant it, he would go for days without eating—such was his moral authority that the British *raj*, the government itself, trembled that he might die, and they would give in. Thus, he had harmed no one and brought about truth.

Ultimately, his moral authority played the role, one, in Britain's decision to let India go free, and two, the decision of so many Indians to come together and form political parties that could achieve that freedom under a constitutional government.

But his bitter disappointment came in 1947 and 1948, when India gained its independence but allowed itself to be divided between a largely Muslim Pakistan and a largely Hindu India. "That is to undo all that we have tried to do. That is to say that we are not all one in God," for Gandhi believed that God has fashioned, just as the *Bhagavad Gita* said, "many roads to the truth." The Hindu, the Christian, the Jew, and the Muslim—they were all on that same path. All religions teach the same fundamental values. We are all one. Do not have a Muslim and a Hindu India. But it came to pass.

Civil war broke out over disputed territory, and thousands were killed. And this poor, frail, now very old man walked from little village to village, staying with Hindus, staying with Muslims; trying to bring them together. And his very moral authority had become a threat, and radicals who wanted a truly separate Hindu India set out to assassinate him. One day, walking along in the midst of this civil war, a young man stepped from the crowd and shot him.

And the last word that Gandhi spoke was, "*Ram.*" "God." And we think of the *Bhagavad Gita*—that, "He who dies with my name upon his lips is freed forever from the cycle of life and joins me in bliss."

Lecture Thirty-Five

Churchill, *My Early Life, Painting as a Pastime, The Second World War*

Scope:

In the spirit of Greek tragedy, we believe that we learn the wisdom to live our lives from the study of the successes and failures of the truly great. In the Teaching Company course *Churchill*, we saw why this statesman might well be called the greatest figure in the 20th century. Here, we look at three of the books by this Nobel Prize–winning author and find wisdom to guide us in drawing fundamental lessons for our lives: Our lives are never over and we are never failures as long as we strive in a good cause. Take time for yourself and renew your spiritual being. You have a destiny. Find it. Evil is real and you must resist it where you find it. But ultimately, be optimistic, for the world is becoming better and freedom will one day triumph.

Outline

I.   This lecture closes our discussion of three great individuals who made history and wrote books that can be read today for their wisdom and guidance. We have discussed Cicero, Gandhi, and now, Winston Churchill.

II. Churchill played a role in the parliamentary debates of the 1920s and 1930s about Indian independence and whether India should receive dominion status. Gandhi had brought the British Empire and its government to a halt and forced the government to accede to his demands.

   A. Churchill called Gandhi "a fakir of a type well-known in the East. He further said that the sight of Gandhi "striding half-naked up the steps of the Viceregal palace" was "nauseating" and an "encouragement to all the forces that are hostile to the British authority."

   B. Churchill's stand was opposed by the British Liberal Party, as well as by most members of his own party, the Conservative Party.

      1. Churchill was convinced that the British Empire was a great force for good and liberty under the law.
      2. Churchill believed that India could never govern itself.

3. He said that concessions to Gandhi were a symbol of the lack of moral fiber that was eroding Britain and its government and would ultimately destroy its empire, as well as its liberty.

III. Many believe that Churchill was the greatest man of the 20th century, perhaps the greatest man of all history. Although Gandhi and Churchill were different in many ways, both wrote books that touch us. Churchill wrote good books, not great books, but good books can teach a person to love great books and can give profound insights.

IV. By 1930, when Churchill was 56, he had fallen from power and was thought to be finished in British politics. He then wrote *My Early Life*.

    A. This autobiography, called *A Roving Commission* in its American edition, is very different from Gandhi's *Experiments with the Truth*. In *My Early Life*, Churchill, knowing that his public career was over, looks back on his experience with insight.

    B. Both Churchill and Gandhi found their compulsory education not only worthless but counterproductive.

        1. Churchill pondered whether great books should be given to young people. He believed that life experiences were necessary and that exposure to great books would only make students hate literature.

        2. Churchill was a failure in school and was last in his class.

        3. Churchill was accepted at Sandhurst. There, he did credibly and finished eighth in his class, which showed that he could learn when he felt the material was worth learning.

        4. Churchill favored a good, practical education that goes along with what the child learns best.

    C. Churchill loved the army because it satisfied his search for glory. He wanted to be famous and known for his bravery.

    D. *My Early Life* describes Churchill's election to Parliament.

    E. The book also describes, in touching terms, Churchill's relationship with his father. Although his father believed that he would never amount to anything, by the age of 26, Churchill had become a bestselling author, a millionaire from the proceeds of his writings and lectures, a war hero, and a member of Parliament.

F. In 1915, Churchill was dismissed from government because he was blamed for the destruction of the British forces at Gallipoli.

V. After his dismissal, Churchill took up painting. In 1932, he wrote a magazine article, which he later expanded into *Painting as a Pastime.*

A. In this book, Churchill says that at every stage of life, the individual must be willing to try something new. The greatest relief from stress is to take up a vocation that is different from one's ordinary activities.

B. Churchill describes the sheer joy of translating nature from the eye to the canvas and raises the question of how we relate to nature. He worshipped nature, traveling as far as Morocco to paint landscapes.

C. Churchill was a successful artist. In 1924, only eight years after taking up painting, he won prizes for works submitted anonymously.

D. The paintings give us insight into the character of this statesman. An autobiography can be crafted, but Churchill's paintings offer a glimpse into his soul—a soul of great optimism. Optimism also percolates through *My Early Life*, despite Churchill's failures to that time.

VI. Britain turned to Churchill again in 1940. On June 4, 1940, he delivered a stirring oration in Parliament, in which he declared, "We shall never surrender." As we know, he was turned out of office after he led his country to victory and then wrote *The Second World War.*

A. This work won the Nobel Prize and made history. It shows World War II as Churchill saw it. The first volume is a lesson for us today. It shows us a soul that has greatness.

B. Churchill's motto for the book—"You should be resolute in defeat and magnanimous in victory"—is a statement of Cicero's moral qualities.

C. Churchill called World War II the "unnecessary war." He believed that it would never have happened if Britain had shown the moral resolve to make the proper peace at the end of World War I. Instead, excessive reparations were exacted from Germany, and it was allowed to regain its power after being dishonored and humiliated.

D. Step-by-step, Churchill traces how failure to meet Hitler's aggression led to World War II.

1. Britain's acceptance of Hitler's rise to power came back to haunt the nation. Like Gandhi and Cicero, Churchill believed in absolute evil in a struggle with absolute good. For Churchill, Hitler was absolute evil.

2. Churchill realized that passive injustice was as wrong as active injustice. Before the war, Britain lacked the moral fiber to take up the fight. If the Conservative Party stood up to Hitler, it would have to raise expenditures, and a balanced budget was essential for the party to stay in power. Thus, passive injustice and the false notion of British self-interest allowed Hitler to gain power.

3. Britain did not understand the value of bringing large and small powers together into a working coalition that would have the moral authority and strength to overthrow Hitler. The British initially dismissed the possibility of coalition. With the collapse of France, Britain was alone.

4. Britain allowed Hitler to move into the Rhineland, considering this action to be in its own self-interest. After all, Hitler was only moving into his own backyard.

5. Britain's false conception of where its interests lay proved ruinous. Self-interest, Churchill says, is always in doing what is right.

6. When Hitler threatened Czechoslovakia, Britain moved from passive to active injustice. Without allowing Czechoslovakia at the bargaining table, Britain, France, Italy, and Germany decided its fate.

E. The British progressed from allowing wrongs to be done to actively doing wrong themselves, because they lacked a sense of true justice. According to Churchill, the concept of true justice harks back to Cicero. It consists of keeping one's world; it is the *fides*, the honor of a nation.

1. *The Second World War* breathes an air of old-fashioned honor. The generation of the 1940s did not understand the concept of honor, and Churchill seemed to be a relic

of a bygone age. As Cicero, Gandhi, and Churchill understood, honor is at the heart of justice, because it rests on integrity and courage. Justice and courage were fundamental to Churchill's view of history and the world.

2. Churchill also exhibited moderation. No one was more resolute in pursuit of the war than Churchill, and no one was more willing to rebuild Germany at the end of the war.

F. Churchill showed wisdom gained not in school and not from a series of great books. He read few books but absorbed those that he read. Churchill's writing, for example, reflects the power of Gibbon's prose. He made the books that he read part of himself—and therein lies true wisdom.

VII. Churchill approached life always willing to change. Like Gandhi, his life was a series of experiments with the truth. He was never afraid to say that he had been wrong or to seek redemption. For Gandhi, Cicero, and Churchill, the ultimate lesson is to never give in.

Essential Reading:

Churchill, *My Early Life*.

———, *Painting as a Pastime*.

———, *The Second World War*, vol. I.

Supplementary Reading:

Manchester, *Churchill*, vols. I and II.

Questions to Consider:

1. Churchill thought that great books are frequently wasted on the young. College students do not have the life experience to appreciate these books. Do you agree?

2. Churchill disliked Gandhi in life. Do you think, upon reflection, he would appreciate the comparison?

Lecture Thirty-Five—Transcript
Churchill, *My Early Life, Painting as a Pastime, The Second World War*

In this lecture we continue with our discussion of three great individuals who themselves made history, who also wrote great books, books that you can continue to read today for wisdom and guidance. We talked first of Cicero, and then in our last lecture we talked of Gandhi. Mohandas Gandhi. Mahatma—the Great-Souled One. To understand him a little better, as well as our third figure, I would ask you to turn your eyes to London, to Parliament, during the very height after the First World War, in the 1920s and '30s, to the debate over the independence of India, and whether that great subcontinent should be given dominion status, like Canada.

In the course of his struggles to achieve the independence of his nation, Gandhi has once again brought the British Empire and its government to a halt, and has required the British Government to concede to the demands put forth by this tiny little man. This has outraged one of the leading members of the Conservative Party, an older man, short and balding. He stands up in Parliament and says, "The sight of this fakir—and that is what he is, a fakir, in the Middle Eastern tradition—striding half-nude up the steps of the Viceregal palace there in New Delhi, and of the Viceroy of His Majesty meeting with this fakir and conceding to his demands is repugnant to all that the British Empire stands for."

That man is Winston Churchill, and his stand opposing dominion status for India is opposed not only by the Liberal Party, but also by most of the members of his own party, the Conservative Party. This will gradually force him "into the wilderness," out of favor with his own party as well as with the opposition party. But he is absolutely convinced: one, that the British Empire is a great force for good, that it is a force for liberty under law; secondly, that India can never govern itself; and, thirdly, that concessions to this Gandhi are the symbol of all the lack of moral fiber that is eroding Britain and its government, and will ultimately destroy not just its empire, but its liberty itself.

Well, you know my admiration for Winston Churchill. I devoted a whole lecture course to him, and I think he is the greatest man, perhaps in history, and certainly of the 20th century. He and Gandhi I both admire. And I must think that speaks to a kind of nobleness of soul to find great men and women and admire them who are so utterly opposed. And how could you be more opposed than Gandhi and Churchill? First of all, just sheer weight. Churchill weighs around 215 pounds. Gandhi weighs little more than 100 pounds. Gandhi, who will not eat meat, who eats not only a vegetarian diet—but at one point stops eating cereals, like wheat and only eats beans and peas, and has a long internal debate with himself about drinking milk, and finally, only at the urging of his doctor that he cannot survive without some form of protein, begins to drink a little bit of milk—and Churchill who loves red meat and beefsteaks. In fact, when he is Prime Minister, flying back and forth between England and America, he says, "My stomach never got used to those time differences, so I would just have a steak served to me every four hours." Gandhi, who never drank; and Churchill, who begins every day with a Scotch. Gandhi, who is a profound believer in God; and Churchill, who says, "Pretty early on in my life I reached an arrangement with God. I thought most of the rituals devoted to him were a lot of nonsense, but I thought he was a pretty benign old fellow, and we would just leave it at that."

But both of them very great men, and for our purposes in this course, writers of books that can touch us. It is to Churchill as an author, as an author perhaps not of great books like the *Bhagavad Gita*, like the *Divine Comedy*, like Goethe's *Faust*, but of good books. I would ask you to consider that there are very many good books. Books that can teach you to love great books. Books that at various points in your life can give you very profound insights into yourself. Churchill was an author who won the Nobel Prize, and at least one of his books that we will discuss, his *History of the Second World War*, made history in that it shaped the way people viewed what had happened in the Second World War.

But let's start by taking him back to 1930. He is living in his magnificent estate at Chartwell, and most people believe he is finished in English politics. He is done for. He has fallen from power and from grace with even his own party. He will never be Prime Minister. He sits back and writes a study of his early life. It is an autobiography, and so, very different in many ways, at first sight, from Gandhi's *Experiments With The Truth*.

Churchill's is *My Early Life*, or *A Roving Commission,* as it would be called in its American edition. It is the work of a man looking back on what has happened to him. And really, the work of someone who knows that their public career is over. And yet, like Gandhi, Churchill reveals many insights that we might ponder. First of all, both Churchill and Gandhi found education—their compulsory education—not only worthless, but also counterproductive. Churchill describes his early education as being like a cave into which he was forced, and from which he never learned anything worthwhile.

"They wanted me to learn Latin, and they handed me a Latin textbook, and they said, 'Learn this conjugation. Learn this declension. *Memsa, Memsai. Memso. Memsa. Memsa.*' And the headmaster came back and said, 'Young Churchill, do you know them?' And I said, 'Yes I do. But I have a question.' 'Yes?' 'You know there are all these "*memsa, memsa, memsa.*" There are a lot of "*memsas*" there. Just *m-e-m-s-a*. What does that mean?' 'They are various uses, various forms. Like this is "*memsa*" when it is a subject. This is "*memsa*" when it is evocative.' '"Evocative" sir?' 'Yes.' 'What is "evocative?' 'It is used when you address a table, when you speak to a table, "O, table".' 'But sir, I never speak to a table.' 'Are you going to be a lot of trouble for me?'"

And that was just the start of his problems with school. He would write, "I ponder whether great books should be put in the hands of young people. Maybe you need a life's experience. All this will really do to a young person is to make him hate this book and make him never want to see it again."

So Churchill instead is a failure in school. And to make sure that people know what a failure you are in school, the way you parade across when parents' day is, is in the order of your rank in class. There is poor little red-headed Churchill, he describes himself in his autobiography, "stepping across, always the last. People looking at one another and saying, 'Isn't that Randolph—his father—Randolph's son?' 'Oh, yes. Dumb little blighter, isn't he?'"

So you know, if you or your child is not doing very well in school, ponder that maybe some great minds cannot be trammeled by school. They cannot be kept in the close confines of school. Instead, Churchill said, "I finally got into Sandhurst." And we talked about the difficulties in that, and three examinations finally to get in. "But once I was there, I did quite credibly. I passed out eighth in my class, which went to show that I could learn when it was worth learning."

So maybe what we want to learn from this is a good, practical education. Find out what your child best loves and let them go along with that. He loved the army. And his *Early Life*, his autobiography, describes with great glee his search for glory. He was never abashed in his search for glory. He wanted to be famous, and his bravery. It describes, in touching tones, his relationship with his father, and how perhaps the only intimate moment he had in his entire life while his father was alive—his father died when he was twenty-one—was on one occasion when his father shouted to him, and said, "Will you please shut up and stop making so much noise!" And then turned to him and said, "I'm sorry boy. Sometimes older people don't have the patience they need with younger people. Forgive me."

So he grew up, he said, a solitary tree, rather like Gandhi, who, at the age of 18, was sent off on his own to England to make his own way—so, the solitary child. "The solitary tree," Churchill wrote, "grows up, if it survives at all, to be strong."

Churchill describes how he finally made it into Parliament, and at the end of that *Early Life*, you understand that this boy, whose father said that he was never going to amount to anything, had, by the age of 26, become a best-selling author, a millionaire from the proceeds of his own writings and lectures, a war hero; and there he was in Parliament. Now, I'd call that a pretty good achievement, would you not? And in that quiet, good book, *My Early Life*, I think we find a little inspiration for ourselves. Particularly reading it now, when we know that 1930 was not the end of Churchill's life.

Take him back to another period in his life. It is 1915-1916, and he has been dismissed from government. He was the author of the great catastrophe at Gallipoli. He was blamed for the utter destruction of the British force, the loss of 120,000 men in an attempt to storm the beaches and to drive the Turks out of the war. They had never given his idea a fair chance, he said. But there he was, out of government. People convinced that he was a failure.

"There I was," he said, "wondering what I would do." His wife would say, "I thought the grief would kill Winston." "But I decided I would take up painting, and I bought myself a canvas and I got myself some paints, and I was simply standing there, peering at this blank canvas. Suddenly a friend of mine drove up, and she was herself a painter, and she said, 'What are you doing, Winston?' And I said, 'I don't know how to start.' And she said, 'Just start.' She took that paintbrush and stuck it in a spot of blue paint and began to paint that canvas. And I went after it, too. I took up painting."

In 1932, he wrote a magazine article that was then reprinted as a book, called *Painting as a Pastime*. It is a marvelously good book, for he tells you that at every stage of your life, you must be willing to try something new, and the greatest relief from stress, the kind of stress he felt when he had been thrown out of the government, is to take up a vocation that is totally different from what you ordinarily do. In other words, if you read books for a living, if you're a professor or even an attorney, don't read for a hobby. Release a whole different section of your mind. "And that is what painting was for me," he said.

He talks about the sheer joy of translating nature from your eye to your palette. Churchill raises for us that question of how do we relate to nature. He worshiped nature. He painted landscapes. He would travel as far as Morocco to paint landscapes, and during the Second World War, he would urge President Roosevelt and finally convince him to go with him, take one day out of their busy schedules. Have Roosevelt carried up to the rooftop of a hotel so that Roosevelt could just witness that sunset that Churchill felt was so beautiful. So, to rejoice in nature.

But unlike almost any artist I know, he could capture this in print. Moreover, he became a success. Already in 1924, only eight years after taking up painting, he was winning prizes for paintings that he submitted anonymously. More than that, these paintings of Churchill's—which hang now in some of the great museums of the world—give us a unique insight into the character of a statesman. You see, the autobiography of a statesman—the autobiography of President Clinton or the autobiography of Ulysses S. Grant or any statesman—that can always be crafted, can it not? A certain spin can be put upon it. But nothing can intervene between what you see in those paintings of Churchill's. They are a glimpse into his soul, and that soul is one of great optimism.

I would suggest to you that perhaps one of the most powerful lessons you can learn from the great books and from life is optimism—I say this as a confirmed pessimist—but I believe that optimism is the key to success. And those paintings of Churchill, those bright, broad landscapes that he describes and paints so magnificently—those are a key to his fundamental optimism. An optimism that percolates through his *Early Life*, that autobiography in which, "Even if my life is over, it has been a good one. It has been a lot of fun. And I look back not on the sad aspects of it, but on the happy aspects." Is that what you do? Look back just on those happy aspects.

In his *Painting as a Pastime*, which by the way his wife urged him not to do—I don't know whether that's a key to success or not, not to do what your spouse tells you—but his wife said, "Do not write that little magazine article. You're not an art critic. All you are is this little part-time painter who goes out and puts down dabs. You're a serious statesman, and that will make you look un-serious." Well, he went ahead and wrote it, and it's a little masterpiece, I tell you. In it he says, "I plan to get to heaven." That's optimistic for a statesman who has had to do many bad things. "I plan to get to heaven, and when I do, I expect to spend the first million years there painting, and vermilion will be the dullest color on my palette, and that is how I see the world, in bright, beautiful colors."

So his *Painting as a Pastime* is a wonderful little book just to sit down with and say, "You know, maybe I am too stressed. Maybe I ought to pick up something absolutely new and pursue it with that kind of complete devotion that marked a Churchill."

Everybody blamed Churchill for everything. After all, in 1930 when he wrote *My Early Life*, he was blamed for the Great Depression. After all, he had been Chancellor of the Exchequer in 1928. He had been Chancellor of the Exchequer when England went back on the gold standard. The best minds of the time, the best economists of the time had told him England should go back on the gold standard, but when the Depression came, everybody said, "Churchill's to blame for it. He put us back on the gold standard. So there it is."

He was always being blamed; but this never got him down. It never depressed him ultimately. And these people who talk about Churchill being a manic-depressive—they absolutely miss the true meaning of that man's life: his optimism. Because, like Gandhi and like Cicero, he believed his whole life was planned by God—that benevolent old fellow—and that he was moving in a course with destiny. So would it be that this man who was finished in politics in 1930, in 1940 would see his country turn to him again.

He would deliver that great oration in Parliament on June the 4th, 1940, declaring that, "We shall never surrender." and lead his country to victory. And no sooner had he led his country to victory, than he is turned out of office. The election is held in July—an election he could have postponed—and he is turned out of office. England wants its experiment with socialism.

So he will sit down and not grieve at this, although it is a bitter personal disappointment, and write his *History of the Second World War*. That is the book that will win him the Nobel Prize. If the Nobel Prize is worthy of anything, then it certainly marks a great book, and that is a book that made history. For he portrays the Second World War as he saw it. He puts his stamp upon that great struggle, and, in particular, its first volume. It's a lesson for us today, and it can still be a book that made history.

It shows us a soul that has greatness. His very motto that he chooses for the book, that you should be "resolute in defeat and magnanimous in victory" is a statement of those moral qualities that Cicero tells us about. Even those who have done wrong to you need to be punished in just moderation. He describes the Second World War as "the unnecessary war." It was the war that never needed to come about had the British had the moral resolve to make the proper peace at the end of the First World War.

"Instead," he said, "we acted in excess, laying these very heavy taxes upon the Germans, these reparations, and yet, at the same time, having dishonored and humiliated them, allowed them to grow back in power." And then, step-by-step, Churchill traces the lessons that could be applied today, how the failure to meet the aggression of Adolf Hitler led to the Second World War.

First of all, the very fact that the British allowed Adolf Hitler to come to power and to put in place a series of evil laws that stripped one segment of the German people, the Jews, of their rights, was a wrong that would come home to haunt the British. Churchill, just like Gandhi and just like Cicero, believed in absolute evil in a struggle with absolute good. And for him, Adolf Hitler was absolute evil. This, too, is a theme that has run all the way through our course, and we have seen already when we looked at the *Book of Job*, that evil is a topic that we do not want to deal with today. We do not want to believe that there is a Devil. We do not want to believe that some things are absolutely evil. Well, Churchill said, "You are wrong. The world can be seen as a struggle between the good and the evil, and that Hitler was absolutely evil." So you committed, Churchill would say, drawing upon our Cicero, passive injustice. And Cicero was absolutely correct that passive injustice is just as bad as active injustice. Hitler was doing the wrong, and you were allowing it to happen. Why? Because you thought it was in your self-interest. Remember Cicero telling us that that is one reason you allow passive injustice to occur. The British thought it was in their own best interest. They could not and would not fight another war. They lacked that moral fiber.

Moreover, it was in the self-interest of the Conservative Party to stay in power, and if they stood up to Hitler, they would have to raise the budget, and a balanced budget was crucial. So your passive injustice in the false notion that it was in your self-interest allowed Hitler to gain power and to commit the first of these wrongs. Then—this is interesting for us today—"You British statesmen and British people would not understand the value of a coalition. You would not work to bring together all those powers. And not just the Soviet Union, not just France, but the little powers of Europe, like Czechoslovakia; bring them together into a working coalition that would have given you the moral authority as well as the strength to overthrow a Hitler. And time and time again you allowed that to slip away until you found yourself finally, with the collapse of France, absolutely alone. Then you allowed Hitler to move into the Rhineland, and once again you thought this was in your self-interest. After all, he was moving only into his own garden, his own back yard, putting armaments in his own back yard. So again, this false conception of where your self-interest lay was ruinous. Because I am going to tell you something: Your self-interest is always in doing what is right."

"And once again, when Czechoslovakia was threatened by Hitler, you passed from passive injustice to active injustice. Because you, with the French and the Italians and the Germans, not even allowing the Czechs into the room, gave away a vital part of their country, that was an active wrong. So do you see how, step by step by step, you passed from allowing wrongs to be done to actively carrying out those wrongs?"

"And why? Because we lacked a sense of what is true justice." And true justice, Churchill said, through his study of history, takes us right back to Cicero. It is keeping your word. It is the *fides*, the honest and the honor of a nation. Churchill's *History of the Second World War* breathes an old-fashioned air of honor, and he talked to a generation already in the 1940s that no longer actively understood what honor was. Churchill seemed a relic of a bygone age. But as Cicero understood, as Gandhi understood, and as Churchill understood, honor is at the heart of justice, because honor rests upon integrity. And it rests upon your having the courage to put that integrity into place. So justice and courage, those are fundamental to how Churchill saw the world, and how he saw the history leading up to the Second World War.

Finally, there was that sense of moderation, and no one was more resolute in the pursuit of that war than Churchill. No one was more willing to rebuild Germany at the end of that war.

It's a wisdom that Churchill gained, not in school. He gained it, not from a series of great books. He was one of those people who read a few books and absolutely absorbed them—the way he read and memorized whole pages of Gibbon's *Decline and Fall of the Roman Empire*. And you can read, in his *History of the Second World War*, the power of Gibbon's prose flowing through his own pen. He read a few books—a few great books and some very good books. He made them a part of himself, and he says that's what you ought to do. Therein lies true wisdom. That was the wisdom he gained from books, but from a willingness to approach life always willing to change. That again is why he was like Gandhi, even though he would shudder at the comparison. His life was a series of "experiments with the truth." He was never afraid—Churchill, just like Gandhi—to say, "I have been wrong." Indeed, his life was a series of redemptions, and the greatest redemption of all coming when he was called by his nation to lead it. It came with a sense of destiny. "My whole life was marching with destiny."

For Churchill, the ultimate struggle with India would show also his moderation. There is no more touching scene than described by Indian politicians, when finally India had been granted its independence. One of them was speaking with Churchill, and they said he was still just Mr. Winston Churchill, and out of office, just a Member of Parliament, "Will you continue to oppose us?" He said, "No. No. You have now gained your independence. And I only ask this of you: Can you come back to me and will you, in five years, and in ten years—that again is optimism, because he's already pretty old—and tell me that the ordinary Indian is better off. And if that is true, then I will say it has all been worthwhile and you were right and I was utterly wrong."

So never afraid to admit that he was wrong, even as you should never be afraid to admit that you are wrong. And ultimately, that sense that if you live your life, follow that destiny, always struggle for what is right—for Gandhi, for Cicero and for Churchill, for all three—the ultimate lesson is "Never give up." You remember the scene? Churchill, late in life, going to speak to his old school, Harrow. Again his wife telling him not to go, he's not up to it. And looking out over those boys at their commencement address, and telling them, "Never give up. Never. Never. Never."

That was the Cicero who stood up there in the Roman Senate in 44 and 43 B.C. and spoke out for freedom. That was the Gandhi, beaten on the stagecoach in South Africa, beaten in the mines of South Africa, starving himself. Seeing India torn by religious and ethnic strife, and yet never giving up. That is the ultimate lesson of the great books: Never give up.

Lecture Thirty-Six
Lessons from the Great Books

Scope:

A great book can lead us from information and facts to knowledge and on to wisdom, the ability to apply information and knowledge to living our lives. That has been the purpose of our course. In the first place, we have explored some of the greatest and most influential works ever written. We have learned facts about their authors and the times in which they were written. We have gained knowledge about what these books say. But our ultimate goal has been the search for wisdom. Can we find in these books wisdom to understand and change our individual lives? This gives us our true definition of a "great book." It is a book of good ideas. It is book not just to read but to ponder. It is a book with ideas that makes us better, better as individuals and better as citizens of a democracy. This is a definition as true and vital today as it was in the age of Socrates and Cicero.

Outline

I. As we approach the conclusion of this course, we must ask ourselves why we should read great books.

    A. At the beginning, this course defined a great book as having a great theme, being written in noble language that elevates the soul, and speaking across the ages, that is, possessing universality.

    B. Any discussion of great books must involve values. People cannot learn from great books unless they are willing to enter sympathetically into the mind of the author.

II. This course has discussed books that made history.

    A. One example, of course, is Machiavelli's *The Prince*.

        1. Lord Acton argues that the modern world began with Machiavelli's idea that the state has no sense of moral judgment and politics has no moral dimension whatsoever.

        2. Machiavelli believed that Socrates and Cicero were wrong. A state and its leaders are judged by different criteria than those used for private individuals. There is a complete separation between public and private morals.

3. In addition to *The Prince*, several other works discussed in this course reveal the soul of a tyrant.

B. *Beowulf, Gilgamesh,* and the *Iliad* all discuss ambition and the desire to leave behind a reputation that will be remembered forever. In the epic of *Gilgamesh,* for example, Gilgamesh recognized that he would not live forever; however, he had built the walls of Uruk, and men would talk about them forever.

C. *The Divine Comedy* is a story of redemption, but it also clarifies ideals that led people from across Europe to take up the Cross and go to the Holy Land to wage war against the infidel. The justification for the crusades can be found in the ideals of the *Divine Comedy.* Although it is a story of divine love, that love must be spread by the sword and by men who believe that they are undertaking the work of God.

D. John Stuart Mill's *On Liberty* looks back at the founders of the United States. Mill represents the continuation of ideas found in the Declaration of Independence. Lord Acton says that the American Revolution is the only revolution in history that was fought for a principle, liberty. Mill's work embodies ideals that led Churchill to stand up and say, "We shall never surrender."

E. The Book of Exodus is still alive in newspapers today. It propounds the idea that one religion has its sanction in a holy book and that sanction must be worked out politically and militarily.

F. The Koran, like the Book of Exodus, made spiritual and political history. It presents a worldview that is total and complete.

III. Some books we have read in this course have made spiritual history.

A. The Gospel of Mark is one such book.

B. In the *Bhagavad Gita*, Gandhi found a statement that truth is God and is the salvation of a soul.

C. Confucius is both a spiritual and a political guide who laid the foundation for more than 2,000 years of Chinese history.

IV. Can these books change our lives today?

    A. Many of these values seem irrelevant to contemporary Americans.

        1. The *Iliad* embodies values of a heroic age of honor, in which warfare was significant. That era was an age of the duel. The concept of honor cannot exist in a society that lacks the duel. Honor may be an outmoded concept.

        2. The age of Dante believed that all of life is preparation for death.

        3. Goethe's *Faust* asks whether absolute standards of beauty exist. For contemporary Americans, the answer is that they do not.

        4. *Walden* deals with nature and the environment, which are certainly major concerns today. Contemporary Americans, however, have difficulty taking seriously the values of a man who left everything behind and ignored correspondence with others.

    B. The values embodied in these great books can change the lives of people today.

        1. The Koran changes lives every day, winning converts to Islam.

        2. The Book of Mark still speaks and changes people's lives, as does the *Bhagavad Gita*.

V. One of the first people to grapple with the question of what makes a great book was Aristotle.

    A. Aristotle died in 322 B.C. He was the tutor of Alexander the Great and a pupil of Plato. He was a professor who was interested in science, the natural world, politics, and empirical evidence.

    B. Aristotle wrote *Poetics,* which has been called the only work of literary criticism that is absolutely indispensable.

    C. Aristotle asserted that a great book should be judged by its moral impact. Thus, a tragedy arouses fear and pity and achieves a catharsis.

VI. In *What Is Art?* Tolstoy says that a great book can be judged not only by the feelings that it arouses but by the quality of those feelings.

A. To take the most obvious example, *Mein Kampf*, although written after the time of Tolstoy, appeals to all that is evil in human emotions. On the other hand, a work such as Dostoyevski's *Notes from the Underground*, which is about the soul in prison, is horrifying to read but imparts the message that even in the midst of terror, torture, and suffering, what is good in people lives on.

B. For Tolstoy, Goethe's *Faust* is not a great book because it is too complicated for ordinary people to read, too much a product of its own time, too full of allusions to Greek and Roman mythology, and too full of philosophical allusions. If a reader has to spend much effort trying to understand what the author is saying, his emotions are not touched.

C. However, others believe that such books as the *Aeneid*, *The Divine Comedy*, and Goethe's *Faust* are worth the struggle. After deciphering the obscure references, the reader sees that these are soul-elevating works. That is why it is worth reading to *Gilgamesh*, with its complicated references to Mesopotamian religion, or the *Iliad*.

VII. Aristotle and Tolstoy's requirement that a great book must arouse good moral feelings begs the question of whose morality is important. One lesson of this course is that a universal set of values exists and that these values can be found throughout these great books.

    A. Books from China (*The Analects*), India (the *Bhagavad Gita*), the Christian Middle Ages, and pagan classical Greece, along with the Koran and *1984*, all reveal a belief in the common set of values defined by Socrates: wisdom, justice, moderation, and courage.

        1. Confucius said that he was happy to meet a good man, a man who practices justice, moderation, and courage.

        2. In the Koran, the Book of Exodus, and the Book of Job, the fear of the Lord is the beginning of wisdom. Some great books link wisdom with belief in God.

        3. Although Cicero understands that natural law must be founded in God, he describes his moral approach to life in purely practical terms. He believes that the person who practices justice, moderation, and courage based on wisdom will be successful and morally good. Some books teach that even without a belief in God, the individual can still lead a moral life.

B. We may not want to accept this universal set of values, but in reading great books, we learn that such a set of values exists.

VIII. How do these books touch our lives? They touch us only if we are willing to use the wisdom that comes from these books to live our lives. That wisdom is broader than a set of values. It is an education for freedom; these great books educate us to live our lives freely and responsibly.

IX. What role does reading play in today's society?

    A. A movie or video game has a more attractive and compelling appeal than a book today.

    B. We may be entering an age that is radically different from the previous 5,000 years. The invention of writing transformed the mind because knowledge could be stored and transmitted in a different fashion.

    C. The past 25 years have seen another radical transformation. The printed word in a book has been replaced by a computer screen, video games, and movies.

    D. These innovations might transform the character of education.

X. What is the meaning of "education for freedom"?

    A. As previously mentioned in this course, *education* comes from a root meaning "to lead out from yourself."

    B. Education is a three-stage process.

        1. Education begins with information—a collection of facts and data. Our era is so overwhelmed with facts and data that we scarcely have time to think.

        2. The next step is to weave these facts and data into knowledge. Knowledge is the ability to see the pattern in a particular subject.

        3. The next step is to apply that pattern, to live one's life by it. This step is what Socrates, Cicero, Dante, and Goethe all meant by wisdom.

C. Wisdom is ultimately an act of meditation. We can come to wisdom only by sitting alone and thinking about what we have learned.

   1. The contemplative life was considered the highest calling in the Middle Ages. The monk would cut himself off from human society to devote his mind to the contemplation of God.

   2. In the *Bhagavad Gita*, the highest calling is seen in those who devote themselves to meditation.

   3. Gandhi talks about those who have the freedom to cut themselves off from all human ties to meditate as a way to achieve wisdom.

   4. Although meditation is essential in transforming knowledge into wisdom, contemporary Americans lack the ability and the time to meditate.

   5. Reading a great book means sitting down with the book and allowing it to speak. It will speak to us only if we open our minds, which we can do only through meditation—the final step to wisdom.

   6. Wisdom is ultimately a source of freedom. As long as people read great books, they can have insights that lead them to freedom.

D. In a commencement address at Harvard, Solzhenitsyn pointed out a danger. People today are flooded with such a wealth of books and information that they are in danger of losing the truth. A great thinker may have ideas that can save the country, but unless that work is picked up by the media or a publishing house, people will remain unaware of it.

E. Some great books have been written and ignored until times and values changed and people were willing to return to them.

   1. *Walden* created little stir when first published. After about 100 years, people began reading it and saw in Thoreau's love of nature a challenge to our destruction of the environment.

   2. Although Gandhi was well known, Martin Luther King first learned about Gandhi in a theological seminary. He recognized that Gandhi's *satyagraha*, his steadfastness in truth, was key to overthrowing an evil system that had paralyzed the moral fiber of this country. Martin Luther King, like Gandhi and Solzhenitsyn, exhibited the sense of justice, moral fortitude, and moderation that comes from wisdom to transform society.

XI. We can all change our lives in small ways and in grand ways as long as we accept the fundamental premise that life is about the individual and as long as we are willing to learn, are willing to make mistakes and admit them, exhibit the ability to redeem ourselves—in an individual sense, not in a theological sense—and never give up. The ultimate lesson of the great books is to never give up. The individual must live his or her life and realize—as both Homer and Thoreau say—that every day offers an opportunity to begin again.

Essential Reading:

Aristotle, *Poetics*.

Supplementary Reading:

Leo Tolstoy, *What Is Art?*

Questions to Consider:

1. How, at the end of our course, would you define a great book?
2. Which of the books we have discussed would you say was once a great book but now no longer speaks to us or our moral values?

Lecture Thirty-Six—Transcript
Lessons from the Great Books

We come now to the end of our course on great books—*Books That Have Made History: Books That Can Change Your Life*—and we ask ourselves, "Why read great books?"

We began our course, as Socrates told us we should, with definitions. How do we define a great book? Remember, you cannot get anywhere in any discussion unless you know what you are talking about, and I gave you a very clear definition: A great book has a great theme; it is written in noble language, language that elevates your soul, raises your soul to the sublime; and it speaks across the ages. A great book must speak across the ages. It has a universality to it. And you see right there I am already loading the discussion, because I have said that this noble language will elevate your soul. That is perhaps something that we would not all accept—that we even have a soul, much less that it can be elevated.

So any discussion of great books must involve values, and I would suggest to you that you cannot read a great book and learn from it— you can read it, but you cannot learn from it—unless you are willing to enter sympathetically into the mind of the author. You cannot learn from the *Koran* unless you are willing to enter sympathetically into the mind of Islam. You cannot read *Job* unless you are willing to enter sympathetically into the mind of the Hebrews and the prophets. You cannot read and learn from Plato unless you are willing to enter into the mind that said that the soul is immortal.

So great books. We have our definition, do we not? Great theme, noble language, speaks across the ages. I am going to tell you we have read some very great books. We have read books that have made history. We have read books like Machiavelli and his *Prince* that has made history. That is to say, as Lord Acton tells us, the beginning of the modern world is with Machiavelli with his ideas that the state has no sense of moral judgment. There is no moral dimension to politics whatsoever, and that Socrates was absolutely wrong. That Cicero was absolutely wrong. We judge the state and the men and women who lead it by categories absolutely different from that of private individuals, and that there is a complete separation from public and private morality. That is Machiavelli. That is why Adolf Hitler kept a copy of Machiavelli beside his bed table.

Machiavelli is not the only work that tells us about the soul of a tyrant. *Beowulf, Gilgamesh*, the *Iliad*—these seemingly innocuous little books. Do they not talk about ambition and a desire to leave behind a reputation that will be remembered forever? Yes or no? And what great statesman does not want to leave behind that kind of a reputation, so that, centuries later, we still talk about a Genghis Khan. Centuries later we will still talk about a Joseph Stalin or Adolf Hitler. How many movies and books and documentaries go back again and again to the horror of the Nazis? Isn't that just what Achilles wanted? To die young but to leave behind a reputation that would endure forever. What about Gilgamesh? No, he was not going to have eternal life, but this is what he had built: Uruk. Those walls were good, and men would talk about them forever.

So the desire to be remembered; the ambition; the courage; a willingness to undergo and do great evils to leave behind that reputation, that is there in some of our books, like the *Gilgamesh* and the *Beowulf* and the *Iliad*.

Political history. In the *Divine Comedy* of Dante, we not only read a story of redemption, we see those ideals that led men from all over Europe—and women in some cases, and children in some cases—to take the cross and go to the Holy Land and wage war. In the *Divine Comedy*, there is Muhammad, down in Hell, as a sower of dissension. The Crusades have their justification in the ideal of Dante's *Divine Comedy*, a story of love; but that divine love must be spread by the sword, and that was the story of the Crusades and the men who believed that they were undertaking the work of God. "God wills it," they cried as they took the cross.

In John Stuart Mill, in his *On Liberty*, we look back to the values of the founders of our country. He is the continuum of the ideas in the Declaration of Independence, the liberty of the individual. Again, as Lord Acton, our guide, tells us, the American Revolution was the only revolution in history that was fought for a principle, for an idea: Liberty. John Stuart Mill's book *On Liberty* embodies those ideals that would also lead a Churchill to stand up and say, "We shall never surrender." So we have read books that have made political history, and continue to make it.

The *Book of Exodus* is still alive in newspapers today. And the idea that one religion or another religion has its sanction in a holy book, and that sanction must be worked out politically and militarily—that is right there in the *Book of Exodus*, when the children of Israel are given the Holy Land, as *Exodus* tells us.

The *Koran*, that magnificent work, like the *Book of Exodus*, it not only made spiritual history, it made political history and continues to make political history. You do not understand the Middle East, you do not understand that vast geographical and political area stretching from Afghanistan out to Morocco and all the way up to the Danube, including the Balkans, unless you know the *Koran*, for it is a worldview that is total and complete.

And we have read books that have made spiritual history. *The Gospel of Mark*. The *Bhagavad Gita*—Hinduism, a religion of more than 600 million people still today. Or Gandhi, who finds in that magnificent *Song of God* a statement of the belief that truth is God and the salvation of your soul.

Confucius. He is both a spiritual guide to us and a political guide that laid the foundation of more than 2,000 years of Chinese history.

I would say that those are books that have made history.

Are they books that can change your life? They certainly embody ages long past. The *Iliad* is a work that embodies the values of a heroic age. An age of honor in which warfare is the greatest value you can have, an age of the duel. How many of us today are going to go out and fight a duel? You cannot have honor without a duel. You snicker at that, but it is true. The concept of honor exists truly only in the society that has the duel. Like an Alexander Hamilton and an Aaron Burr, who would fight over the question of honor. So that is so outmoded, can the *Iliad* still speak to you today?

Or again, the age of Dante. The age of a belief that your whole life is but a preparation for death. We saw Socrates tell us that in the *Phaedo*. Is that how you live your life? As though your whole life is but a preparation for death? Just the opposite. Our whole life is spent trying to avoid death. To live as long as we can, or to come back from it. So, such an alien set of values.

Or let's take Goethe—Goethe in his *Faust*. He is deeply concerned with the question of "Are there absolute standards of beauty?" That is something that just doesn't engage us today. We accept that each individual has some standards of beauty, that "I don't like those paintings. I know what I like. I don't know anything about art. And that's how we accept it. And, well, I don't know if our highways are ugly. They have all these fast-food places, but you know, they get the job done. I would rather not have a beautiful building and have a fast-food place, where I could pull in and have a little hamburger or a taco."

So we just don't worry about beauty. But to Goethe, everyone must come to terms if they are thoughtful, with the concept of beauty.

And nature? Well, we have a great deal of political discussion about nature and the environment. But *Walden*—Henry David Thoreau, he is so extraordinarily eccentric. How can we really enter into the values of someone who leaves everything behind and goes off and just lives in a cabin, and tells us "do not look at our e-mail?" He says don't get your postage, but don't look at your e-mail. We're just not going to do that. So are these values so far removed from us that even though these books have made history, they cannot change our lives today?

Well, we know at the outset that's wrong. They do change lives. The *Koran* certainly changes lives every day, winning converts for Islam. The *Book of Mark* still speaks and changes people's lives. We know about that. The *Bhagavad Gita* is still read and changes lives all through the Indian world in the subcontinent and other places where Indians have gone.

So these spiritual books certainly can still speak to us. But what about a Cicero *On Duty*? *On Moral Obligations*? What makes them a great book and can they still speak? Can they still educate us? Well, let's go back to our ideal of a great book. How are we so confident in saying that a great book has a great theme, is written in noble language and speaks across the ages, has a universality to it?

One of the first to grapple with the question of what makes a great book is Aristotle. He died in 322 B.C. He was the tutor of Alexander the Great, and the pupil of Plato. If Plato was an intellectual and Socrates a searcher after the truth, Aristotle was a professor. Very interested in science. Very interested in observations of the natural world, observations of politics. Interested in empirical evidence. So a very hardheaded thinker. And yet, in his book on *Poetics*, which has been called perhaps the only work of literary criticism that is absolutely indispensable—that work that gave us our definition of a tragedy. We looked at the *Oresteia* or the *Bacchae*. Aristotle says that we judge a great book by its moral impact. A great book is a book that arouses in you moral feelings, and they should be good feelings, ultimately, feelings that lead you to wisdom. Thus a tragedy arouses in you the feelings of fear and pity. These are necessary emotions and thereby achieves that purging, that catharsis of fear and pity.

So a great book, for Aristotle, is one that has a moral impact upon you. So once again, if we are going to talk about great books, we cannot separate the question of morality from them. Leo Tolstoy, the author of *War and Peace*, of *Anna Karenina*; whose book on *The Kingdom of God Is Within You* so touched Gandhi; left us one of the most remarkable works on what makes a great book. Again, it is a book that scholars pay little attention to. They will send you to read *War and Peace*, but for Tolstoy it was the justification of his entire life, *What Is Art?* It is called, *What Is Art?* Tolstoy says we judge a great book not only by the feelings it arouses in you, but the quality of those feelings. A great book, art, a painting as well, a sculpture as well, architecture as well, must arouse in you good feelings. It must create a good morality.

Thus, by definition, to take the most obvious example—written after Tolstoy, of course—*Mein Kampf*. That is an evil book. It is evil because it appeals to all that is evil in human emotions. So it is evil. But, says Tolstoy, take a work like Dostoevsky, *Notes from the Underground*, a precursor of Aleksandr Solzhenitsyn, written about the soul in prison. That is a horrifying book to read, but it rouses in you the good feeling that even amidst terror and torture and suffering—what is good in men and women lives on. That is why it is noble, Tolstoy tells us.

Then there is a work like Goethe's *Faust*, Tolstoy says. Now, I believe it's a good book. I believe it is a great book. But Tolstoy says it is not a great book because it is too complicated for ordinary people to read. It is too much a product of its time. Too filled with allusions about Greek and Roman mythology, too full of philosophical allusions. And so, a book like it—or the *Divine Comedy* today or Virgil's *Aeneid*—if they are so complicated that you spend all of your time trying to understand what the author is saying, then the emotions cannot speak to you. I would disagree there. I think there are books like the *Aeneid*, like the *Divine Comedy*, like Goethe's *Faust* that are worth the struggle.

They are worth finding out, first, what does the author mean by this mythological reference.—who was Forchis, for example. But once you do this, they are soul-elevating works. That is why it is worth going back to the *Gilgamesh*, with its complicated references to Mesopotamian religion, or why it is worth wading through the *Iliad*.

Because we see in them the simple passages, like "When Dawn broke forth with her rosy fingers." You don't need any mythological allusions to understand there. Homer is speaking directly to you from the heart about the beauty of every day. Like Thoreau, "the Sun is a morning star." So, if a book is too complicated, don't let that put you off. Go into it and read it and study it and think about it.

But for both Aristotle and for Tolstoy and for me, a great book must arouse in you good moral feelings. Now, you ask, "Whose morality?" Wasn't that the question at the beginning of our course? That was the question whenever we began to talk about teaching morality in the schools. Whose morality? And it has been the lesson of this course, and the books that we have read, that there is a universal set of values that we find throughout these great books. I do not say that as a dogmatic statement. I say it simply as an empirical one that we have taken from this course—did we look at books from China, Confucius; did we look at the *Bhagavad Gita* from India; did we look at works from the Middle Ages; did we look at them from Classical Greece, from the Christian Middle Ages and pagan Classical Greece; did we look at the *Koran*; and do we look at a work even like *1984*—in which we see that there are a common set of values that were already defined by Socrates. What are they? Wisdom, justice, courage and moderation.

We found that for Confucius these were the lynchpin of human society—justice or, as he called it, benevolence; courage; the wisdom that you strive for. Remember that he said, "I have never met a wise man. I wish I could. But what I am happy to meet from time to time is a good man. Somebody who practices justice, moderation and courage."

And there in the *Koran*, we are called to justice, moderation and courage, and we are told in the *Koran*, along with the *Book of Exodus* or with *Job*, that fear of the Lord is the beginning of wisdom. So in some of our great books we have found wisdom linked directly to a belief in God.

But Cicero, although he understands that natural law must be founded in God, nonetheless describes his entire moral approach to life, his way to live your life, what he tells his son in pure, practical terms. If you practice justice, moderation and courage, based on wisdom, then you will be successful, and you will understand that no successful person ever does anything that is morally wrong.

So, some of our books teach us that without a belief in God you can still have a belief in morality and practice a moral life. We may not want to accept this universal set of values, but one of the things we come away from in reading the great books is that such a set of values exists.

How then do these books touch our lives? They will only touch our lives if we are willing to use the wisdom that comes from them, in order to live our lives. That wisdom is broader than just any set of values. That wisdom is an education for freedom. And ultimately, that's what these great books are. They educate us to live our lives in a free and responsible way.

It is a question for me and I think it should be a question for you, as well, "What role does reading even play in today's society?" I mean—we have far more effective ways of reaching people. A movie, a video game has an impact upon the mind far more attractive and compelling than a book today. In fact, we might very well deal—as I am afraid our schools have not yet—with the possibility that we have reached an age radically different from the last 5,000 years. We told ourselves, or I told you, that around 3,000 B.C., civilization began in Egypt and in Mesopotamia. It began with the invention of writing, and that transformed the mind, because knowledge could now be stored and transmitted in a vastly different fashion than before, when everything relied upon memory. I would suggest to you that the last 25 years have seen, in terms of our technology, exactly such a radical transformation, in which the printed word in a book has been replaced by whatever appears on a computer screen and even far more by what appears on a video game, or through movies. That could absolutely transform the very character of education.

So will we, a hundred years from now, still read these great books, and will they still have a message to speak to us?

What do I mean when I tell you that a book like that is an education for freedom? How do I define education? What did we say "education" was? *Educo*—to lead out from yourself. An education is a three-stage process, and it begins with information. It begins with collecting a lot of facts and data, just what you find on the Internet every day. In fact, we live in a world in which we are so overwhelmed by facts and data that we have barely time to think. The data become so overwhelming that it is difficult to take the next step, which is to weave this into knowledge.

What is knowledge? Knowledge is what you ought to take away from a good Teaching Company course. It's an ability to see the pattern in a particular subject.

But there is a third step, and that is taking that pattern and living your life by it, applying it. And that is what Socrates, and that is what Cicero, and that is what Dante, and that is what Goethe all meant by "wisdom." Wisdom is ultimately an act of meditation. You only come to wisdom by being able to sit down by yourself and think about all this material. That is why, for the Middle Ages, the contemplative life, the meditative life, was the supreme life. The monk cut himself off from all human society so that the mind could be devoted entirely to the contemplation of God.

That is why, in the *Bhagavad Gita,* the highest forms are those who absolutely devote themselves just to meditation—and that is still alive in India today. Gandhi talks about those who have the freedom just to cut themselves off from all human ties to meditate, as a way to achieve wisdom. So meditation is essential to transforming knowledge into wisdom.

And it is just such an ability and a time to sit down and meditate that we do not have today. That is what a great book is all about. It is not reading it in a hurry. Digesting it for a class. It is sitting down with that book and allowing it to speak to you. And it will only speak to you if you absolutely open up your mind, and that can come only through this meditation. That is the final step to wisdom, that wisdom is, ultimately, a source of freedom. That is why, as long as people read great books; as long as they can sit down, take this book in their hand and contemplate it on their own, they will have these insights that will lead them to freedom.

But there's a danger, and Aleksandr Solzhenitsyn pointed it out to us, in the speech he gave at Harvard, in his commencement address. In which he talks about, "You now have such a wealth of information, such a wealth of books that floods you, that you are in danger of losing the truth. In other words, you are so surrounded by what comes out through journalists, let us say, so overwhelmed with all of that, that you are under the illusion of knowing what is going on. You are under the illusion when you go to a bookstore and see the shelves filled with works of history, with works of classics, that you have everything at your disposal.

"But there might be," Solzhenitsyn says, "out there somewhere, uncovered by the media, unpublished by a major publishing house, some thinker." He says, "From time to time I get a letter sometimes from professors of little liberal arts colleges way out in your Midwest, and I see there a person who has ideas that could save your country. But they will never be heard of, because the media don't pick them up. Major publishing houses don't pick them up."

There, too, is a lesson from our great books. There have been great books that have been written, authors that have been absolutely ignored, who have lain there for centuries, until time and values were willing to scoop them back up. Thoreau is an interesting indication of that. His *Walden* created very little stir when it was published. In fact, it made no money whatsoever. It would take 100 years before society was able to pick it up and to read in that love of nature a challenge to our own destruction of the environment.

Or take Gandhi. Now, yes, he was a well-known figure. But it would be in theological seminary where blacks were allowed to attend—not in the South, but in the North—that Martin Luther King would first learn about Gandhi, take that book in his hand, and see that Gandhi's steadfastness in the truth, his *Satyagraha*, was a key to overthrowing an evil system that had paralyzed the moral fiber of his country. And it was a Martin Luther King, like a Gandhi, like a Solzhenitsyn, who had the justice; this ingrained sense of what is right, had the moral fortitude and had the moderation that comes out of wisdom, to transform society.

Now you too can change your lives, in small ways or in grand ways, as long as you accept the most fundamental premise that life is all about you as an individual; your willingness always to learn; your willingness to make mistakes; admit those mistakes; redeem yourself—not in a theological sense, but in an individual sense—and never to give up.

That is the ultimate lesson of these great books—never give up. Live your life and realize that every day, just as Thoreau told you and just as Homer tells you, every day you can begin again. That is why I find the first book of the *Iliad*, with which we began our course, one of the most noble statements of what a great book is about. There is Zeus, with all the problems and cares, going back home, having a meal, spending time with his wife, and taking a long rest and sleep. Knowing that the next day will be a chance, even for a god, to begin all over again.

Timeline

312	Conversion of the Roman emperor Constantine to Christianity, which became the official religion of the Roman Empire
476	Fall of the Roman Empire in Western Europe
800	Charlemagne establishes what became the Holy Roman Empire of the German Nation
1066	Norman Conquest of England
1194–1500	Gothic art and architecture dominate Europe
1215	Magna Carta
1304–1527	Renaissance
1517–1648	Reformation
1558–1603	Queen Elizabeth I of England
1648–1789	Age of the Enlightenment
1775–1789	American Revolution and Constitution, "The Founding"
1789–1815	French Revolution and Napoleon
1860–1914	Golden age of the British Empire
1861–1865	American Civil War
1914–1918	World War I
1929–1953	Joseph Stalin rules the Soviet Union
1933–1945	Adolf Hitler rules Germany
1945–	Scientific and technological revolution
1990–	United States as the world's only superpower

Glossary

Akkad: The geographical term to describe the northern portion of ancient Mesopotamia. The Akkadians and their descendants, the Babylonians, spoke a Semitic language and were much indebted culturally to the neighboring Sumerians.

Aryan: A term derived from the Sanskrit word for "noble." *Aryan* was much used in the 19th and first half of the 20th centuries to describe the Indo-European invaders of India, who conquered the peoples of the Indus Valley civilization and developed the literature and culture of classical India. The term was misused by the Nazis but still retains its value as a collective designation for use in discussing the early history of India.

Asia Minor: Classical term to describe the area now known as Turkey.

birth of civilization: Rise of complex political structures, writing, monumental architecture, and use of metal. These advances occurred simultaneously in Egypt and Mesopotamia.

city-state: A term to describe a sovereign political unit based on a walled city and surrounding territory. *City-state* is frequently used to describe the political units of early Mesopotamia, Greece and Italy, Phoenicia, and medieval and Renaissance Italy.

classical antiquity: The Greek and Roman world from roughly 800 B.C. (Homer) to 476 A.D. (fall of the Roman Empire in Western Europe).

classics: Conventional term for the writings of classical antiquity, now used in general to describe great books from all periods and cultures.

Communism: An ideology maintaining that society should be constituted so that the means of production and subsistence are held in common and labor is organized for the common benefit of all. This ideal was maintained by Plato. However, as a modern political system, communism has been marked by the creation of the totalitarian state and party apparatus to subordinate all aspects of the individual, the society, and the economy to the control of the state.

determinism: The antithesis of free will, determinism argues that humans have no control over decisions, actions, and events, which are the inevitable consequences of forces independent of the human will.

Enlightenment: Term to describe the epoch in European history from 1648 (Descartes and the end of the Wars of Religion) to 1789 (the French Revolution). The age of the Enlightenment was marked intellectually by faith in reason and progress and admiration for the legacy of classical antiquity.

Founders (Founding Fathers): Collective term for the American statesmen who signed the Declaration of Independence, waged the Revolutionary War, and established the Constitution.

free will: The idea that humans make their own choices, unconstrained by necessity or external circumstances.

Gentile: A non-Jew.

Gestapo: *Geheime Staatspolizei*, the secret state police of Nazi Germany.

ideology: A complex set of ideas and values that unifies a community, directs its actions, and validates its decision making. For example, democracy is the ideology of the United States.

Indo-European: A linguistic term to describe a number of related languages, ranging geographically from India to North and South America. These include Sanskrit and the derived languages of India (such as Hindi); Persian; Greek and Latin; the Romance languages, such as French and Spanish, derived from Latin; the Germanic languages, including English; the Slavic languages, including Russian; and the Celtic languages, including Irish. The original home of the Indo-European speakers seems to have been in southern Russia, from which they migrated east and west, beginning around 2200 B.C.

law (Jewish): The complex code of laws and regulations, based on the Ten Commandments and elaborated in the first five books of the Old Testament (the Pentateuch) and later Jewish tradition.

Marxism: An ideology based on the ideas of Karl Marx (1818–1893) and Friedrich Engels (1820–1895) and the intellectual foundation of modern communism.

Mesopotamia: "Land between the rivers." A geographical term used historically to identify the region, now largely in Iraq, between the Tigris and Euphrates Rivers. Location of early civilizations of Sumer, Akkad, and Babylonia.

Middle Ages (medieval period): The period in European history between the fall of the Roman Empire in Western Europe (476) and the fall of the Roman Empire in the East at Constantinople in 1453.

National Socialism (Nazism): The ideology of Germany under Adolf Hitler, based on racism, nationalism, and socialism and espousing a totalitarian state in which the individual and all aspects of life were absolutely subordinate to the state.

Pharisee: Member of an influential Jewish group in Judaea at the time of Jesus. The Pharisees were trained in the Jewish law and insisted on a strict interpretation of that law. Their role in society might be compared to that of professors in our own day.

Renaissance: The beginning of the modern age, marked by the Renaissance ("rebirth") of interest in classical antiquity. As is true of most historical designations, such as *Middle Ages*, it is difficult to define precisely the chronological limits of the Renaissance. It began in Italy, then spread to Northern Europe. Defensible dates are from the career of the Italian poet and lover of antiquity Petrarch (1304–1374) to Martin Luther and the beginning of the Protestant Reformation (1517).

Roman Empire: The Roman world from 48 B.C.–476 A.D. Used in this way, the term *Roman Empire* describes the political system of monarchy established by Julius Caesar and his successors to rule over territory ultimately stretching from Britain to Iraq. However, starting in 246 B.C., long before Caesar, the Roman Republic began to conquer an overseas empire. Thus, historians commonly, if confusingly, speak of the Roman Republic ruling the Roman Empire. The Roman people permitted Caesar and his successors, especially Augustus, to transform Rome from a republic into a monarchy in order to continue to rule this overseas empire.

Roman Republic: Rome from 509–48 B.C., marked by political liberty and a balanced constitution.

Sadducees: Members of an influential group in Judaea at the time of Jesus. Sadducees tended to be wealthy and insisted on the Temple as the focus of Jewish religion.

Semitic: Linguistic and cultural term used to describe certain related languages and cultures of the Middle East in antiquity and the modern world, including Babylonian, Hebrew, Phoenician, Syriac, and Arabic.

Socialism: A term that first appears in English in 1832 to describe an ideology opposing laissez-faire economics in favor of some form of communal ownership of productive assets.

Soviet Union (Union of Soviet Socialist Republics): The political entity that in 1922 replaced the Russian Empire. In 1991, this communist state fragmented into numerous nations, including the Russian Federation.

Sumer: A nation composed of a number of city-sates in ancient Mesopotamia, speaking the same language and sharing the same culture. The Sumerians influenced greatly the later history of the Middle East. The Sumerian language seems to be unrelated to any other known language.

Third Reich: Name given by Hitler to Germany under National Socialism (1933–1945).

Biographical Notes

Aristotle: Greek philosopher (386–32 B.C.). Not an Athenian by birth, Aristotle spent much of his life teaching in Athens. He was the pupil of Plato and founded his own university in Athens, the Lyceum. Far more than Plato, Aristotle focused on empirical studies, including natural science and history. He was perhaps the most profound mind of classical Greece as Plato was the most intellectual and Socrates the noblest. He was the tutor of Alexander the Great. Aristotle was the most influential intellectual figure in both the European and the Islamic Middle Ages. His *Poetics* is the first book on literary criticism to come down to us from classical antiquity. It provides us with a working definition of a great book as one that has a beneficent moral impact on its audience.

Augustus Caesar: Roman statesman (63 B.C.–14 A.D.). Born Gaius Octavius, he was the great-nephew and adopted son of Julius Caesar. Modern historians generally refer to him as Octavian during his early political career and rise to power (44–27 B.C.), from his adopted name of Gaius Julius Caesar Octavianus. Building on his relationship with the popular Julius Caesar, Octavian, at the age of 19, raised an army on his own initiative. With extraordinary political skills, he achieved absolute mastery over the Roman world, winning a decisive victory over Marc Antony and Cleopatra at Actium in 31 B.C. He then carried out a series of political, military, social, and economic reforms that successfully transformed Rome from a republic into a monarchy and inaugurated two centuries of peace and prosperity throughout the Roman world. In 27 B.C., he marked the inauguration of the new order by adopting the name Augustus, which means "messiah." Augustus is rightly regarded as the greatest statesman in history, the model of the good Roman emperor. He was celebrated by Vergil in the *Aeneid*, and during his reign, Jesus was born. He is discussed at length in The Teaching Company course *Famous Romans* (Lectures Fourteen–Sixteen).

Brown, John: American opponent of slavery and terrorist (1800–1859). Born in Connecticut and Puritan in background, Brown was a failure in business. Deeply convinced of the immorality of slavery and profoundly influenced by the Bible, he took his sons to Kansas and Nebraska in 1845 in a violent effort to oppose the supporters of slavery. On October 16, 1859, funded by respected New England abolitionists, Brown, along with his sons, formed a small group that seized the federal arsenal at

Harpers Ferry. The goal, which failed, was to start a slave rebellion. Brown was captured, tried, and hanged for treason.

Cato, Marcus Porcius the Younger: Roman statesman and opponent of Julius Caesar (95–46 B.C.). Far more than Brutus, Cato was the noblest Roman. He loved liberty, which he defined as the political freedom of the balanced constitution of the Roman Republic. He saw Caesar as the preeminent threat to that liberty. Thus, Cato opposed Caesar at every step of the rise to power. Ultimately, Cato chose civil war rather than allow Caesar to become despot. Defeated in that war, Cato chose suicide rather than accept the clemency of Caesar. In *The Divine Comedy*, Dante paid tribute to his own love of political liberty by placing Cato as the guardian of the gates of Purgatory. Cato is discussed at length in *Famous Romans* (Lecture Twelve).

Gladstone, William Ewart: British statesman (1809–1898). Gladstone was four times prime minister of Britain during the golden age of the British Empire (1868–1874, 1880–1885, 1886, 1892–1894). He embodied the ideals of the Liberal Party. He believed in free trade and a broad franchise of voters. He believed in democracy, and he believed that democracy was only viable if ordinary citizens were educated and had economic opportunity. It was the role of the government to provide education and economic opportunity. Gladstone believed that the British Empire was a great force for good, but he was opposed to wars of aggression. He was much influenced by Lord Acton in his views of history and served as a model for Winston Churchill. For us, in addition, Gladstone is a model for how a statesman shaped his life and values around the lessons of the great books. Gladstone believed that all we need to know about ethics can be learned from Homer, and he himself wrote scholarly volumes on Homer and the historical context of the *Iliad* and *Odyssey*.

Hammurabi: Babylonian king (1728–1686 B.C.). Hammurabi is one of the most important figures in the early history of the Middle East. His reign marked the high point of Babylonian civilization and political power. He ruled over an extensive empire, including modern-day Iraq and parts of Iran and Turkey. Babylonian civilization reached new levels in astronomy and literature. The government was marked by a well-trained bureaucracy. Hammurabi issued a major code of laws that influenced the subsequent legal systems of the ancient Middle East, including the Old Testament. He is important both for our understanding of the historical background of the Ten Commandments and for the transmission of the Gilgamesh epic.

Hitler, Adolf: German dictator (1889–1945). Born an ethnic German in the Austro-Hungarian Empire, Adolf Hitler was a failed artist who discovered the meaning of his life in World War I. Determined to lead Germany back to greatness after the defeat of 1918, Hitler became leader of the National Socialist Party. He transformed a fringe political group into the dominant force in the chaotic democratic politics of Germany in the 1920s and early 1930s, the Weimar Republic. In jail, he wrote *Mein Kampf*, which stated clearly his determination to destroy the Jewish people of Europe and to begin another world war. He became chancellor of Germany in 1933 by legal means. He moved swiftly to establish a totalitarian system as complete and as evil as that of Stalin. True to his promise, he led the world into World War II. That war, as Winston Churchill said, would never have happened except for Hitler. In the name of his crackpot ideas of racism and nationalism, Hitler ordered the murder of more than 6 million people in concentration camps. The total number of people who died as a result of Hitler's war and policies is estimated at 50 million. He committed suicide in the last days of World War II, leaving his nation and Europe in ruins.

Julius Caesar: Roman statesman (100–44 B.C.). Julius Caesar is one of the most influential figures in world history and one of the most gifted individuals in history. Beginning his career as a rather shady politician, he grew into a figure who transformed history. A military genius, Caesar conquered Gaul (France), successfully invaded Britain, and defeated his rival Pompey, reputed to be the best general of the age. Caesar used this military success and the loyalty of the army to establish himself as dictator of the Roman Empire. He understood that a republic could no longer rule this empire and that the Roman people wanted authoritarian rule. He described his victories in Gaul and in the civil war against Pompey in *Commentaries*, which became the model for history and Latin prose. Such generals as Napoleon, Robert E. Lee, and George Patton have paid tribute to the military brilliance of Caesar. Caesar undertook a series of economic, political, and social reforms at Rome and in the provinces of the Roman Empire, which laid the foundation for the next 2,000 years of European history and civilization. Jealousy of Caesar and his own lack of patience led to Caesar's assassination by a conspiracy of 63 senators, headed by Brutus and Cassius. Among the great books we study, Vergil's *Aeneid*, Dante's *The Divine Comedy*, and Shakespeare's *Julius Caesar* all pay him tribute.

King, Martin Luther, Jr.: American civil rights leader (1929–1968). A minister and son of a minister, King was a man of profound faith and courage. He stood up against a corrupt social and political system in the American South, which denied to U.S. citizens their constitutional rights on the basis of race. King led nonviolent resistance to segregation that resulted in major legislation and the collapse of segregation. His political and social views evolved into a strong resistance to the American war in Vietnam and an increasing focus on economic reform. His assassination in 1968 remains a mystery. King was profoundly influenced in his beliefs by the Bible, Thoreau, and Gandhi, as well as a number of great books, which he quoted in his profoundly moving *Letter from a Birmingham Jail* (discussed in *A History of Freedom* [Lecture Thirty-Five]).

Lenin, Vladimir: Soviet Russian revolutionary and dictator (1870–1924). Lenin was a convinced follower of Karl Marx who instituted one of the most brutal tyrannies in history in order to transform the Russian Empire into a Marxist state. Lenin came from a middle-class background and was well educated. His plots against the tsarist regime forced him into exile. By the agency of the German government, he returned to Russia in 1917 at a critical moment in the beginning of the revolution. Lenin had a powerful intellect and an utterly ruthless drive for power. He masterminded the Bolshevik seizure of power and victory in the civil war. He crushed all opposition and established the main features of the communist dictatorship in the Soviet Union, including the use of terror as a state policy and the concentration camps. In addition to his political leadership, Lenin also made fundamental contributions to Marxist theory, and subsequent generations of communists all over the world have called their ideology Marxism-Leninism.

Marx, Karl: Economic thinker and intellectual founder of communism (1818–1883). Marx was one of the most influential figures of the 20th century. Born in Germany, he was educated in philosophy and the classics. He developed an all-encompassing philosophy based on economic determinism. He believed that ideas were the product of economic conditions. He was a political activist who sought to drive the workers to revolution through such publications as *The Communist Manifesto*, written with his close collaborator Friedrich Engels. Marx spent his last years in London, writing his massive work *Das Kapital*. Marx is important to us to show the different lessons that can be drawn from a study of the great books. He is also one of the preeminent examples to contradict his own view. Marx shows that history is indeed made by ideas, as the long and unfortunate history of the Soviet Union, communist China, and other communist regimes has shown.

Sophocles: Athenian writer of tragedies (496–406 B.C.). Along with Aeschylus and Euripides, Sophocles was one of the three greatest playwrights of the golden age of Athenian tragedy. Aristotle considered his *Oedipus the King* to be the perfect tragedy. He is discussed at length in *A History of Freedom* (Lecture Four) and *Famous Greeks* (Lecture Fourteen).

Stalin, Joseph: Dictator of the Soviet Union (1879–1953). Born a Georgian in the Caucasus, Stalin's birth name was Iosif Dzhugashvili. He took the name Stalin during his early career as a political activist for Marxism and the overthrow of the regime of the tsar in Russia. Stalin means "man of steel," and Stalin was one of the hardest and most ruthless figures in history. A protégé of Lenin, he played an important role in the Russian Revolution and the civil war of 1917–1924. After Lenin's death, Stalin secured by brute force and cunning absolute mastery of the Soviet Union. From 1929–1953, he ruled by terror the most complete despotism the world has ever seen. Some 20 million of his own citizens died in his concentration camps. Despite this terror, he was genuinely loved by millions of Russians and was hailed as the savior of his country for the victory over Germany in World War II. Stalin is the model for Big Brother in George Orwell's *1984*. Stalin is discussed in *A History of Freedom* (Lecture Thirty-Four).

Thucydides: Athenian historian (died c. 400 B.C.). Thucydides was an admirer of Pericles. During the Peloponnesian War, he was exiled by his fellow Athenian citizens for his failure on a military assignment. This left him with an abiding hatred of democracy but gave him the time and opportunity to write his monumental *History of the Peloponnesian War*. This is one of the most influential works of history ever written. The Founders of the United States regarded Thucydides as a guide for political decision making in the new republic. Thucydides and his history are discussed at length in

Famous Greeks (Lecture Fifteen). He is important in this course as our source for the *Funeral Oration* of Pericles.

Tolkien, John Robert Reuel: British author (1892–1973). J. R. R. Tolkien was the creator of a fantasy world based on the ideals and values of the Anglo-Saxon and Scandinavian heroic age of the early Middle Ages. He was a scholar of medieval English literature and a specialist on *Beowulf*. He was professor at Oxford University from 1925–1959. But he is remembered and important for his novels, above all *The Lord of the Rings*, which continues to grow in popularity and has been the source of one of the most successful and critically acclaimed series of films in movie history.

Bibliography

Note: The Essential Readings focus on the books we are discussing. I have recommended editions that are available and offer guides to further reading on the book and the author. I have recommended as Supplementary Reading books that put our works into a broader context or that I find especially useful in understanding the text. This means that on several occasions, I recommend books and essays that are older and more traditional simply because I think they will be more useful than the most recent scholarship on our book and author.

Essential Reading

Aeschylus. *Oresteia.* R. Lattimore, trans. Chicago: University of Chicago Press, 1953, numerous reprints. The best translation of this compelling tragedy.

———. *Prometheus Bound, The Suppliants, Seven against Thebes, The Persians.* P. Vellacott, trans. Baltimore: Penguin, 1961, numerous reprints. A convenient and good translation.

Aristotle. *Poetics.* W. Fyfe and W. Roberts, trans. Cambridge, Mass.: Harvard University Press, 1932, numerous reprints. A good translation and valuable for its inclusion of other classical works on literary criticism.

Beowulf. S. Heaney, trans. New York: Farrar, Strauss, and Girard, 2000. A brilliant translation by a highly regarded modern poet.

Bhagavad Gita. J. Mascaro, trans. London: Penguin, 2003. An accurate and sensitive translation.

Bible. I prefer the majesty of the King James Version. Of the modern revised versions, the best, for translation and notes, is the New Revised Standard Version of the New Oxford Annotated Bible, New York: Oxford University Press, 1991.

Bonhoeffer, Dietrich. *Letters and Papers from Prison.* New York: Simon and Schuster, 1997. A moving testimony to the courage under trial of a remarkable intellectual and man of action.

Churchill, Winston S. *My Early Life.* New York: Simon and Schuster, 1996. A recent and in-print edition of Churchill's autobiography, written in 1930, when the British political world and the press thought he was finished.

———. *Painting as a Pastime.* Delray Beach: Levenger Press, 2003. Churchill's masterly essay on how to stay young, giving unique insights into the paintings of Churchill, which themselves give unique insight into Churchill the statesman.

—————. *The Second World War*. Boston: Houghton Mifflin, 1986. A masterpiece of historical writing, filled with the lessons of history for our own day.

Cicero, Marcus Tullius. *On Duties (De Officiis)*. W. Miller, trans. Cambridge, Mass.: Harvard University Press, 1913, numerous revisions. By far the best translation, in print, of this fundamental work on education and morality.

Confucius. *The Analects*. D. C. Lau, trans. New York: Penguin, 1979. The best translation into English, with a valuable introduction.

Dante. *The Divine Comedy*. R. Sinclair, trans. New York: Oxford University Press, 1961. Of the many English translations, I prefer that of Sinclair for accuracy and for the clarity of its notes.

Euripides. *Bacchae*. P. Vellacott, trans. Baltimore: Penguin, 1972, numerous reprints. A convenient translation of this last tragedy of Euripides.

Fears, J. Rufus. *Selected Writings of Lord Acton*, vol. I, *Essays in the History of Liberty*. Indianapolis: LibertyClassics, 1985. Part of a three-volume edition, the most complete collection of the writings, published and unpublished, of this seminal figure in the liberal tradition and in the great books tradition.

B. Foster and D. Frayne, trans. *Gilgamesh*. New York: Norton, 2001. A good. recent translation, with useful supplementary material.

Gandhi, Mahatma. *An Autobiography: The Story of My Experiments with the Truth*. Boston: Beacon, 1993. A recent edition of the autobiography of a great and original man of action and thought. The biography is as idiosyncratic—I use the word in a most positive sense—as was Gandhi himself.

Gibbon, E. *The Decline and Fall of the Roman Empire*. New York: Random House, 2000. This complete edition in three volumes is to be preferred to the various abridged versions in print.

Goethe, Johann Wolgang von. *Faust: A Tragedy*. W. Arndt, trans. New York: Norton, 2000. A convenient edition and translation, with useful supplementary material.

Homer. *Iliad*. R. Lattimore, trans. Chicago: University of Chicago Press, 1951, numerous reprints. This has rightly been called "the finest translation of Homer ever made into the English language."

Koran. The best translation is that of A. J. Arberry, *The Koran Interpreted*. New York: Simon and Schuster, 1996.

Lincoln, Abraham. *Speeches and Writings*. New York: Library of America, 1974. The fullest collection of Lincoln's words and, of course, containing the Gettysburg Address (vol. II, p. 536).

Machiavelli, Nicolo. *The Prince*. New York: Penguin, 2003. A convenient translation of this fundamental work in the great books tradition.

Malory, Thomas. *Morte d'Arthur*. New York: Norton, 2003. An excellent edition, with useful supplementary material, of this work, celebrating the central medieval values of loyalty, chivalry, love, and religion.

Marcus Aurelius. *Meditations*. M. Staniforth, trans. Baltimore: Penguin Books, 1964. A good, convenient translation of this enduring guide to how to live your life with Stoic courage.

Mill, John Stuart. *On Liberty*. New York: Penguin, 1974. One of the seminal books on the history of liberty.

Orwell, George. *1984*. New York: Penguin, 2003. The masterpiece of insight into the mentality of totalitarianism.

Plato. *Euthyphro, Apology, Crito, Phaedo, and Phaedrus*. Harold North Fowler, trans. Cambridge, Mass.: Harvard University Press, 1990. A good translation of the dialogues focusing on the trial and death of Socrates.

————. *Republic*. D. Lee, trans. New York: Penguin, 2003. A convenient and accessible translation of this book, which we have called the embodiment of the values and ideals of classical Greece.

Remarque, Erich Maria. *All Quiet on the Western Front*. A. W. Wheen, trans. New York: Spark, 2003. The brilliant novel of World War I that is a powerful indictment of the folly of modern wars.

Shakespeare, William. *The Complete Works*. New York: Oxford University Press, 1986. This is a superb complete edition.

————. *Julius Caesar*. New York: Penguin, 2000. A convenient edition with good notes, part of the Penguin Shakespeare Series.

————. *Othello, the Moor of Venice*. New York: Simon and Schuster, 2004. An excellent edition of the single play, valuable for its explanatory notes. Part of the Folger Shakespeare Series, from the famous library in Washington, D.C.

Solzhenitsyn, Aleksandr. *The Gulag Archipelago, 1918–1956: An Experiment in Literary Investigation*. New York: Harper and Row, 1974–1978. The massive indictment of Soviet communism by the Noble Prize-winner and survivor of the labor camps of Stalin.

Thoreau, Henry David. *Walden and On Civil Disobedience*. New York: Penguin, 2004. A convenient edition of these classic works by one of America's most original thinkers.

Thucydides. *The History of the Peloponnesian War*. Rex Warner, trans. New York: Penguin, 1954, numerous reprints. The monumental work of history; contains the *Funeral Oration* of Pericles.

Vergil. *Aeneid*. R. Fitzgerald, trans. New York: Knopf, 1990. The best translation into English, done by a noteworthy American poet. More than other versions in print, Fitzgerald's edition has a feel for the poetry of the Aeneid.

Supplementary Reading

Achtemeier, P. "Mark, Gospel of." In *The Anchor Bible Dictionary*, D. Freedman, ed., vol. IV, pp. 541–557. New York: Doubleday, 1992. A useful introduction to contemporary views on the composition and context of the Gospel of Mark.

Adler, Mortimer. *How to Think About the Great Ideas: From the Great Books of Western Civilization*. Chicago: Open Court, 2000. A traditional defense of the great books.

Andrewes, A. *The Greek Tyrants*. New York: Harper and Row, 1963, numerous reprints. The best study of tyranny among the Greeks and of the intellectual and political context in which the audience of Aeschylus responded to *Prometheus Bound.*

Barker, E. *Greek Political Thought: Plato and His Predecessors*. London: Methuen, 1960. This remains the best introduction to Plato for the general reader.

Barth, K. *The Word of God and the Word of Man*. New York: Harper, 1957. An extremely influential and provocative approach to reading and understanding the Bible.

Bethge, E. *Dietrich Bonhoeffer: Man of Vision, Man of Character*. New York: Harper and Row, 1970. The best biography of Bonhoeffer, by a close friend and confident.

Brooke, Rubert. *Rupert Brooke and Wilfred Owen: Selected Poems.* New York: Sterling, 2003. Poets of World War I who help us understand the impact of *All Quiet on the Western Front.*

Brown, J. *Gandhi: Prisoner of Hope.* New Haven: Yale, 1991. A standard and good biography of Gandhi.

Burckhardt, Jacob. *The Civilization of the Renaissance in Italy.* New York: Random House, 2002. A masterly interpretative study of the age of Machiavelli by a true humanist, a work that might well be called a great book itself.

Carrithers, M. "Hinduism." In *Cambridge Encyclopedia of India*, F. Robinson, ed., pp. 333–339. Cambridge: Cambridge University Press, 1982. A good orientation for the general reader on the Hindu religion, so vital for understanding the *Bhagavad Gita.*

Carrithers, M., M. Cook, H. Carpenter, and R. Dawson. *Founders of Faith: The Buddha, Confucius, Jesus, and Muhammad.* New York: Oxford, 1990. Recent accounts of these four central figures in the great books tradition and in the history of ideas.

Chadwick, H. Munro. *The Heroic Age.* Cambridge: Cambridge University Press, 1912, numerous reprints. A classic study of the values of *Beowulf* and the *Iliad.*

Champakalakshmi, R., et al. "History to Independence." In *Cambridge Encyclopedia of India*, F. Robinson, ed., pp. 68–85. Cambridge: Cambridge University Press, 1982. A good introduction to the history of early India and the context of the *Bhagavad Gita.*

Conquest, Robert. *Stalin: Breaker of Nations.* New York: Viking, 1991. The best biography of Stalin in English.

Coomaraswamy, A. *Hinduism and Buddhism.* Westport, Conn.: Greenwood Press, 1971, rep. New Delhi: Indira Gandhi National Centre for the Arts, 1999. A sensitive and compelling interpretation by a distinguished scholar. Very important for understanding the *Bhagavad Gita* and its message.

Crenshaw, J. "Job, Book of." In *The Anchor Bible Dictionary*, D. Freedman, ed., vol. IV, pp. 858–868. New York: Doubleday, 1992. A good introduction to recent scholarly views on the Book of Job.

Dill, S. *Roman Society from Nero to Marcus Aurelius.* London: Macmillan, 1904, numerous reprints, including New York: Meridian Books, 1964. This is by far the best book written on the intellectual history of the Roman Empire of Marcus Aurelius. It remains a classic.

Dodds, E. R. *The Greeks and the Irrational*. Berkeley: University of California Press, 1951, numerous reprints. Remains a highly influential treatment of the broader context of the ideas presented in the *Bacchae* of Euripides.

Eliot, T. S. *On Poetry and Poets*. New York: Faber and Faber, 1985. A collection of essays by the most famous 20th-century poet in English and a major literary critic, well-versed in the classics. It contains his essay on "What Makes a Classic," celebrating the *Aeneid* as the greatest European poem.

Esposito, J. *The Oxford History of Islam*. New York: Oxford University Press, 1999. A good, current reference work for understanding the Koran, Muhammad, and Islam.

Everitt, A. *Cicero: The Life and Times of Rome's Greatest Politician*. New York: Random House, 2003. A recent, popular biography, sympathetic to Cicero.

Fadiman, Clifton. *The New Lifetime Reading Plan*. New York: HarperCollins, 1997. A traditional defense of the great books.

Fears, J. Rufus. "Antiquity: The Model of Rome." In *An Uncertain Legacy: Essays in Pursuit of Liberty*, Edward McClean, ed., pp. 1–38. Wilmington: Intercollegiate Studies Institute, 1997. This places Vergil's ideas in the *Aeneid* into the political context of the age of Augustus.

———. "The Roman Experience." In *Preparing America's Foreign Policy for the 21st Century*, David Boren and Edward Perkins, eds., pp. 369–372. Norman: University of Oklahoma Press, 1999. The lessons of the Roman superpower for the American superpower.

———. *Selected Writings of Lord Acton*, vol. I, *Essays in the History of Liberty*. Indianapolis: LibertyClassics, 1985.

———. *Selected Writings of Lord Acton*, vol. II, *Essays in the Study and Writing of History*. Indianapolis: LibertyClassics, 1985.

———. *Selected Writings of Lord Acton*, vol. III, *Essays in Religion, Politics, and Morality*. Indianapolis: LibertyClassics, 1985. This three-volume edition is the most complete collection of the writing of this fundamental figure in the great books tradition, including much unpublished material.

Frankfort, H., et al., *Before Philosophy: The Intellectual Adventures of Ancient Man*. Baltimore: Penguin, 1964, numerous reprints. A classic study on speculative thought in the ancient Near East and Egypt, of great value for understanding *Gilgamesh*.

Gibbon, Edward. *Memoirs of My Life and Writings*. New York: Columbia, 1998. One of the best autobiographies in the English language, carefully crafted to present a public image of Gibbon.

Greene, W. *Moira: Fate, Good and Evil in Greek Thought*. New York: Harper and Row, 1963. Originally published in 1944, this remains the best treatment of these ideas so fundamental to understanding Greek tragedy.

Hallo, W., and W. Simpson. *The Ancient Near East: A History*. Fort Worth: Harcourt Brace, 1998. The best short history of the ancient Near East and the historical context of *Gilgamesh*.

Hogan, J. *A Commentary on the Complete Greek Tragedies*, vol. I, *Aeschylus*. Chicago: University of Chicago Press, 1984. Helpful for understanding some of the more difficult passages in the *Oresteia* and *Prometheus Bound*.

Horne, A. *The Price of Glory: Verdun 1916*. Harmondsworh: Penguin, 1978. Vivid account of the battle that for many epitomized the folly of World War I.

Huizinga, Johan. *The Waning of the Middle Ages*. Mineola: Dover, 1998. A brilliant discussion of the values that lay at the heart of the *Morte d'Arthur*. A classic of historiography.

Kallen, H. *The Book of Job as a Greek Tragedy*. New York: Hill and Wang, 1959. Originally published in 1918, this is a provocative comparison of Job and Greek tragedy. Few have accepted its thesis, but the book encourages thought about how we compare great books.

Kitcher, K. "Exodus, The." In *The Anchor Bible Dictionary*, D. Freedman, ed., vol. II, pp. 700–708. New York: Doubleday, 1992. A good introduction to recent scholarly views on the historical context of the Book of Exodus.

Kramer, N. *History Begins at Sumer*. Garden City, N.Y.: Doubleday, 1959. An engaging discussion of Sumerian civilization and the historical context of *Gilgamesh*.

Lewis, R. W. B. *Dante: A Life*. New York: Viking, 2001. A recent biography of the great poet.

Manchester, William. *The Last Lion: Winston Spencer Churchill; Visions of Glory 1874-1932*. Boston: Little, Brown and Company, 1983.

————. *The Last Lion: Winston Spencer Churchill; Alone 1932-1940*. Boston: Little, Brown and Company, 1988.

Matthews, John. *King Arthur, Dark Age Warrior, Mythic King*. New York: Random House, 2003. A recent study of the historical background of the legend of King Arthur.

Mill, John Stuart, *The Autobiography of John Stuart Mill*. New York: New American Library, 1964. Mill's account of his intellectual development.

Murray, G. *Aeschylus: The Creator of Tragedy*. Oxford: Clarendon Press, 1940. A penetrating study of the tragedies of Aeschylus by a great humanist. Far more valuable to the general reader than most contemporary scholarship on Aeschylus, which is written for specialists.

Nietzsche, F. *The Birth of Tragedy and Other Writings*. R. Geuss and R. Speirs, trans. Cambridge: Cambridge University Press, 1999. In this early work of the philosopher Nietzsche, written while he was still a professor of classics, the idea of the "rational" Greeks was exploded. Such a challenge to conventional scholarly ideas destroyed Nietzsche's academic career, but his essay laid the foundation for much of 20th-century interpretation of Greek tragedy.

Orwell, George. *Animal Farm*. New York: Penguin, 2003. Orwell's satire on communism in action, valuable for the light its throws on his views in *1984*.

————. *Homage to Catalonia*. San Diego: Harcourt, 1969. Orwell's account of his experiences in fighting on the socialist (Loyalist) side during the Spanish Civil War, giving us valuable insight into the ideals that motivated many of Orwell's generation in Britain.

Platt, Michael. *Rome and the Romans According to Shakespeare*. Lanham, Md.: University Press of America, 1983. The best scholarly study of Shakespeare's use of the lessons of Roman history but no longer in print.

Plutarch. *The Lives of the Noble Grecians and Romans*. New York: Modern Library, 1992. This complete edition of Plutarch's *Lives* is much preferable to various editions of individual lives, which wrench them from the literary context of the work as a whole. Plutarch is invaluable for understanding Shakespeare's *Julius Caesar*. Plutarch himself is a great author, who served as the basis for The Teaching Company courses *Famous Greeks* and *Famous Romans*.

Rohde, E. *The Cult of Souls and Belief in Immortality among the Greeks*. New York: Harper and Row, 1966. The classic account of the intellectual and religious context of Plato's *Phaedo*.

Rose, H. J. *Religion in Greece and Rome*. New York: Harper, 1959. Remains the best introduction to Greek religion for the general reader.

Rutherford, R. *The Meditations of Marcus Aurelius*. Oxford: Clarendon Press, 1989. The best recent scholarly interpretative study.

Salway, P., and J. Blair. *Roman and Anglo-Saxon Britain*. New York: Oxford University Press, 1992. A good brief introduction to the historical context of *Beowulf*.

Sarna, N. "Exodus, Book of." In *The Anchor Bible Dictionary*, D. Freedman, ed., vol. II, pp. 689–700. New York: Doubleday, 1992. A good introduction to modern scholarly views on the composition and content of the Book of Exodus.

Sassoon, Siegfried. *War Poems of Siegfried Sassoon*. Mineola: Dover, 2004. A favorite poet and friend of Winston Churchill and one who gives us insight into the impact of *All Quiet on the Western Front*.

Schoeck, H. *Envy: A Theory of Social Behaviour*. New York: Harcourt, Brace and World, 1969. A sociological study of this key element in human nature, portrayed with such brilliance by Shakespeare in *Othello*.

Schweitzer, A. *The Quest for the Historical Jesus*. New York: Macmillan, 1910, rep. 1968. A remarkable scholarly book that transformed the life of its author, who became a humanitarian compared by many to Jesus.

Sharpe. L. *The Cambridge Companion to Goethe*. New York: Cambridge, 2002. A compendium of material to help in understanding *Faust*.

Solzhenitsyn, Aleksandr. *One Day in the Life of Ivan Denisovich*. New York: Dutton, 1963. Solzhenitsyn's first book, a fictional but gripping account of life in a Stalinist labor camp.

Spivack, B. *Shakespeare and the Allegory of Evil*. New York: Columbia University Press, 1958. A scholarly study of this central aspect of *Othello*.

Taylor, H. O. *The Medieval Mind*. London: Macmillan, 1914, numerous reprints. This remains the most readable account of the intellectual context of *The Divine Comedy*.

Thoreau, Henry David. *Political Writings*. New York, Cambridge, 1996. This edition contains Thoreau's essay on John Brown, giving a very different view—at first sight—of Thoreau's ideals.

Tolstoy, Leo. *What Is Art?* L. Volokhonsky, trans. New York: Penguin, 1996. The author of *War and Peace* writes one of the most stimulating books on the meaning of art and the beautiful.

Watt, W. Montgomery. *Companion to the Qur'an*. London: Allen and Unwin, 1967. A good reference guide to the Koran by a distinguished scholar.

Weston, Jessie L. *From Ritual to Romance*. Princeton, 1993. A brilliant interpretation of the legend of King Arthur. A classic work of literary and anthropological interpretation that influenced T. S. Eliot in *The Wasteland*.

Willcock, M. *A Companion to the Iliad: Based on the Translation by Richmond Lattimore*. Chicago: University of Chicago, 1976. Very useful for understanding the numerous mythological and other references that can make the *Iliad* difficult to access for modern readers.

Wills, Garry. *Lincoln at Gettysburg: The Words That Remade America*. New York: Simon and Schuster, 1993. A well-reviewed and detailed study of the *Gettysburg Address*.

Wright, G., and R. Fuller. *The Book of the Acts of God*. Garden City, N.Y.: Doubleday, 1960. A traditional and clear introduction to the historical and theological aspects of the Bible by two distinguished scholars, Wright, a biblical archaeologist, and Fuller, a New Testament theologian.

Wyatt-Brown, B. *The Shaping of Southern Culture: Honor, Grace, and War, 1760s–1890s*. Chapel Hill: University of North Carolina Press, 2001. An excellent discussion of the ideal of honor as a real force in human behavior, affording us a valuable comparative insight into the role of honor in Shakespeare.

Yao, X., ed. *The Encyclopedia of Confucianism*. New York: Routledge/Curzon, 2003. Authoritative articles on all aspects of the teaching and influence of Confucius.

Zimmern. Alfred. *The Greek Commonwealth*. Oxford: Oxford University Press, 1911, numerous subsequent editions and reprints. A highly sympathetic account of the Athenian democracy and Pericles, written by a scholar and a man of affairs.

Notes

Notes